The French Revolutionary and Napoleonic Wars

The French Revolutionary and Napoleonic Wars

Strategies for a World War

Jeremy Black

ROWMAN & LITTLEFIELD
Lanham • Boulder • New York • London

Published by Rowman & Littlefield
An imprint of The Rowman & Littlefield Publishing Group, Inc.
4501 Forbes Boulevard, Suite 200, Lanham, Maryland 20706
https://rowman.com

86-90 Paul Street, London EC2A 4NE

British Library Cataloguing in Publication Information Available

Library of Congress Cataloging-in-Publication Data
Names: Black, Jeremy, 1955– author.
Title: The French revolutionary and Napoleonic wars : strategies for a world war / Jeremy
    Black.
Description: Lanham : Rowman & Littlefield, [2022] | Includes bibliographical references
    and index.
Identifiers: LCCN 2021042824 (print) | LCCN 2021042825 (ebook) | ISBN
    9781538163696 (cloth) | ISBN 9781538163702 (paperback) | ISBN 9781538163719
    (epub)
Subjects: LCSH: Napoleon I, Emperor of the French, 1769–1821—Military leadership. |
    Strategy—History—19th century. | France—History, Military—1789–1815. | Napole-
    onic Wars, 1800–1815. | France—History—Revolution, 1789–1799.
Classification: LCC DC220.1 .B53 2022 (print) | LCC DC220.1 (ebook) | DDC 944.04—
    dc23
LC record available at https://lccn.loc.gov/2021042824
LC ebook record available at https://lccn.loc.gov/2021042825

For
Alexander Mikaberidze

Contents

Abbreviations

Add.	additional manuscripts
AE.	Paris, Ministère des Affaires Étrangères
Ang.	Angleterre
AP.	*Archives parlementaires de 1787 à 1860: Recueil complet des débats législatifs et politiques des chambres françaises*, 127 vols. (Paris, 1879–1913).
BL.	London, British Library, Department of Manuscripts
Cobbett	William Cobbett, ed., *Cobbett's Parliamentary History of England . . . 1066 to . . . 1803*, 36 vols. (London, 1806–20).
Consortium	*The Consortium on Revolutionary Europe, 1750–1850. Selected Papers.*
CP.	Correspondance Politique
CRO.	County Record Office
FO.	Foreign Office Papers
NA.	London, National Archives
NAM.	London, National Army Museum
Napoleon	*Correspondance de Napoléon Ier* (Paris, 1858–60)
SP.	State Papers
WO.	War Office Papers

Preface

My name is Ozymandias, king of kings:
Look on my works, ye Mighty, and despair!

The inscription on the pedestal of the ruined statue encountered by the traveller in Percy Bysshe Shelley's poem *Ozymandias* (1818) was a comment on the rise and fall of empires, and more specifically on the fate of Napoleon. Indeed, a sense of futility is captured by Shelley:

Nothing beside remains. Round the decay
Of that colossal wreck, boundless and bare.
The lone and level sands stretch far away.

Possibly the specific inspiration for Shelley was the announcement by the British Museum that it had acquired a fragment of a statue of the powerful Rameses II of Egypt (r. 1279–1213 BCE), and the name Ozymandias is a Greek version of part of his throne name. That was a reasonable prelude to reflection on Napoleon, and indeed it captured a cyclical character to history, one in which war devoured its products and brought down pride. I cannot better Shelley.

The wars between 1792 and 1815 saw the making of the modern world, with Britain and Russia the key powers to emerge triumphant from a long period of bitter conflict. This book focuses on the strategic contexts and strategies involved, and does so in order to explain their significance, both at the time and subsequently. This is a reinterpretation of Revolutionary and Napoleonic warfare, strategy and their consequences.

That is a massive task for the space allocated, and, in approaching it, I have to prioritise between issues, questions and methods, and all this against the background of a massive relevant literature on the topic. Specialists may well have differing views on the significance, then and later, of particular combatants and issues, and such debate is all to the good. Indeed, this book is very much offered in the spirit of a contribution to a debate rather than as any misleading suggestion of a definitive account, to which this study certainly does not lay claim.

I have chosen to focus on the long-term significance of the period, and notably so to include the United States as a player in the resulting international order in 1815. I also seek both to keep footnotes to a strict minimum and to limit references to those that are likely to be read by non-specialists.

It is necessary at all stages to remember the human cost. Colonel Hudson Lowe, later Napoleon's jailer on St. Helena, noted of a Russian attack on the French in the Battle of Leipzig in 1813: "The dead and the dying absolutely obstructed the passage in the gates and streets."[1] And so also for civilians. In newly occupied Barcelona, the French garrison maintained order in 1808 under pressure by shooting all suspects and confiscating the properties of the wealthy and the Church. Also in Spain, the hard-fought 1808–9 French siege of Zaragoza led to the deaths of thousands of civilians.

Throughout, I have benefited from the outstanding quality, quantity and range of the scholarship on the period. I would particularly like to note the pleasure of friendship of a number of scholars on the period, both alive and dead, including Gordon Bond, Mike Duffy, Charles Esdaile, Ole Feldbaek, Alan Forrest, Edward Ingram, Herb Kaplan, Mike Leggiere, Ciro Paoletti, Rick Schneid and Dennis Showalter. I also benefited from the opportunity to lecture alongside a number of scholars, notably Nick Lipscombe and Alan Rooney, on ten campaign tours of Napoleonic warfare. Some of the ideas for this book were developed in a speech to the Masséna Society's 2021 conference. I would like to thank Leopold Auer, Stan Carpenter, Bruno Colson, Philip Cuccia, Mike Duffy, Charles Esdaile, Alan Forrest, John Gill, Lothar Höbelt, Virgilio Ilari, Caleb Karges, Mike Leggiere, Nick Lipscombe, Ciro Paoletti, Ken Weisbrode and Neil York for commenting on earlier drafts of all or part of this book. They are not in any way responsible for any errors that remain. I would like to thank the Earl of Elgin for permission to consult his family archives. It is a great pleasure to dedicate this book to Alexander Mikaberidze, who has done so much to illuminate the period and to refocus our understanding of it, and who is also a thoroughly pleasant individual and a most generous host.

NOTE

1. Lowe to Colonel Bunbury, October 20, 1813, BL. Add. 37051 fol. 162.

ONE

Introduction

A series of wars—at least, depending on how they are delimited, six main ones in Europe, each with different contexts, courses and consequences[1] —poses obvious problems for us as we decide how best to analyse and consider them. There is the temptation to approach them in order, and to devote as much attention as is available to each, bringing forward, as a consequence, the particular and the detailed. There is also the contrary temptation, one driven by the exigencies of explication and space, to search for one consistent pattern and explanation, or, at least, to look for repeated patterns, a method that leads to a focus on France as the only consistent combatant from 1792 to 1815.

Neither approach is satisfactory. In particular, the past was planned, experienced, understood, and recalled in, and as, a series of moments. Conversely, contemporaries also had a sense of interest, continuities and patterns, each sustaining the other, even if they might struggle to impose this sense on events. To fit our analysis into one pattern is also too simple, not least when there were so many independent forces playing a signifi-cant role. The complexity of these forces, however, helps explain the temptation to focus on what might seem a consistent element—French strategy, the focus suggested by the title of this book. However, such an emphasis risks underplaying the importance of the strategies of the other powers, notably Britain and Russia, both of which made peace with Na-poleon, but neither of which France, then or subsequently during the war, was able to subjugate. To a degree, indeed, French strategy was a response to those of these powers, and, more particularly, French fears about what these strategies and related assumptions might be. Understanding these strategies gives us a context that was global, for that was the strategic scan, scope and significance of Britain.

At the same time, as the narrative chapters will make clear, the strategic context changed greatly over the period, not least with the impact of both domestic events and those in international relations. These events changed hopes and fears and thus strategies accordingly, with the context, course and implementation of strategy all linked. Far from a "system," however defined, dominating events and strategies, these events helped reset strategies in a reactive and contingent fashion, and also in part comprised the "system."

The political cultures that affected responses also changed greatly. In the early 1790s, there was the development of a revolutionary/counter-revolutionary dichotomy. In turn, even while that language continued, the dichotomy was to be superseded under Napoleon by more conventional great power confrontation. Yet, the situation varied, with the continued validity of the dichotomy being particularly apparent in Spain, while an abiding fear of revolution continued to be the case across Europe. Not only was this true for France's enemies but also for her allies, for example those in the Confederation of the Rhine in 1813.

The changes in political culture and, separately, the abiding significance of contingency had significant implications for strategy; and not least, in the first case, with a sense that domestic and international politics were interwoven such that strategy did not stop with the movements of armies and navies. The latter is very much a limited conception of strategy,[2] and, moreover, one that does not in practice explain the movements. Aside from the interweaving of domestic and international politics, and the role of both for military moves, a continuing strategic element that it is overly easy to slight today was that of a belief in the role of Providence. This was seen not only with the role of religion (and irreligion) in exacerbating hostility and distrust but also with the use of prayers in conflict, for example on British warships where many captains were Evangelicals. George III of Britain (r. 1760–1820) responded to the failure in 1803 of an Irish insurrection that had looked for French support: "Every man that reflects must feel the interposition of Divine Providence which has hurried on this daring insurrection before enough consolidated to the effect the mischief intended."[3] Other rulers were apt also to see the same, although the irreligious Napoleon focused his sense of Providence directly on his destiny, which was an aspect of the hubris of his personal instability.

If strategic context was therefore wide-ranging, the sense of strategy was far from fixed, and to a degree the events of this period strengthened the need for the term "strategy" in order to explain what happened.[4] Indeed, as discussed in chapter 9, the use of the word was both new and still very limited. It was only just entering into the professional military lexicon, and our subsequent taxonomy (tactical, operational, strategic), although today still very fuzzy and somewhat situationally dependent, did not yet exist. To a considerable extent, therefore, what is understood as strategy for this period is, as for earlier periods,[5] a matter of the application of later definitions. Moreover, both despite, and because of, a very extensive literature, these are far from fixed, varying considerably within and between countries and by author.[6] For, both then and now, a degree of what can be criticised as imprecision in practice about the meaning of "strategy" arose from the range of political cultures, their disparate views, as well as the difficulties of definitions, and the issues posed by the available vocabulary.

There is also the need to be wary of fixing on the period subsequent assessments, including some current ones. In particular, in the aftermath of World War II (1939–45), there can be a tendency to measure strategy by the criteria of that conflict, especially that of total victory. Linked to that, but also separate, is a tendency, in much discussion of military history, to treat battle as the key medium and measure of success and significance. This approach, one to which Napoleon was especially prone, underplays other aspects of military activity, from protection and deterrence to threat. Moreover, returning to the specifics of the period 1792–1815, Austria, although frequently defeated in battle, was always resurgent, and was eventually one of the victorious powers, in both 1814 and 1815.

Protection and threat were particularly, but not only, seen in naval warfare, where battle avoidance was frequently a key theme. As a result of such avoidance, there was a fundamental asymmetry between navies seeking battle—notably, at pretty well all stages, and even when outnumbered, the British—and those that did not. This contrast in turn reflected, at least in part, the multitude of tasks that warships were expected to fulfil. Thus, two of the biggest battles, the Nile (1798) and Trafalgar (1805), arose not from two sides seeking battle, but, instead, from the

British attacking French fleets with the intention of preventing French invasions: of Egypt and Naples respectively.

There was also the often crucial naval strategic goal of blockade, with each side seeking to cut the trade of the other. Moreover, this goal added to strategic complexity. Thus, much British naval activity rested on a defensive strategy, in the shape of the prevention of enemy attack, both by British action, such as convoying merchantmen, and keeping squadrons at sea to discourage invasion attempts, and by a continuous high level of preparation. As a consequence, where best to send ships was unclear, as it was not obvious what the French would do.[7]

As a reminder of the multifaceted character, both of strategy and of the response to it, the effect of such British defensive activity was in practice an offensive situation that gave Britain far more maritime control than her rivals and, with that control, an unprecedented degree of usage. In particular, the articulation of other empires was ruptured by British naval strength and deployment, and amphibious action, which was a strategy that increased the disruption cost of breaking with Britain, as Denmark discovered in 1801.

This was seen more comprehensively when Spain joined France in 1796, as the strategic response was clear and successful. Although it was not possible to attack Spain's capital, the British navy cut Spain's links with her colonies. The absence of aerial surveillance and rapid communications ensured that this could not be achieved on the extensive seas of the Atlantic. Instead, the strategy was implemented by means of blockading positions near Spain's Atlantic ports, a task that extended the blockade of France. On October 16–17, 1799, four British frigates captured two Spanish frigates off Cape Finisterre, each bearing bullion from the New World. The following April, the British blockading squadron off Cadiz captured nearly all of a large Spanish convoy. In October 1804, the British squadron blockading Cadiz took three large Spanish frigates carrying a valuable cargo of bullion.

This capability provided Britain with a strategic advantage, and France, correspondingly, with a strategic disadvantage. The combination ensured a fundamental asymmetry throughout the period, albeit one that the French sought to bridge, not least through winning, often coercing, the support of other naval powers. This was a key and continuing aspect of the strategic context, and one that has to be kept in mind given the usual tendency to focus heavily on the conflict on land. Indeed, this is a mistake, and not just at the global level, for the situation at sea also very much affected the situation in Europe.

There is no one way to view strategy, and, instead, a need to consider a variety of approaches. The traditional one, a focus on the movements of large units, is now best handled not as strategy but, instead, as the operational level of war. Indeed, Napoleon's use of the *Grande Armée*, notably in 1805–6, is very much seen in that light,[8] and profitably so. In part, instead, strategy relates both to overall goals and to the prioritisation necessary for their implementation, for instance Napoleon's decision in 1805 to focus on Germany and not Italy. Goals and prioritisation are a measure of the processes and views of the entire political system, and one in which domestic drives and objectives play a major role, as do domestic perceptions of the international situation.

Related, but separate to this, comes the question of how much of a priority should be given to the international system as a whole, as opposed to the individual powers. In short, was the former the sum and product of the latter; or did the system have a dynamic that affected, even dictated, the strategies of individual powers? Scholarly views sharply differ on this matter, and it would be foolish to pretend that there is a consensus underlying the particular approach that is taken by any individual writer. Indeed, readers need to consider these points and be aware that there is value to be gained from a range of analytical methods.

So also with such issues as the respective weight to place on particular conflicts and individual powers. Another area of uncertainty surrounds how far to emphasise success as the measure of strategic quality, and how far success had to be sustained in order to be treated as evident. If to 1815, or indeed 1814, then Napoleon failed totally; but that argument, while pertinent, has also to be employed with some care. Yet, there is clearly a difference between a Soviet success in 1942–45 that lasted until 1991, and that of Napoleonic France, which ultimately proved more transient, really lasting only from 1800 to 1812. This appears even more apparent if Napoleon's continually unsatisfied sense of his own position is emphasised, a sense that suggests both anger and anxiety.

Again, an analytical question arises from how far that transience of French power is to be treated as inevitable, how far likely, and how far contingent. The notion of the balance of power as a self-righting mechanism would suggest the first. However, such a notion can be seen as a mechanistic assumption that does not match the behavioural reality that many look to success and ally with it, as occurred with Napoleon. If the latter factor is emphasised, then victory in battle has lasting value by encouraging such a quest to ally with France. If, conversely, the former factor, self-righting, is stressed, then the successful strategy is one in which seeking consent and a harmonious peace is foremost.

From this latter perspective, the French were consistently bad strategists from 1792 to 1815. In contrast, France had stabilised its position after 1748 by negotiating frontier agreements with neighbouring states and by not engaging in aggressive expansionism in Europe. It had still made two significant gains, Lorraine (1766) and Corsica (1768), both of which have lasted to the present, unlike those under Napoleon. However, the first, Lorraine, was the peaceful bringing to fruition of a 1738 peace treaty with Austria, and the second a purchase in which the seller, Genoa, was content, even if many Corsicans were not. Their rebellion left an unsettled legacy in which Napoleon grew up.

Again, in contrast to 1792–1815, if France from 1816 intervened elsewhere in Europe, beginning with Spain in 1823 and Belgium in 1831–32, this was with the consent of other key powers; in 1823, Ferdinand VII of Spain, and in 1831–32 with the British. So also with French forces in the Papal States from 1849 to 1870, and France's role in the Crimean War against Russia (1854–56) and the 1859 war with Austria in Italy. Thus, in terms of strategy, France proved far more successful than in 1792–1815, and it is rather that later period that should be studied if considering France.

Looked at differently, France failed, in western Europe, both under the *ancien régime* and in 1792–1815, to match Russia's success in creating a hegemony in eastern Europe and, prior to that, the hegemony of the Ottoman (Turkish) Empire in the Balkans, and Austria in east-central Europe and, subsequently, northern Italy as well. Between 1450 and 1720, Russia both took territory from other empires (Sweden, Turkey and Poland) and conquered hitherto independent territories, both Russian ones, such as Novgorod and Pskov, and Islamic ones, such as Kazan and Astrakhan. This process continued both during the years 1721–91 and thereafter. Thus, Poland was partitioned (1772–95), with Russia getting most of the territory, while the khanate of Crimea was annexed in 1783 and the kingdom of Georgia in 1801. The latter two steps were important to Russia becoming a major power both on the Black Sea and in the Caucasus. The Napoleonic years saw this experience taken forward, with gains in

Finland from Sweden (1809), in Bessarabia from Turkey (1812), and in Poland (1814–15).

It was France that ultimately and totally failed to match Russia's expansion within Europe and Britain's without, a commitment that became a simultaneous double one that Napoleon could not master. To an extent, France appeared to come close to success, in 1800–1801 when cooperating with Paul I of Russia; and from 1807 in agreement with his successor, Alexander I, notably in 1810–12. Then, at the height of Napoleonic power, much of western Europe was part of a France, or rather French empire, that thereby, as redefined, reached as far as to include Lübeck on the Baltic and Dalmatia (the Illyrian Provinces) on the Adriatic. Moreover, client states, such as the new kingdoms of Bavaria, Italy, Saxony, Westphalia and Württemberg, were similarly expanded. Yet, all this was compromised in 1812 when Russia was invaded, before French power was swept aside in 1813–14, and the client states as a result had to align with the expanding list of Napoleon's enemies.

More generally, if the distribution of territorial power was far from fixed, that created opportunities for expansionist rulers, and also the risk of being subsumed or subordinated to the expansionism of another. Far from seeing the *ancien régime* or 1792–1815 French governments as being bound to fail because of some supposed self-righting mechanism within an inherently multipolar European balance of power, it is appropriate to note the fluid state of European international relations. This necessarily directs attention to the strategic choices made, both in asking why French governments were not more successful, and also why they were unable to sustain the high points of their achievements.

Indeed, the idea of a balance of power related not only to Europe, but also to how far such a balance was seen to be able to encompass, let alone restrict, British maritime pre-eminence. The French played successfully upon European fears of British commercial dominance from the late 1790s. Separately, key European powers were still prepared to leave Napoleon in power as a balance to Britain in 1813. However, Napoleon rejected the opportunity, and in 1813, and again in both 1814 and 1815, he played the gambler's chance on outright victory. The result was a warning against the quest for such a victory.

In chronological terms, a sequence of falls in French fortunes are notable alongside the rises, significant instances of the first being found in early 1793, early 1799 and, more dramatically, 1813–14. The extent to which these were the successes of others, or the failures of France, and, if both, in which ratio, deserves attention and is important in the analysis.

So also with a more fundamental question of strategic priority. France's earlier strategies can be seen as setting a context of assumptions that made later success unlikely. In the 1630s, 1640s, 1650s, 1660s, 1670s, 1680s, 1690s, 1700s, 1710s, 1730s and 1740s, French armies had advanced into the Low Countries, Germany and/or Italy; but, after 1748, it had not done so in the Low Countries or Italy, while in the Seven Years' War (1756–63), France had only done so in Germany in alliance with Austria. After that war, French forces had not advanced into Germany. From that perspective, the resumption of expansion in 1792 was, irrespective of the Revolutionary goals, a challenge to the assumptions of others. Indeed, it was necessary, through repeated victories, to change the latter, and that was not really done until 1801, in so far as western Europe was concerned, and until the successive treaties of 1805–7 for central Europe. Thereafter, the situation could be seen as potentially stable in the form of an acceptable Russian dominance in eastern Europe, but with this stability overturned in 1812 due to Napoleon's determination to replace that dominance. Even so, it was the subsequent strategic plays of 1813, by Russia, Prussia, France (in rejecting Austrian terms) and Austria, in that order, that destroyed the Napoleonic dominance of central Europe, and, in 1814, these four were also the key strategic actors on land in the case of western Europe. There was no inevitability at play in the course or sequencing of developments.

For strategic routes not taken, there was a bigger one that in a sense was the key choice throughout. It was possible with a modest outlay of effort to make major gains, in territory, resources or influence, outside Europe in at least some areas. Even more clearly than within Europe, there were no obvious bounds to the ambition of powers. There was no inherent reason why France should not have been as successful as Britain, or indeed more so, a situation that had seemed in prospect in the early and mid-1750s, and again in the early 1780s. Oceanic power did not depend on being an island, as Portugal, Spain and the Netherlands showed.

France's global position was a matter of relations with non-European powers, with competing European powers that also had a global presence and with European powers without such a presence but whose competition within Europe absorbed French energies. France was far from the sole player, and, arguably, it was Britain's successful counterstrategies that thwarted the potential France gained through cooperation with Spain and the Dutch. But strategic priorities played a role. In 1778, France had chosen not to involve itself in the Austro-Prussian War of the Bavarian Succession, but, instead, to intervene in the War of American Independence, which ultimately helped ensure Britain's defeat, although also hitting French finances. With his focus on Europe and the army, a land bias that was to be repeated by later commentators, notably Antoine-Henri Jomini, Napoleon probably would not have made that choice, or possibly have understood it. This is an ironic measure of his failure, one notable considering that he came from Corsica, an island, albeit a Mediterranean one, where Atlantic trade and power politics were far distant.

The choice of 1778 was also a reflection of the more "progressive" ability of *ancien régime* France to develop into making more apt strategic choices based on a more acute reading of the situation. A different aspect of that was the skill and success of *ancien régime* French commanders, such as Luxembourg, Villars, Berwick and Saxe. Their achievements, including the invasion of northern Italy in 1733–34 and the conquest of Belgium in 1745, qualify some of the bolder claims made for French proficiency from 1792.

For reasons of space and succinctness, I, like others, speak of France, Britain, etc., but that can suggest a unity and consistency of purpose and clarity of interest that is misleading. Simply in terms of the leader, there were marked variations. Few states indeed matched Naples and Austria in each having the same ruler throughout. However, from 1799, France and, from 1801, Russia each had the same ruler. The changes seen in France prior to Napoleon ceased and, from late 1799, he controlled the country until 1814 and again in 1815. In William Pitt the Younger, Britain had the same first minister until 1801, with his returning to power from 1804 until his death in 1806. George III was king throughout, although, due to ill health, with a regency from 1810 under his elder son, the future George IV.

Dynasticism, however, led to unpredictability, both in the shape of possible changes in the views of the monarch and with reference to the prospect of a new one. This would indeed have happened had Napoleon remained emperor. In 1789, the French envoy in Berlin drew attention to past transformations in Russian policy when rulers died and warned about the danger of constructing systems on the basis of Catherine the Great's long period as monarch.[9] Born in 1729, she ruled from 1762 and lived until 1796, but her unpredictable successor, Paul I, was assassinated in 1801, aged forty-six.

In a brilliant 2008 piece, Charles Esdaile commented on the commonplace flaw in writing on Napoleonic strategy, that of conceiving of it "very much in operational terms." As a consequence, while there is detail on the positioning of troops during campaigns and on the means by which battles were won, there is less concern with Napoleon's broader purpose.[10] This is correct, and so also for other players. Much of the discussion is indeed highly operational and frequently adopts misleading or decontextualised accounts of strategy. That is not the intention here. The focus, throughout, will be on strategy, not on operational art, however much the latter is misunderstood and misdescribed as strategy.

NOTES

1. The War of the First Coalition (1792–97) and Second (1798–1802) are clear, but the Third, which began in 1803, is sometimes separated from a Fourth of 1806–7, the latter different because Austria had left the war while Prussia entered it. The wars of 1809, 1813–14 and 1815 then see subsequent coalitions.

2. For my discussions of meaning, see Jeremy Black, *Plotting Power: Strategy in the Eighteenth Century* (Bloomington: Indiana University Press, 2017), and *Military Strategy: A Global History* (New Haven, CT: Yale University Press, 2020).

3. George to Thomas, Lord Pelham, Home Secretary, July 31, 1803, BL. Add. 33115 fol. 153.

4. Black, *Plotting Power*.

5. Jean-Philippe Cénat, *Le roi stratège: Louis XIV et la direction de la guerre, 1661–1715* (Rennes: Presses Universitaires de Rennes, 2010).

6. Black, *Military Strategy*.

7. George to Henry Dundas, Secretary of State for War, October 25, 1794, BL. Add. 40100 fol. 145.

8. John Kuehn, *Napoleonic Warfare: The Operational Art of the Grand Campaigns* (Santa Barbara, CA: Praeger, 2015).

9. AE. CP. Prusse 210 fols 9–10.

10. Charles Esdaile, "Napoleon as Anti-Strategist," *Journal of Strategic Studies* 31 (2008): 516.

TWO

Strategic Contexts

I have no great idea of the proposed crusade against France; there exists few examples in history of these leagues against particular nations having produced anything like the end for which they were instituted, and for this plain reason that the parties concerned in such leagues are subject to every impression that can tend to disunion, and the party attacked becomes on the other hand more united than ever.
—William, Lord Auckland, British diplomat, 1791 [1]

Assessing the strategy of any period involves looking both forward and back. For the first, there is not only what the conflict of the period led to, but also the future that contemporaries were seeking to create, shape, respond to, or at least affect. But there are also the continuities, notably established structures, and the weight of past commitments and ideas. The interaction of the two, future and past, provides the dynamic, but also the complexity, of history. It does so not only for those at the time, but also for us trying to understand the respective weight of past factors.

With our subject, there is a tremendous temptation to focus on the process of creating the future, and to start history, as it were, anew. This owes much to the idea of revolution, a dramatic change involving a rejection of past and present, and to the particular ideology and vocabulary at play. Moreover, time is organised, then and in retrospect, with the notion of an inherent break between the pre-Revolutionary *ancien régime* and new practices and circumstances. This situation is seen in the discussion of politics, both international and domestic, ideology and warfare, and each is presented as contributing to the other. [2] Thus, the strategic context apparently becomes that of imposing or, in stark contrast, resisting novelty. Praise and criticism are directed accordingly, because standing out against the teleology of history appears particularly remiss, at once a failure of perception and an inability to respond.

Conversely, while being aware of the fallacies involved in much discussion of revolutionary change and modernisation, it is separately important to note the extent of continuity, and not least, but not only, in strategic terms. This is apparent in resources, ideas, methods and outcomes, all of which interacted to produce a degree of continuity in the context that repays attention, not that there was only a simple contrast between change and continuity.

As far as resources were concerned, the societies involved in the warfare remained, by the standards of 1850, let alone 1890, largely pre-industrial. Low-efficiency agriculture dominated economies, and in power generation, industry and transport, coal-fired steam engines remained relatively unimportant, and notably so outside Britain, compared to more traditional sources of power, especially wood, wind and water. On both land and sea, transport systems were pre-steam, and, like agriculture and industry, they remained greatly affected by the weather. So also with the seasonality of conflict, which continued to be less common in winter, although that factor did not prevent such campaigns, just as it had not prevented them prior to 1792. The efficiency and talent pool of societies were affected by their discriminatory treatment of women. For men, there were also major limitations on social mobility, not least a widespread lack of education and literacy. Furthermore, in ideas, the point of reference was often the past.

In contrast, the French Revolutionaries, followed by Napoleon, who was very much a product of the Revolution, adopted, both in France and in the territories they conquered and organised, a more meritocratic approach, and a cult and practice of self-conscious modernisation which was advanced as explaining the logic and value of their systems. A greater use of statistics was an aspect of this modernisation.[3] Yet, there was not the comparable transformation of technology or economic processes. Instead, the French Revolutionaries, Napoleon, Britain and Russia, all somewhat differently, but also within the same constraints, sought to maximise the potential of a pre-industrial society for war.

War is frequently seen as affected by a transformation as a result of the French Revolution. However, in practice, continuity was to be particularly apparent in warfare, a theme we will consider at greater length.

Alongside interest in new ideas, techniques and technologies, conflict still involved long-established essentials. Armies were dominated by infantry, who relied on firepower from low-accuracy, slow-firing musketry, while cavalry was the other contact arm. Artillery provided support, but, as with muskets, the range of its smooth-bore pieces was limited compared to what rifling was to bring. The emphasis was on direct fire. Warships were still built of wood, powered by the wind as marshalled by sails through a large crew, and relied, like armies, on close-quarter fire, followed by an advance into the opposing position, in the case of ships by boarding them.[4]

There was also continuity with pre-1792 warfare, for, in contradiction to the argument sometimes made that the French Revolutionary Wars saw the working out of earlier peacetime developments and ideas, Austria, Britain, France, Prussia, Russia, Turkey and Spain had all been at war since 1778. This provided many commanders, such as the Russian Alexander Suvorov, with valuable experience, and was the context in which new concepts were advanced and considered.[5]

Not least with reference to the American War of Independence, the problems posed by a new type of politics, and by the related insurrectionary warfare, were highlighted in January 1792. This was prior to the outbreak of the French Revolutionary War and, in the aftermath of a failure of confrontation with Russia in 1791 that encouraged a withdrawal from Europe, a luxury that Britain had, as an island, when William, Lord Grenville, the British foreign secretary, signalled his wish not to become involved with the defence of the Austrian Netherlands (Belgium) against rebellion:

> Surely if mere military force is sufficient to maintain the Emperor's sovereignty his 50,000 or 60,000 men will answer that purpose without trouble or expense on our part, and without committing the Republic and us with the Enragés[6] of France. If there is such a rooted hatred to the Emperor's government there, that not even that army can keep them quiet, will 20 or 30,000 men from England and Holland do it? Or if not why should we have the disgrace of being involved in his failure? . . . I feel very strongly that this is not a time for embarking in gratuitous or unnecessary guarantees, particularly of forms of Government.[7]

These elements need to be recalled when we discuss the particular changes in warfare in the period, whether those of tactical method, army organisation or scale. The last, a product of the introduction or intensification of conscription systems,[8] was very clear. Alongside battles of hitherto unparalleled scale—Wagram in 1809, with 341,000 troops and 1,022 cannon; Borodino in 1812 with about 233,000 troops and 1,227 cannon; and Leipzig in 1813 with about 560,000 troops and 2,070 cannon—there were also simultaneous deployments of large numbers, both in the same campaigning zone and across a full range of zones. This was not new, and Louis XIV (r. 1643–1715) had done the same with some success, but the scale from the 1790s was unprecedented in Europe.

Multiple-front wars placed a great emphasis on strategic skill, as it was necessary to consider how best to allocate resources between zones, which may be the most appropriate term, as "fronts" suggests a linear coherence that was commonly absent. This decision-making involved both military and political considerations, the latter set in large part by the extent of coalition warfare. Napoleon's determination to ignore his allies helped give him a degree of advantage in this respect, but also was an aspect of the weakness of his position.

Commitments and interests showed considerable continuity at the level of strategic geography, in the sense of the areas and interests of particular concern. Moreover, these have proved a way for commentators to consider continuities over the divide of the French Revolution.[9] Thus, there is interest in how far French strategists, if such an anachronistic term can be employed, continued to think of a "natural boundary" on the Rhine, with this supposedly representing a continuation from the *ancien régime*. There were also rivalries that continued across the divide, notably those between Britain and France, and between Russia and the Ottoman Empire, which will henceforth be referred to as Turkey.[10]

Moreover, particular areas remained in dispute. Thus, 1795 saw the third and final partition that ended Polish independence, but this process of Austrian, Prussian and Russian aggrandisement had begun in 1772 with the First Partition. Furthermore, the struggle over Poland continued to be an issue in the power politics of eastern Europe, one in which France intervened. From this perspective, the Congress of Vienna of 1814–15 brought a new partition that persisted, despite two Polish rebellions, until World War I, with a new partition thereafter in 1939 in the shape of the Nazi-Soviet Pact.

These themes of continuity can be repeated at the level of smaller territories, for example the attempt by Bavaria to make gains from neighbouring Austria, and the ambition of German secular rulers to control ecclesiastical (Church) principalities, a process seen since the Reformation. The territorial imperative, the quest to acquire more land, was crucial to the competitive power politics of the period. Bavaria was successful until Napoleon failed in 1813, when it changed sides and held on to most of its gains. The ecclesiastical principalities were allocated to the secular rulers.

At the level of conflict, the goal was along the continuum from conquest to defence, with victory the common mediator. Sieges were important, and some, notably of Mantua, Saragossa and Danzig (Gdansk), were lengthy. In addition, in effect, Lisbon and Cadiz were both besieged by the French during the Peninsular War, although the French could not cut their British maritime supply routes.

However, battles were generally more significant, and strategies did not tend to focus on sieges. Defensive plans were swept aside by the advance of armies. Indeed, strategy, on both land and sea, was frequently a matter of forcing the pace to battle and then exploiting the consequences. This has been contrasted with a supposedly less intensive and decisive warfare of the *ancien régime*, which, however, is misleading, as, alongside sieges, there were numerous battles then, and some were decisive, for example the Russian victory over Charles XII of Sweden at Poltava in 1709 or the Spanish victory over the Austrians at Bitonto in 1734, one that ended the Austrian attempt to rule southern Italy.

Despite talk of a new age of revolutionary warfare, systems and processes of command did not alter with the onset of the period or during it. Command and control were very much affected by the absence of the successive technological possibilities that were to come with steamship, locomotive, telegraph, telephone and radio. Instead, messages essentially were reliant on the speed of a courier and that of a ship, and these were heavily dependent on weather.

Developments that offered possibilities, including submarines and mines,[11] but, more notably, manned balloon flight from the 1780s and semaphore networks from the 1790s, could not transform the situation. The former was not persisted in for military purposes, which was understandable given its limitations, notably the time required to inflate and dependence on the wind, although, in 1794, a balloon helped French reconnaissance at the battle of Fleurus and, in 1805, Marshal André Masséna used a captured Austrian balloon to observe Austrian positions near

Verona. Developed by the French from the early 1790s, the semaphore offered more possibility, but, although capable of long-distance links, the French network, which reached Amsterdam in 1810 and Mainz in 1813, remained limited.

This situation greatly affected not only the dispatch of instructions to units, but also coordination by allies. Thus, in 1794, having sailed from England on November 29 and having "had a favourable passage to the mouth of the Elbe," Morton Eden was able to reach Vienna on the night of December 13.[12] That was a good outcome, but not a process that eased planning the 1795 campaign against France. In 1798, Thomas Grenville was sent to Berlin on a mission to Frederick William III to try to recruit Prussia to the Second Coalition. The Cabinet decided on this mission on November 16. He tried to sail from Yarmouth on December 18, only to be held up by fog and then an east wind. Grenville sailed on the 21st, but was prevented from reaching Cuxhaven by ice in the approaches to the river Elbe, and returned to Yarmouth and London. Trying again on January 27, 1799, Grenville was held up by fog. He got away on the 29th, but the frigate *Proserpine* was wrecked on a sand bank amidst ice flows off the Elbe on February 1. On the 2nd, all of those on the ship left it and walked to the island of Neuwerk, wading through icy water. Fourteen of the 187 died. Grenville reached Berlin on February 17, but had no success.

This difficulty with communications gave a major advantage to states on interior lines, which was France's position when facing a coalition, and also states that had one major field army which was under the direct command of the ruler. Napoleon was the quintessential example of the latter, and his strategic grasp was therefore of particular importance due to the possibility he had of implementing his views from the strategic to the operational and even tactical level. However, far from this being new, it was in many respects a very traditional and, indeed, outdated approach. Frederick II, "the Great," of Prussia (r. 1740–86) had brought this system to a successful outcome, but his strategic task and range was far narrower than that of Napoleon who, from 1799, was controlling armies across Europe, as well as navies. This was not an easy process to achieve when based in command of a field army.

To a degree, however, there was a prudential need for Napoleon to act in this fashion. As he demonstrated, power came from the barrel of a gun, and his most basic strategy was to stay in power and to use whatever means necessary, or, rather, that he could understand in that light. This may appear a given, as he was only to be overthrown twice, and each time in the aftermath of serious defeats by foreign powers. Yet, the lesson of the 1790s was that governments were vulnerable and that they could be assailed, or at least thwarted, and both by ambitious generals or by rebellious citizens. There was no reason to believe that this situation would not persist, and, indeed, Napoleon ensured his safety in terms of further change between 1799 and 1804 by transforming the Consulate and then creating the empire. However, his falls, in both 1814 and 1815, indicated the extent to which support for him from within his system was conditional on success. Focusing therefore on the field command of the main army both prevented its being used by another and provided a way to generate the necessary success.

At the same time, there is the question of Napoleon's psychology. While this subject has been much discussed, it has generally attracted insufficient attention from those assessing his strategy, as the two subjects have somewhat been separated by some commentators. However, from the outset, there were themes of violence and revenge in his writing, indeed violent fantasies reflecting at least in part his disquiet about his own father and also the recent violent history of Corsica, from which he came.[13] The command of the army was a way to fulfil these fantasies, as well as his desire for safety and his quest for control. Throughout, there was a degree of adventurism,[14] but one that focused on violence and sometimes thuggery. Work on other figures of the period, including Wellington, Castlereagh, Jefferson and Clausewitz, has also argued for the significance of their formative years.[15]

At one level, control from the field army worked if strategy could be "shrunk" to sequential conflict with the main field army of his opponents, but that process had its limitations, as we shall see. Indeed, it led to an operationalisation of strategy, prefiguring that of Germany in the two world wars, one in which bigger questions of strategy were treated as if they could be settled by battle. To a degree this could work, as it also was to do for Germany against France in 1940. However, as for Germany in that world war, Napoleon was to discover the limitations of this strategic method when competing in 1805–7 and, even more, from 1812, with both Britain and Russia.

Linked to this, there was the problem for French strategy of a weakness at the global level. In large part, this was a continuation from the situation during the *ancien régime*. During the Seven Years' War

(1756–63), France had lost a struggle for oceanic and colonial mastery, and although Britain, in turn, had been weakened thanks to French entry on the American side in 1778 into the War of American Independence (1775–83), Britain had ended that conflict still with the largest navy and the strongest European presence in India. Moreover, in confrontations with France in 1787 (the Dutch Crisis) and 1790 (the Nootka Sound Crisis), the French had backed down, in 1790 in failing to support its ally Spain.

Furthermore, the Revolutionary crisis restricted strategic options. In 1790–92, France did not act to support its major Indian ally, Tipu Sultan of Mysore, when he was at war with Britain, instead withdrawing its garrison from its major Indian base of Pondicherry. In 1791, a major slave rebellion broke out in France's largest and richest Caribbean colony, Saint-Domingue (Haiti), and it proved impossible to suppress the rebellion, although that was not apparent until total failure in 1803. In 1793, the basis of France's global (and Mediterranean) strategy since 1700, alliance with Spain, ended when Spain joined the powers fighting the Revolution.

Militarily weak, the French turned to idealistic hopes. These were neither the basis for any realistic strategy nor the context for its discussion. Thus, in January 1792, the attention of the National Assembly was directed by its Colonial Committee towards Madagascar:

> not to invade a country or subjugate several savage nations, but to form a solid alliance, to establish friendly and mutually beneficial links with a new people. . . . Today it is neither with the cross nor with the sword that we establish ourselves with new people. It is by respect for their rights and views that we will gain their heart; it is not by reducing them to slavery. . . . This will be a new form of conquest. [16]

Such hopes came to nothing. Similarly, in October 1794, the National Convention was told that France would gain influence in India if it stood for justice and liberty. However, that year, Tipu was not interested in an alliance, and France, in truth, could offer little to him. [17] Thus, the strategy of weakening Britain in the Indian Ocean as it had already been harmed in North America could not be repeated. Indeed, this was one of the most serious failures in French strategy throughout the period, and one that is overlooked due to the focus on campaigning in continental Europe. Very differently, France also failed in Ireland. In part, this was due to politics there, but the limitations of intervening overseas given the naval situation were also very important. So also was a French focus on the Continent.

Even solely on the Continent, French strategic management was seriously flawed. This was the case at a number of levels. Thus, the French expectation that their armies could seize the required supplies was militarily rash as well as politically inopportune, as the French fully showed while campaigning in Portugal in 1809–11. Napoleon's determination to control was frequently proven inappropriate in terms of the management of strategy, but was a consequence of his unwillingness to have a powerful Ministry of War, a situation that was to be matched under Hitler.

It was not only Napoleon's attitude that undermined any emphasis on an institutional management of the war effort. There was also the attitude of the generals, many of whom earlier under the Directory (1795–99) had become used to following their own head. They sought a personal relationship with Napoleon, and not least in order to cut through his contradictory remarks and gain personal rewards for their service. These benefits could not be provided by the War Ministry, which indeed was in some disorder in 1800, when both Napoleon and General Louis-Alexandre Berthier, the talented minister of war, went into the field. Berthier was replaced by Lazare Carnot, who had held the job earlier and who both distrusted Napoleon and failed to provide adequate coordination at the ministry. Carnot resigned that October, to be replaced by Jean-Gérard Lacuée, although the latter did not gain the title. Instead, Berthier resumed his role in 1801, retaining it until 1807.

In combination with major changes in subordinate personnel and bureaucratic structures, the French situation was not the basis for a coherent system able to generate strategic assessments. The directing, supervision and arbitrating focus was very much placed on Napoleon. This was a situation he sought, but he failed to appreciate the disadvantages. With too much of a focus on Napoleon's views, the lack of clear lines of authority was a major problem within the army. In the United States of America, in contrast, the decentralised nature of the armies' command system, with the generals in the nine (later ten) military districts reporting directly to the secretary of war,[18] lacked coherence and could not provide integrated operational planning or activity. Indeed, in the War of 1812 with Britain, the American army proved poor as an offensive force, although the Americans were crucially successful on the defensive in 1814–15.

The French system faced major problems, not least communications, a constant issue that became a greater difficulty when the theatre of war was more distant. Couriers could generally go no faster than the standard speed of a horse, ten miles an hour, and only exceptionally, in daylight, good weather, and with a fresh horse, at eighteen miles. Until the wire electric telegraph was introduced in the 1840s, this was very much a traditional system. And this situation made micromanagement worse. This situation concentrated Napoleon's reliance on continued interference from a distance, a practice decried by George III.[19] This reliance proved especially flawed, in the case of Napoleon, with the Peninsular War, which he did not understand. When he went there in 1808, he went with overwhelming force and was able to command the initiative. However, he did not appreciate the nature of campaigning there or the topography, and was unable to work with the politics within Spain. The latter reflected Napoleon's poor strategic ability. In Napoleon's absence, there was no *de facto* overall "supreme" commander, and, given Napoleon's leadership style, he left his commanders to keep him and his staff in Paris up to speed. That was, to all intents and purposes, a green light for the great individualists who were Napoleonic marshals to circumvent the chain of command via king Joseph I in Madrid. Napoleon failed to give the latter sufficient authority. Catalonia, and increasingly the east coast operations under Marshal Louis-Gabriel Suchet, were, in the main, controlled by Henri Clark in Paris and Berthier. However, the other French army commanders considered that they had operational freedom and were not constrained by Joseph, or needing to report to him.

Linked to his micromanagerial direction from a distance, Napoleon was consumed with his own projects and jealous of his subordinates. He could seek to leave discretion to his commanders,[20] but the latter knew that that would not protect them. Moreover, this discretion was frequently absent. In 1810, he tried to micromanage Masséna's campaign, ordering him to take the Spanish-Portuguese border fortresses, Ciudad Rodrigo and Almeida, first before driving on Lisbon, a delay that gave Wellington time to develop the Lines of Torres Vedras to protect the city. Furthermore, Napoleon's misguided attempt to direct plans through written instructions was compounded by the absence of a clear command structure within the French army in Spain. Thus, in 1810, Masséna had serious disputes with his subordinates, Jean-Andoche Junot and Michel

Ney, disputes that compromised operational activity. This situation was not the way to implement a strategy.

Yet, control over the military was a key issue of political strategy, one affecting both the domestic sphere and the international one. Napoleon's coup in 1799 was but part of the most prominent instance of this in France. Haiti was repeatedly to demonstrate the same, while successive *caudillos* were to make it apparent as Spanish America became independent. In contrast, legitimacy could limit this risk, as across most of Europe, but also in Brazil once it became independent under a branch of the Portuguese royal family.

As a reminder of the role of contingency rather than the assumption of a consistent strategic culture and context, America was also affected by the problems of military independence. General James Wilkinson, governor of the Louisiana Territory in 1805–7 and the senior officer of the army from 1800 to 1812, was heavily involved with plans for a western secession. Drawing on a political and intellectual inheritance from Britain, there was, more generally, a strong fear of military force subverting the republic, which contributed, in America, to opposition to a large standing (permanent) army, a strategy that France could scarcely follow. Jefferson and the Democratic-Republicans, who gained power after the bitterly contested election of 1800, limited its peacetime size to 3,284 men.[21]

There was no doubt of Napoleon's energy, and that included his attempt to get to grips with the geography, which led him to devote considerable attention to maps. Campaigning in northern Italy in 1796, he was keen to obtain maps, while, in 1799, the *Bureau Topographique* of the Ministry of War was attached to his field headquarters.[22] In 1813, Baron Odeleben, describing Napoleon's headquarters in Germany, wrote:

> In the middle . . . was placed a large table, on which was spread the best map that could be obtained of the seat of the war. . . . This was placed conformably with the points of the compass . . . pins with various coloured heads were thrust into it to point out the situation of the different *corps d'armée* of the French or those of the enemy. This was the business of the director of the *bureau topographique* . . . who possessed a perfect knowledge of the different positions. . . . Napoleon . . . attached more importance to this [map] than any want of his life. During the night [the map] was surrounded by thirty candles. . . . When the Emperor mounted his horse . . . the grande equerry carried [a copy] . . .

attached to his breast button . . . to have it in readiness whenever
[Napoleon] . . . exclaimed "la carte."[23]

Napoleon was highly critical of what he saw as the failure of many of
his generals to understand maps, although Masséna showed good situational awareness in Italy in 1805. These, however, were references to the
use of the map for operational reasons, rather than for strategic purposes.
Indeed, the contrast is instructive.

It was possibly significant that Napoleon himself did not employ the
term "strategy" until after he was exiled to St. Helena in 1815, and then
very infrequently,[24] although, in addition to the usual term of the period,
"art of war," "strategy" has been a term often applied to him, and that
remains the case. Much of the literature of the period discusses what can
be seen as strategies, notably in terms of priorities, although without
generally using the term.[25]

A focus on Napoleon can imply a lack of strategic skills on the part of
other commanders and rulers. There were certainly deficiencies, with
Alexander I of Russia (r. 1801–25), for example, combative towards allies
and prone to a failure to notice his limitations. Yet, Napoleon did not
have a monopoly of talent, and his victories do not mean that failure on
the part of others proves their inadequacy. Indeed, working with circumstances was the key strategic skill, and for most commanders and rulers
that meant playing with a weak hand. Indeed, avoiding war or accepting
a bad peace might well be the best strategy, even if it can appear inglori-
ous and a failure as far as posterity is concerned. From this perspective,
Prussian strategy in 1796–1805, with its emphasis on neutrality, had
many advantages. Moreover, campaign experience did not necessarily
define strategic skill. Thus, George III of Britain had never fought, but,
unlike the leading ministers of the Napoleonic period, he had experience
in directing a war, including in 1780–83 against France, Spain and the
Dutch, all again opponents of Britain in the late 1790s. Prioritisation, a
central issue in strategy, was to the fore in both wars.

In addition, Britain had important advantages in strategic formulation, not least an active system of intelligence gathering, on which there
was a willingness to spend formidable sums. Indeed, William, Lord
Grenville, foreign secretary from 1791 to 1801, spent £841,901 on such
intelligence gathering.[26] Intelligence was a key element in strategy, for
the latter was framed in accordance with military and political goals and

purposes, and these depended heavily on assumptions about the possible moves of others.

At the same time, guiding the response to intelligence, preconceptions about interests, responses and attitudes all played a role. A key preconception was the frequent belief, certainly greater than in previous eighteenth-century wars, that regime change was required, and for both political and ideological reasons. This process culminated with the removals of Napoleon in 1814 and 1815. When pursued, the overthrow of regimes required a very different strategy to that of simply gaining an advantage over them. This was a reminder of the dynamic and, certainly, unfixed character of strategy.

NOTES

1. Auckland, British envoy in The Hague, to Sir Robert Murray Keith, his counterpart in Vienna, August 23, 1791, Edinburgh, National Library of Scotland, Department of Manuscripts, Acc. 9769 72/2/7.

2. David Bell, *The First Total War: Napoleon's Europe and the Birth of Warfare as We Know It* (New York: Houghton Mifflin, 2007). See the important critique by Eugenia Kiesling, "'Total War, Total Nonsense' or 'The Military Historian's Fetish,'" in *Arms and the Man: Military History Essays in Honor of Dennis Showalter*, ed. Michael Neiberg, 215–42 (Leiden: Brill, 2011); and reviews by Peter Paret in *American Historical Review*, 112 (2007): 1489–91; Charles Esdaile in H-Diplo, December 2007; and John Shy on the website of the Michigan War Studies Group.

3. Jean-Claude Perrot and Stuart Woolf, *State and Statistics in France, 1780–1815* (London: Harwood Academic Publishers, 1984); Marie-Noëlle Bourguet, *Déchiffrer la France: La statisque départmentale à l'époque napoléonienne* (Paris: Éditions des Archives Contemporaines, 1988).

4. Jeremy Black, "Naval Power in the Revolutionary Era," in *War in an Age of Revolution, 1775–1815*, ed. Roger Chickering and Stig Förster, 219–41 (Cambridge: Cambridge University Press, 2010).

5. Jonathan Abel, *Guibert: Father of Napoleon's Grande Armée* (Norman: Oklahoma University Press, 2016).

6. Royalist exiles.

7. William, Lord Grenville, Foreign Secretary, to Auckland, January 17, 1792, BL. Add. 34441 fol. 162; Robert Walpole, envoy in Lisbon, to Grenville, October 1, November 2, 12, 1791, March 14, June 9, 1792, Grenville to Walpole, October 18, 1791, NA. FO. 63/14–15.

8. Donald Stoker, Frederick Schneid, and Hal Blanton, eds., *Conscription in the Napoleonic Era: A Revolution in Military Affairs?* (Abingdon: Taylor and Francis, 2009).

9. Frederick Schneid, "Kings, Clients and Satellites in the Napoleonic Imperium," *Journal of Strategic Studies* 31 (2008): 571–604.

10. John LeDonne, *The Russian Empire and the World, 1700–1917: The Geopolitics of Expansion and Containment* (New York: Oxford University Press 1997).

11. Robert Fulton to William, Lord Grenville, Prime Minister, September 2, 1806, BL. Add. 71593 fol. 134; Alex Roland, *Underwater Warfare in the Age of Sail* (Bloomington: Indiana University Press, 1978).

12. Eden to Grenville, December 18, 1794, NA. FO. 245/4, p. 423.

13. Philip Dwyer, "Napoleon Bonaparte and the Search for a Sense of Self: Clues to Behavioural Patterns in His Early Writings, 1785–1795," *Consortium, 2000,* 181–90.

14. Guglielmo Ferrero, *Avventura, Bonaparte in Italia, 1796–1797* (Milan: Corbaccio, 1996); Patrice Gueniffey, *Bonaparte, 1769–1802* (Cambridge, MA: Harvard University Press, 2015).

15. Peter Paret, "The Impact of Clausewitz's Early Life on His Theories and Politics," *Journal of Military History* 84 (2020): 35–50.

16. *AP.* 37, 152.

17. Siba Pada Sen, *The French in India, 1763–1816* (Calcutta: K. L. Mukhopadhyay, 1958), 530.

18. William Skelton, "The Commanding Generals and the Question of Civil Control in the Antebellum U.S. Army," in *The Vistas of American Military History, 1800–1898,* ed. Brian Reid and Joseph Dawson (Abingdon: Taylor and Francis, 2007), 18.

19. George to Dundas, October 9, 1799, BL. Add. 40100 fol. 235.

20. Napoleon to Berthier, in command in Germany, March 30, 1809, *Napoleon,* 18, 406.

21. Theodore Crackel, *Mr. Jefferson's Army: Political and Social Reform of the Military Establishment, 1801–1809* (New York: New York University Press, 1989).

22. Vittorio Scotti, ed., *L'Europa scopre Napoleone, 1793–1804* (Alessandria: International Napoleonic Congress, 1999), 1:85; *The Bonaparte Letters and Despatches* (London: Saunders and Otley, 1846), 1:106; Everett Dague, "Building the Ministry of War: The Consular Period, 1799–1801," *Consortium, 2000,* 130.

23. Erhard von Odeleben, *A Circumstantial Narrative of the Campaign in Saxony* (London: John Murray, 1820), 1:145, see also 265–66; Michael Leggiere, *Napoleon and the Struggle for Germany: The Franco-Prussian War of 1813,* vol. 2, *The Defeat of Napoleon* (Cambridge: Cambridge University Press, 2015), 180.

24. Napoleon, *De la Guerre,* ed. Bruno Colson (Paris: Perrin, 2012), 147–49.

25. Frederick Schneid, ed., *European Armies of the French Revolution, 1789–1802* (Norman: University of Oklahoma Press, 2015).

26. Grenville, secret service accounts, NA. Audit Office 1/2121/3. For examples of intelligence material, see NA. FO. 38/5–15.

THREE

The Shock of the New? 1792–97

The war that started in 1792 was born in the crucible of ideological suspicion and hatred. France declared war on Austria on April 20 in part due to incompatible views on particular issues, notably jurisdictional disputes over territories near the French border, in which the traditional rights of German princes were challenged by the newfound claims of the French state. More serious, however, was a mutual lack of sympathy and understanding and a shared conviction that the other power was weak and would yield to intimidation. In a clear instance of a major driver of strategy, that of internal politics, Jacques Pierre Brissot and the other supposedly moderate Girondin leaders saw war as a means to unite the country behind them. What, however, this would mean for the rest of Europe was unclear. The Jacobins were more concerned with containing counter-revolution at home, and Maximilien Robespierre, a leading Jacobin, explicitly opposed the declaration of war as a device to help Louis XVI.

For both sides, there was no strategy made inevitable either by clearly predicted events, nor, indeed, by the changing goals of Revolutionary France in the highly febrile atmosphere of its strategic discussion. On the part of the revolutionaries, the habitual bases of legitimate rule were renounced from 1792 in favour of popular will and the ideology of liberation, which provided a potent claim for control and transformation. Ideological challenge, and both revolutionary and counter-revolutionary activity and threats, helped drive strategy.[1] Misleading expectations about the likely response of the other helped lead both France and Austria to war, each, separately, declaring war on the other.

Speakers in the National Assembly returned frequently to what they saw as the nexus of strategic threat, the link between domestic and foreign threats: each allegedly made action against the other essential. The actions of the *émigrés* (the Royalist refugees), the real and rumoured Austrian connections of the royal court, and the obvious hostile sentiments of most foreign monarchs lent apparent substance to this strategy, which was at once rhetorical and practical. In January 1792, the Girondin Pierre Vergniaud declared, in a vociferous speech in which the threat to the Revolution was stressed and the call "*aux armes*" reiterated, that the breaking of the treaty with Austria was as necessary as the destruction of the Bastille, stormed on July 14, 1789, was for France's internal regeneration.[2]

Indeed, the gathering crisis led to a division that belies the use of the term "France" as a ready signifier of unity of purpose. The armed volunteers of the Revolution increasingly identified Louis XVI as an enemy, and the king's dismissal of the Girondin ministers on June 13 helped to unite and radicalise his opponents. Marseilles volunteers marched into Paris on July 30 singing the "War Song" by Rouget de Lisle, better known as "The Marseillaise." A very different strategic context was suggested by a review at Coblenz of the forces of Prussia, which had joined in as the ally of Austria: "The celerity and precision with which all their movements are performed, are inconceivable to those who have not seen them. Every operation they go through is mechanical."[3]

French troops advanced on April 28, 1792, towards Tournai, only to withdraw in a disorderly fashion in the face of an Austrian unit and murder their commander, General Théobald Dillon. A force sent on April 29 to attack Mons also turned back and retreated in panic. In June, the *Armée du Nord* tried again. Under its new commander, Marshal Luckner, it captured Menin and Courtrai on June 19, only to abandon them both on the 30th as it retired to the French fortress of Lille. The military situation in Belgium then stabilised.

At this stage, much of Europe was neutral, but it was also having to consider its likely response to the conflict. William, Lord Auckland, one of Britain's most prominent diplomats, wrote on August 18, 1792:

> If the affairs of France could be separated from the interests of other countries, I should earnestly turn my attention from all French news

which I have long ceased to regard otherwise than with horror and disgust: but the fate of Europe and of mankind may be connected with the French catastrophe.[4]

The Austro-Prussian alliance moved in for what it hoped was the kill. On July 25, the Prussian commander, Charles, Duke of Brunswick, had issued a declaration setting out the aims of Frederick William II of Prussia and Emperor Francis II, the ruler of Austria—to seek the re-establishment of Louis XVI's authority—and warning that Paris would be subject to exemplary vengeance if the king was harmed. This threat, however, helped precipitate a crisis that ensured that the strategy-deciding process in France was transformed. The royal palace was stormed on August 10, and the monarchy was suspended. The theory and, to a limited extent, practice of popular sovereignty was thrust to the fore, which was the very opposite of the strategic outcome sought by the invaders. Brunswick himself was mortally wounded at Auerstädt in the French victory over the Prussians in 1806.

Moving forward on August 19, 1792, the Prussians had rapidly won success, taking the surrender of the frontier fortresses of Longwy on August 23 and Verdun on September 3. Brunswick indeed had swiftly overcome the Dutch radicals with a Prussian invasion in 1787. In contrast, his progress into France in 1792 was to be slow, in part due to the intractable terrain of the Argonne and the effect of rain on the roads, but also due to logistical problems and dysentery. French resistance did not collapse, and this political determination was instrumental in the strategic outcome. Brunswick's army was not prepared for a major campaign, and it was arguably too late in the year to attempt one, but he reached Valmy, only about 108 miles from Paris, on September 20. There, he encountered a larger French army and, after failing to dislodge it, gave up the struggle and, on September 30, began to retreat. In turn, Brunswick ended the siege of Thionville and abandoned Verdun and Longwy in October. Auckland discerned a new strategic context: "An undisciplined rabble of new republicans, greatly inferior in honour, has foiled the greatest armies and best generals in Europe."[5] As a result, the cause of republicanism was strengthened within France.

Informed that the Revolutionaries sought to overturn "all existing governments . . . carrying their principles into all the different countries of Europe," the Portuguese government was pressed to arms by the British.[6] That government had indeed been anxious about the impact of

French developments on domestic opinion,[7] while also initially hopeful that they would lead Spain to break with France and turn to Portugal and Britain,[8] an idea Spain had rejected in late 1789.[9]

In the new military and political environments, the French Revolutionary forces revealed a new capacity which had evaded them in the Austrian Netherlands (Belgium) early in the year, that of mounting a successful offensive. To the south, angered by Victor Amadeus III of Sardinia having earlier provided shelter for Royalist *émigrés*, the French declared war in September 1792, although there was no inherent need to do so as the king wished to avoid conflict. An invasion of Savoy and Nice, parts of the state of Savoy-Piedmont, which was the kingdom of Sardinia, won rapid success, and Savoy was incorporated into France on November 27.

The poorly prepared, outnumbered and dispersed defenders retreated in confusion across the Alps into Piedmont, and the French then threatened to invade Piedmont and Austrian-ruled Lombardy (the Milanese). In response, Victor Amadeus hired Austrian troops. This was an aspect of the extent to which war forced lesser powers, such as Genoa, to seek protection, while, at the same time, this strategy increased their vulnerability to attack by others. The fears of lesser powers were compounded by the competing demands of the combatants.

In providing protection including deterrence, there were also the fundamental asymmetries of the contrasting capabilities of armies and navies. The ability of naval force to influence the situation on land was an issue. Thus, Pope Pius VI approached Britain in 1792 for help in deterring the threat of French attack. In addition to seeking a British declaration that the Papal States were under British protection, there was a request for a British fleet in the Mediterranean to give substance to the declaration. Ferdinand III of Tuscany was keen to see a British squadron anchor at Livorno. The kingdom of Naples was hostile to France, but, on December 17, a large French fleet, fifteen ships of the line and sixteen frigates, arrived off the port of Naples. The threat of attack led the government to agree both to acknowledge the French Republic and to be neutral.

Meanwhile, on the part of the French Revolutionaries there was a determination not to allow foreign powers to interfere or prevent their policies. Thus, in October 1792, arguing that it would compromise French independence, the French government made it clear that it could not guarantee the life of Louis XVI.[10] Strategy was being defined in an ideological context, Pierre Lebrun, the foreign minister, writing in November: "Policy and justice are two ideas that have for too long been separated, but the Republic has firmly decided never to separate them."[11]

Operational considerations could contribute to the same end. On November 16, 1792, the Executive Council decided both that Austrian forces should be pursued wherever they retreated, a threat to neutrals, especially the Dutch and the Elector of Cologne, and that the estuary of the river Scheldt was to be open to navigation, a clear breach of the Peace of Westphalia of 1648, and one that would, against Dutch interests, open rival Antwerp to navigation. On November 19, 1792, in response to appeals from radicals in the German territories of Zweibrücken and Mainz, the National Convention passed a decree declaring that the French people would extend fraternity and assistance to all people seeking to regain their liberty. It was anticipated that "freed" people would supply French forces and seek union with France.[12] This was an instance of politics as strategy, with undermining the bases of power as a means to ensure victory.

Despite their initial success in Italy, or at least Savoy and Nice, in other words Italian territories on the side of the Alps nearest France, the French, in 1792–95, concentrated on operations in the Rhineland and the Low Countries. This was a marked contrast to the situation during the War of the Polish Succession in 1733–35, in which they had focused on Italy due in part to the Low Countries being neutral. No such limitation proved possible in 1792. In late 1792, French forces advanced into Germany, capturing Mainz and Frankfurt.

Most spectacularly, a larger French army defeated the main Austrian force in Belgium at Jemappes on November 6, 1792, in part thanks to the success of its using a formation in columns rather than lines for the attack. That battle, however, shows, from the outset of the war, the problematic nature of explaining victory, and, as a result, the need, both at the time and subsequently, to be cautious in the evaluation of strategic capability. The French fielded 38,000 troops and 100 cannon, the Austrians only 13,200 troops and 54 cannon. Revolutionary enthusiasm may well have played a role in encouraging the repeated assaults by the thirty-eight battalions of French volunteers, but there were also thirty-two battalions of regular infantry, still wearing their white Bourbon uniforms. Both groups had benefited from the intensive training to which General Charles Dumouriez, the talented commander of the Army of the North, had subjected his forces in the summer of 1792. Far from enjoying clear battlefield superiority, the initial French attacks were beaten back by defensive fire. Eventually, the pressure of greater French numbers, and the threat of being outflanked, led the Austrians to retreat, but they had held out for four hours, escaped successfully, and had 1,241 casualties, compared to 4,000 for the French. However, the French could afford such losses and were willing to accept them.

As with many other battles, for example Frederick the Great of Prussia's victory over the Austrians at Mollwitz in 1741, the consequences were considerably more significant than the actual battle was decisive. In this case, the radicals were strengthened within France, while the Austrians retreated towards the Rhineland, as Napoleon hoped to force the Prussians to do in 1815. After Jemappes, Belgium fell far more rapidly than when conquered by the French, again from Austria, in 1744–47. Brussels fell on November 13, 1792, and by December 2, when the citadel at Namur surrendered, Belgium had been conquered. The French pressed on to capture the German city of Aachen, from which they threatened both the Dutch city of Maastricht and an advance to, and across, the Lower Rhine.

Many of the French gains in late 1792 were to be reversed. Indeed, on December 2, the French were driven from Frankfurt by a Hessian force assisted by the citizens, while, in 1793, the Austrians defeated the French at Neerwinden in Belgium on March 18 and drove them from Mainz in Germany in July. Nevertheless, it was clear at the close of 1792 that the war was not going to be a quick pro-Royalist police action in France nor a profitable restoration of order by other powers.

Governments across Europe developed, as their first strategy, measures to limit the possibility of revolution. Concern about the position of insurrection in Britain in November 1792 led William Pitt the Younger, the prime minister from 1783 to 1801 and again in 1804–6, to suggest that it might soon be necessary to call out the militia, which indeed happened the following month, while George, 1st Marquess Townshend, Lord Lieutenant of Norfolk, offered an echo of a baronial past, which, however, still seemed fit for the purpose:

> The method I took on a late occasion and shall endeavour to apply again on any similar, was to summon immediately the high constables and others, and to collect tenants and neighbours to suppress any tu-

mults and riots, to read first the Proclamation and warn them of the consequence of persevering. I armed my tenants and attendants.[13]

In early 1793, the British and Dutch entry into the war altered the international situation, while throwing other elements into the complexities of alliance strategy making. Britain took a major role in expanding what became the First Coalition (1792–97) against France, but, as in her earlier wars with France, notably the Wars of the Spanish Succession (1702–13 for Britain) and Austrian Succession (1743–48 for Britain), she found her allies unwilling both to subordinate their strategies to British wishes and, at least in British eyes, to forget traditional animosities and interests.

Indeed, as the major powers manoeuvred for advantage, the Austrians were concerned about the fate of Poland, and Prussia and Russia even more so. Moreover, Austria feared the animosity of these two powers. Johann Philipp, Count Cobenzl, as chancellor, the leading Austrian statesman in 1792–93, saw the French Revolution as an opportunity to get Prussia to agree to the Belgian-Bavarian exchange: Austria transferring Belgium to the Elector of Bavaria in return for his yielding Bavaria, which would have made the Austrian possessions more coherent. This had long been an Austrian goal, and one Prussia opposed. There were differences over other matters. Thus, Francis II of Austria was unwilling to agree to Catherine II of Russia's demand that they should fight for the restoration of the Bourbons, a conflict in which, due to proximity, Austria would have to be to the fore.

The concerns and requirements of allies varied greatly. Portugal had to be cajoled into the anti-French camp, and this did not happen in 1793 until the summer convoy was in from Portugal's major colony, Brazil, and thereby free from French attack. The Portuguese sent a squadron to cruise in the Atlantic with the British Channel fleet, but it was not until September 10 that a treaty of defence was signed between the two powers. Britain was keen that Portugal come into line on commercial terms. Portuguese ports were closed to the French, and trade with France was restricted in line with British requests, while mutual convoy protection was promised.

In talking about the primacy of the politics of strategy, British radicals had a point in contrasting the Pitt ministry's opposition to the French attempt to create a new political order in the Low Countries with its willingness to accept the Second (1793) and Third (1795) Partitions of

Poland. However, the ministry's earlier determination to influence the fate of eastern Europe had been victim of the Ochakov crisis in 1791, when there had been a climbdown in a warlike confrontation with Russia over its gains from the Turkish empire. Moreover, from 1792, the British concentrated on their traditional area of prime concern, the Low Countries. It was not surprising that Poland was not a focus of attention for Britain, but the British should not have been perplexed that other powers acted similarly in focusing on their regions of prime concern. Where Britain was mistaken was in failing to appreciate this point in specifics as well as generalities, and notably so in the case of Prussia, for which the Low Countries were marginal: Prussian intervention in Holland in 1787 had been exceptional, and Belgium was not a central concern.

In 1793, the British army, assisted by Hanoverian and Dutch forces, was ordered to besiege Dunkirk, a potent symbol of Anglo-French hostility, France's North Sea port, and one whose fortification, prohibited by the Anglo-French Treaty of Utrecht of 1713, had only been permitted by the Treaty of Versailles of 1783, and then only in the aftermath of British defeat in the War of American Independence. Besides capturing a notorious privateering base, the British hoped to use Dunkirk as a bargaining counter to persuade the Austrians to cede part of Belgium to Britain's Dutch ally. As a French possession, furthermore, Dunkirk could be summoned to surrender to George III, rather than to Austria, and thereby to accept a British garrison.

The siege brought up the customary problem of the merits and disadvantages of concentration, one that had both strategic and operational dimensions, not that these necessarily could, or should, be separated. In 1793, it was mistaken to besiege Dunkirk, for it was not a crucial goal, either politically or militarily, and, by failing to remain with the Austrians, the British became a more tempting target for French attack. Once the British had lost the initiative, the French moved up in greater numbers and defeated the British covering force, which led to the abandonment of the siege.

The Austrians, in contrast, made gains after their victory at Neerwinden on March 18, 1793. Victorious very early in the campaigning season, the Austrian commander, Prince Josias of Saxe-Coburg did not seek to follow Brunswick's 1792 attempt of an advance on Paris. Instead, he sought the apparently surer capture of a major French fortress that could also serve as a base. The campaign, however, was frittered away in a series of sieges, notably Condé and Valenciennes, both captured in July, followed by Le Quesnoy in September. In some respects, this was a repetition of the failure to break through the French defensive system in 1709–11 and 1744. Whereas the Austrians had in 1781, when allied with France and concerned more about Germany and eastern Europe, ended the system of the Barrier, forts that had protected the Austrian Netherlands (Belgium), the French had retained their frontier defence system. This meant that it was not possible for the Allies in 1793 to come to the assistance of those rising against the regime within France. Indeed, in June and July, the regime was able to send troops against these rebellions.

Just as the outbreak of war increased the paranoia of French public culture, so the fortunes of war drove the pace of the foreign policy of the French Republic. Once at war, France evolved a new strategy, one distinct from the dynastic politics of the old order, although this strategy proved a muddled strategy, in part because Revolutionary warfare was a matter of the adjustment of objectives to fit with the new realities of the 1790s. Contingency played a role: discourse and reality could differ widely, and the Revolution's proclaimed military aims might be more ideological than its actions on the ground. Indeed, both the course and goals of policy, and the response of other powers, greatly reflected the fortunes of war. Thus, defeat at Neerwinden and the loss of Belgium to the Austrians in 1793 led in France to a more cautious approach to annexation and the spread of revolution, and to a stronger interest in peace. Brissot and the Girondins fell as a result of a coup carried out by the Paris National Guard on May 31–June 2, 1793, a coup that led to dominance by the Montagnards, or radical Jacobins, and to their creation of a new constitution. Initially the dominant figure was Georges Danton, who sought a return to more conventional diplomacy, in contrast to the more radical domestic policies of the Montagnards. In order to get peace, Danton tried to create an alliance system. Prussia, Sardinia, Switzerland and Tuscany were offered terms designed to weaken the relative position of Austria and Britain. In turn, Danton sought a negotiated peace with Britain in late 1793, but French objectives were scarcely ones that would satisfy either her or Austria.

Using the Revolutionary Tribunal established in March 1793, and the Committee of Public Safety founded on April 6, which Maximilien Robespierre joined in July, the Montagnards who had gained power launched a fully fledged Terror in July. The regime denounced all obstacles as the work of nefarious "enemies of the Revolution." The Terror was radical, both in its objectives and in its lower-class connotations. Nevertheless, the cause of the people was employed to keep them in order. Indeed, the people were not trusted. Between the creation of the National Convention in September 1792 and its dissolution in the autumn of 1795, no legislative elections took place; only at the local level were a few assemblies convened for municipal and judicial purposes. Apart from the abortive constitution of 1793, the convention was not prepared to let the people have a direct say in whom they elected as their deputies: elections offered the possibility of democracy, but the new elites thwarted this process with a two-tier procedure intended to filter out popular elements. Moreover, the press was curbed.

The legislation issued by the Revolutionary governments brought no real improvement for the poor because the country lacked the wealth and tax base to support an effective and generous national welfare system. Without economic growth, the secular philosophies of change and improvement were flawed, and it is not surprising that most radical thinkers were sceptical about the appeal of their views to the bulk of the population, were, indeed, whatever their stated belief in the sovereignty of the people, hostile to what they viewed as popular superstition and conservatism. In 1793, Louis de Saint-Just, a prominent member of the Committee of Public Safety, later called the "Angel of Death," stated that "men must be made what they should be." It is not surprising that their imposed public virtue had only limited appeal, as, besides being impractical, it was largely irrelevant to the problems of most people.

Summary justice led in the Terror to the death of many Royalists as well as those Revolutionaries seen as insufficiently radical, including the Girondins, and rival Jacobins, notably Danton (arrested on March 30, 1794, and executed on April 5) and the extreme Jacques-René Hébert, executed on March 24, 1794. The Revolutionary courts passed 16,594 death sentences, although many others died in prison or without trial. Paris and Nantes were particular centres of Revolutionary slaughter. The Terror produced not so much an increase in efficiency by reducing points of political friction as an increase in uncertainty stemming from unpredictable violence. The Terror within the military was accentuated, the Revolutionary commissions attached to the armies being a source of arbitrary punishment.

In late 1793, nevertheless, energetic French leaders, benefiting from the largely uncoordinated nature of their spread-out opponents, drove the invaders back by achieving local concentrations of strength. Using his two-to-one numerical advantage and at the cost of heavier casualties, Jean-Baptiste Jourdan won the battle of Wattignies (October 15–16) with a series of frontal attacks and the outflanking of the Austrian left, tactics that utilised French manpower. The French benefited from the *levée en masse*, the conscription of eighteen- to twenty-five-year-old men, ordered that August.

At the same time, the French were not always victorious. Disciplined Austrian fire initially checked the French at Hondschoote (September 8) and Wattignies (October 15–16), and helped to defeat them at Weissenburg (October 13). The Prussians won victories at Pirmasens (September 14) and Kaiserslauten (November 18–30). Nevertheless, there was no conclusive defeat of the French army.

The reorganisation of the French army in the winter of 1793–94, the *amalgame*, under which professional troops were joined with those from the *levée en masse* in the same formation, helped in fighting quality, although the dismissal of many noble officers in January 1794 led to a loss of experience. The surveillance by government representatives on mission to the army (political commissars) that had been established after Dumouriez's flight in April 1793 also did not help.

The crucial battle turned out to be Fleurus in Belgium on June 26, 1793. The French held off attacks by a smaller Austro-Dutch force, and the Austrians then fell back. A battle that was far from decisive as an engagement had a strategic consequence. The British and Austrians were driven into retreating on separate axes, which greatly helped the French, while the British were angered by what they saw as Austrian and Prussian cravenness and selfishness.[14] Indeed, the political and international situation was transformed by the successes of the Revolutionary armies in Belgium that year. Within France, victory gave war prestige and discouraged compromise. Moreover, government and generals came to require continued warfare in order to fund their activities as well as to sustain their prestige. This remained true whatever the political situation, and thus also for the Thermidorian regime that succeeded the Jacobin Terror in July 1794.

Exploitation by French occupying armies in turn generated resistance in the Rhineland, but Austria and Prussia were increasingly concerned about eastern Europe, while, in alliances with Britain signed in March 1793 and February 1795, Russia promised only warships to the anti-French cause. More seriously, relations between Prussia and Austria had deteriorated, in part because of anger about Prussia's gains under the Second Partition of Poland, and Johann Amadeus Franz von Thugut, an opponent of Prussia, was appointed director general of the Chancery in March 1793, remaining in office until January 1801. Unable to fulfil her long-standing, and recently revived, hopes of exchanging Belgium (the Austrian Netherlands) for Bavaria, Austria began to look for fresh gains in Poland. All three of the partitioning powers (Austria, Prussia and Russia) sent armies to destroy the Polish rising of March 1794, and this commitment entailed Austria withdrawing troops from the struggle with France.

Although tensions between the partitioning powers were foremost, the disunity of the First Coalition was more widespread, including, in particular, major differences between Britain and Austria, and between Britain and Prussia. The Prussians showed only limited interest in fighting France, and, in October 1794, the furious British cancelled their subsidy to Prussia.[15] This provided an opportunity to offer more money to Austria. Tensions between Austria and Prussia were not the limit of divisions between the Allies. In Italy, Austria, which had long been worried about Savoy-Piedmont/Sardinia, distrusted Victor Amadeus III.

Alongside disagreements on the part of the Allies, there was failure. Captured on January 20, 1795, Amsterdam was a target that had eluded the French in previous wars, notably in 1672, although the Prussians had captured it in 1787. Winter campaigning meant that rivers and canals were frozen and could be crossed by the invaders. The timescale, however, does not appear too different to that in the 1740s. If the United Provinces was conquered in 1795, a sign of the success of the French Revolutionaries, on the other hand, in 1748, the Dutch inability under French pressure to sustain their war effort had helped lead to peace, and the French had already taken the major Dutch fortresses of Bergen-op-Zoom (1747) and Maastricht (1748).

The conquered Dutch, on May 16, 1795, accepted satellite status as the Batavian Republic, as well as a massive indemnity; the cession to France of Maastricht, a key fortress and Meuse crossing, Venlo and Dutch Flanders; a French army of occupation until a general peace was negotiated; and a loss of control over the navy. The creation of new dependent sister republics epitomised the use of power to make revolutionary changes elsewhere in Europe. Natural limits and small republics had indeed been aspects of the Girondin plan for Europe, but they were to be introduced under the shadow of a dominant and exploitative France and to display republican imperialism rather than a form of European federalism.

Having overrun the Low Countries in 1794–95, the French were able to negotiate peace with an exhausted Prussia, which was more concerned about Poland. Under the Peace of Basle, signed on April 5, 1795, Prussia accepted French occupation of the left bank of the Rhine (the bank nearest France), while France promised compensation on the right bank and accepted a Prussian-led neutrality zone in northern Germany. This abandonment of the coalition covered France's position in the Low Countries and led other powers to follow. Prussia did not fight France again until 1806. Instead, in 1795, Prussia faced the prospect of war with the newly aligned Austria and Russia over the partition of Poland. Despite no longer having to fight France, Prussia finally yielded, agreeing to terms on October 24.

There were a separate set of strategies at play in the case of the war between France and Spain, which began on March 7, 1793, when France declared war. Iberia was tangential for France at this stage, but Spain was important given its wider and major significance in naval matters, Italy and the transoceanic world. Spain represented, however, a separate war on land, one in which most other powers did not intervene. Already concerned about France as a source of subversion,[16] Spain accepted the war in order to limit French expansionism. Spanish forces initially invaded Roussillon in Pyrenean France, winning a series of victories, although failing either to capture Perpignan or to fire up discontent with the Revolution. In turn, in 1794, the French drove the Spaniards from Roussillon and invaded Catalonia, winning the battle of the Black Mountain. The French pushed on to besiege Roses, which fell in 1795. The Catalans, however, ignored French suggestions of a French-backed independent republic.

In the western Pyrenees, the French were also successful from 1794, capturing San Sebastian that year and Bilbao and Vitoria in 1795. The Spanish government was worried that the Basque region might transfer its allegiance to France in return for respect for its traditional laws and Catholic faith. Negotiations with the French on this basis were indeed held in 1794. This illustrated the hybrid nature of strategy and also looked back to the warfare of the War of the Spanish Succession (1701–15), but there was no parallel at this stage, and no equivalent to the "sister republics" the French established elsewhere, an absence which was a realistic response to the situation.

By its Peace of Basle, of July 22, 1795, Spain only ceded to France Santo Domingo, its half of Hispaniola, now the Dominican Republic. The following year, Spain allied with France. Portugal had deployed six thousand troops alongside the Spaniards in 1793, but it also turned to neutrality in 1795. As a result of Spain, a major naval power, joining France, the British fleet was outnumbered in the Mediterranean and withdrew from it in late 1796.

In contrast to the weakening of its European alliance system, Anglo-American relations improved with the negotiation in 1794 of the Jay Treaty. In turn, American animosity with France led, in 1798–1800, to the Quasi War, in which France attacked American merchantmen for carrying British trade. This attack further improved Anglo-American relations.[17]

Its European treaties in 1795–96 greatly enhanced France's position towards Austria and Britain. Yet, although there was a peace party in Vienna, while hopes of Russian assistance were again disappointed, neither Austria nor Britain were seriously interested in accepting French gains. These were simply the most spectacular instances of France's wider failure of winning consent and support. This failure was international both in terms of the response of other powers and with respect to the loyalty of those who had been conquered. The latter issue obliged French forces at the front to face the continuous strategic risk of the security of their routes back to France, let alone possible rebellion.

At the same time, 1795 did not see the collapse of Austria in the west. That year, the French in Germany were pushed back across the Rhine: Dagobert, Count Wurmser, in command of the Army of the Upper Rhine, and François, Count of Clerfayt, successively defeated Pichegru and Jourdan respectively: Wurmser recaptured Mannheim, and Clerfayt beat Jourdan at Höchst near Frankfurt, and defeated François Schaal at Mainz. These battles indicated the importance of the Rhine river line, which was the case both militarily, as providing France with the opportunity to advance into Germany or to challenge France's control of the left bank of the Rhine, and also politically as a symbol of success.

Meanwhile, prefiguring British strategy after the German successes of 1940, George III pressed the need for resolution and for hoping that something would turn up:

> A steady attention to obtaining our own advantages that we may be gainers by the stand we have made though betrayed by the European powers who ought to have cooperated with us, and if they had the horrid French fabric must before this time have been destroyed, now I believe its own unnatural formation will effect this if we will but be quiet and not by making peace save the [National] Convention.[18]

Failure on land in Europe meant that George had to consider other means to victory, including "stopping all provisions and naval stores" reaching France by using blockade and diplomatic pressure.[19] In a long-standing practice, George's strategic vision towards France indeed combined direct and indirect pressure. Thus, Austrian successes in November 1795 led him to offer an apparent mathematical certainty: "I think no problem in Euclid [the most famous classical mathematician] more true than that, if the French are well pressed in the next year, their want of resources and other internal evils must make the present shocking chaos crumble to pieces."[20]

Separate Austrian and British discussions with France in 1796 proved fruitless. War would continue. The French invaded southern Germany and northern Italy that summer. Meanwhile, a sense of the pressure put on France's opponents can be gained from a report from Leipzig of August 1796. Due to French advances, the British diplomat Ralph Heathcote had left Mergentheim with the Elector of Cologne, to whom he was accredited, for Nuremberg further east:

> But I had scarcely reached the latter place when the accounts of the uninterrupted success of the enemy, both on the Upper and Lower Rhine, became from day to day so alarming, that every hope, of finding a place of security either in that Imperial City or in any other southern place of Germany was necessarily given up entirely. . . . The road was entirely covered by baggage wagons belonging to the Austrian armies.

Once in Leipzig, Heathcote had to think anew of fleeing, this time to Hamburg from which he would be able to sail to Britain.[21]

FRENCH WAR-MAKING

The French benefited in the 1790s from numbers, tactics, command and organisation. Superiority in numbers was important in a number of key battles, including Valmy, Jemappes and Wattignies. The *levée en masse* decreed on August 23, 1793, and the general conscription ordered under the Jourdan Law in September 1798 were significant in raising these numbers, as was the size of the French population. In 1800, excluding the conquests made from 1792 and non-European colonies, this was about 26.8 million. Under the *ancien régime*, France did not have a conscription system comparable to Prussia or Russia, and it had too few troops to confront its now larger opposing coalition in early 1793. In the previous European war in which France had been involved, the Seven Years' War (1756–63), the French had deployed for the army and navy about 2.5 percent of the population at any one time, and in total nearly one million men, about 4 percent of the population.[22] In that conflict, France had benefited from cooperation with Austria, most of the German states (but not Prussia) and Russia, and the neutrality of the Netherlands, Savoy-Piedmont and Spain (until it became an ally in 1762). The situation was very different in 1793. The reality of the resulting system, however, did not measure up to aspirations. In 1797, the army fell to 365,000 effectives, so that, in 1798, the obligatory nature of military service was institutionalised and extended in the Jourdan Law. The new system was designed to produce a more stable system than the *levée en masse*. Thanks to their size, French armies were able to operate effectively on several fronts at once, to sustain heavy casualties, to match the opposing forces of much of Europe, and to put earlier ideas about combat and conflict into practice.[23] The greater scale of the French army was to be organised in the field with the development of the corps system, and this innovation was to pave the way for the development of operational art, at least as understood in the modern West.[24] The corps system offered flexibility but, however, also required large numbers of troops.

Johann Amadeus von Thugut, the leading Austrian minister, complained in 1794, "Reduced to the defensive, we are continually harassed . . . by innumerable [French] hordes. . . . Our army is vastly weakened by [its] partial victories while the enemy repairs its losses with the greatest ease."[25] There were also organisational issues confronting the

Austrians, as also other armies. Colonel Graham, who was accompanying the Austrian army in Italy, reported thence in January 1797:

> Whether owing to the difficulty of finding officers or from reasons of economy, the number of vacancies in the regiments is immense, which leaves the duty severe on the others, and in action is of the worst consequence from the want of a sufficient number of officers to attend to the men.[26]

The large number of inexperienced French soldiers that resulted from mass conscription created a problem of organisation. Independent attack columns were the most effective way to use these soldiers, and this method was also best for an army that put an emphasis on the attack. Column advances were far more flexible than advancing lines. Moreover, the French combination of artillery, skirmishers and assault columns proved a potent *ad hoc* use of tactical elements that was matched to the technology of the time. In a continuation of developing pre-Revolutionary ideas, columns were preceded by skirmishers that disrupted the close-packed lines of opponents, and were supported by massed cannon that weakened them prior to the impact of the columns. There was an emphasis on movement and a flexibility that was linked to this.

At the same time, the details of battles are often difficult to establish because the sources are affected by gaps, uncertainty and serious contradictions,[27] even for famous battles on a well-defined and tight battleground, such as Waterloo, for which the actions of particular units remain a matter for debate. Maps and plans for battles are often unsatisfactory, and many accounts of moves are approximate or conjectural. Particular problems attach to the precise course and condition of roads and tracks, and also to the amount, quantity and density of ground cover in the form of thickets and woods, cover that may have obscured the position of enemy units or delayed the rapid movement of troops. Issues of timing are frequently vexed, which is a problem if moves are to be seen as simultaneous, sequential or consecutive. It is often unclear when an engagement began.[28]

For contemporaries, understanding the battlefield was far more of an issue. The greater dispersal of French units due to the use of columns ensured that command and coordination skills became more important, and, in organising their army anew with a committed professionalism,[29] the French benefited from young and determined commanders. Alongside the disruption of the Revolution, the sudden and huge development of the army helped create a large number of posts to be filled, no matter by whom. This provided an opportunity for talent (as well as mediocrity), and both ordinary soldiers, such as Jourdan, and junior officers, including Napoleon, were able to rise to the top. There was a more "democratic" command structure, at least at the battalion level: the social gap between non-commissioned officers and their superiors was less than hitherto. Seeking to end the friction caused by incompetence, the Revolution emphasised social mobility and created an officer class dominated by talent and connections, as opposed to birth and connections, although the election of officers was rapidly abandoned. The stress on republican virtue, seen in 1792–94, was replaced by an emphasis on professionalism, merit no longer being regarded, as it had been in 1792–94, as a dangerous sign of individualism.[30]

Discussing this in terms of professionalism, however, underrates the political dimension. The use of Revolutionary violence was directed in part against the army, with generals murdered or more formally executed in 1792, 1793 and 1794. Punishment and politicisation helped ensure that, in battle and on campaign, generals were willing to accept heavy losses among their troops, but also that there were indeed traitors. Thus, in 1793, Charles-François Dumouriez, in a vulnerable political position after his defeat at Neerwinden, concluded agreements with Austrian commanders that were intended to allow him to suppress the Revolution in Paris, although he was thwarted by a lack of support within the army and defeated in April.

The armies were systematised by Lazare Carnot, head of the military section of the Committee of Public Safety, who brought a measure of organisation to the military confusion that followed the Revolution. The "Organiser of Victory," and definitely a workaholic, Carnot was a pre-Revolutionary army officer with a strong interest in engineering and mathematics, who was a key figure in military administration from 1793 to 1797, and again in 1800. Success in forming, training and sustaining new armies was instrumental in the transition from a royal army to a nation in arms, although the process of administrative rationalisation was heavily politicised.[31] Carnot himself attributed French successes not to the larger number of troops but to the high proportion of non-commissioned officers,[32] which was certainly a contrast with the Austrian and British armies.

The forces of Revolutionary France, whatever the theory of their logistical organisation and ethos, relied to a considerable extent in the 1790s on seizing food in the areas into which they advanced. Although administered in a rapidly changing fashion, the logistics brought about by the combination of need with the opportunities posed by conquest led to the partial abandonment of the magazine system, the reliance on food depots. Carnot advocated requisitioning, and thus living off the land, as the means to support the large forces he helped mobilise by introducing conscription in 1793. The results, however, were inadequate.

French logistics were linked to the aggressive style of war—in tactics, operations and strategy—of the Revolutionary armies, a style that relied on numbers, enthusiasm and the opportunity to despoil areas. The way was open for the ruthless boldness that Napoleon was to show in Italy in 1796–97, not least in suppressing popular opposition there once opposing Sardinian and Austrian armies had been defeated, notably the Austrians at Castiglione, Arcole and Rivoli in 1797. In command of the Army of Italy, he attacked and developed the characteristics of his generalship: self-confidence, swift decision-making, rapid mobility, the concentration of strength and, where possible, the exploitation of interior lines.

However, this new logistical system faced and created problems. In particular, much of the terrain in which the French operated had only limited agrarian surpluses and these were soon exhausted, so it was difficult in 1799 for France's Army of Italy to find adequate food because it had already devastated much of the countryside in 1796–97. The French forces in Italy in 1796 lacked shoes, uniforms and food, shortages that exacerbated desertion,[33] and the same was the case in Germany.

Moreover, transferring the burden of war to conquered territories undermined the acceptance of French control, leading to violent responses that further helped develop a vicious cycle of exaction and also undermined the universalist and liberal aspirations of France's supporters. The cause of the Revolution became the practice of repression.[34] The brutal exploitation of Lombardy in 1796, as well as anticlericalism and the position and policies of France's Italian supporters, led to a popular uprising that was harshly repressed. There were also serious popular uprisings within Germany in Swabia and Franconia.

Thus, as Dumouriez had realised in the case of Belgium, the very conduct of the army, and the organisation of its supply system, helped to weaken France politically and made it totally reliant on military success, with a spoils system operating to the benefit of both regime and army.[35] Military convenience, lust for loot, the practice of expropriation, ideological conviction, the political advantages of successful campaigning and strategic opportunism all encouraged aggressive action by the French, but were also to invite revenge. In 1815, Major William Turner, part of the British army advancing after Waterloo, wrote from near Paris: "Every town and village is completely ransacked and pillaged by the Prussians and neither wine, spirits or bread are to be found. The whole country from frontier to Paris . . . laid waste." This was linked to a desire for revenge: "That infernal city Paris will be attacked and no doubt pillaged for it is a debt we owe to the whole of Europe."[36]

In Parliament in April 1797, Richard Brinsley Sheridan, the most famous author of English comedies of his days and an opposition spokesman, had mocked governmental assurances about the ease with which the French would be defeated:

> I will not remind those gentlemen of their declaration so often made, that the French must fly before troops well-disciplined and regularly paid. We have fatal experience of the folly of those declarations; we have seen soldiers frequently without pay, and without sufficient provisions, put to rout the best-paid armies in Europe.[37]

That account was both accurate and insufficient. The Russians, although not well paid, had not yet engaged the French, while the success of the French hitherto owed much to the divided priorities of the other powers, notably Prussia. In addition, the other Italian states did not provide much help to Sardinia and Austria, relying instead on the latter to protect Italy from French expansionism.[38] This reflected yet again an unwillingness of powers to be readily grouped into alliance systems, which was in part a product of the widespread dispersal of agency in the international system. This dispersal, however, was a situation that the Revolutionaries could not really accept because of their rejection of other values, and it was also a situation with which the instinctively masterful Napoleon was generally unwilling to act.

While noting links, it is necessary to differentiate between the 1790s and what followed under Napoleon in the 1800s. Focusing on the 1790s, the politics—military, diplomatic, financial and social—of the Revolution were more important than its tactical innovations.[39] It has been argued that the French soldiers were better motivated and, hence, more successful and better able to use the new methods. This is hard to prove, but, initially at least, Revolutionary enthusiasm, drawing on a concept of an assertive nation,[40] does seem, by its nature, to have been an important element in French capability. This enthusiasm was probably necessary for the higher morale required for effective shock action. Patriotic determination was also important to counter the limited training of the early Revolutionary armies. Napoleonic veterans, in contrast, had a high morale that owed much to frequent success. Furthermore, with time, professionalism and unit loyalty had become more significant for French troops. In turn, this professionalism and loyalty was linked to their image as good soldiers, and to interest in promotion,[41] points that were also true for other armies and navies.

REBELLIONS

The political dimension is made doubly important because of the classic flaw in writing about strategy in this period, that of concentrating on foreign war, and notably so in the form of state-to-state conflict. In practice, the most important strategic requirement was maintaining control of the home base against rebellion, but this requirement is seriously underplayed. This requirement was seen, for example, with Britain, notably in Ireland, where a rebellion was suppressed in 1798 by Charles, 1st Marquess Cornwallis, who had earlier, as Charles, 2nd Earl Cornwallis, been defeated at Yorktown in 1781. This requirement was also seen in the deployment of over twelve thousand troops in England in 1812 to deal with the Luddite riots against new industrial technology. An even more serious problem was posed by the naval mutinies of 1797. The Irish rebellion benefited, albeit too late, from a French expeditionary force that was in turn defeated, just as, with a continuation from the *ancien régime*, another French force had been deployed in Ireland in 1690–91, and a Spanish one in 1600–1601. In the 1790s, there was no effective coordination between disaffection in Britain and French support. So even more with Napoleon, who, in general, avoided international populism, although, on a pattern seen earlier with the French, notably in 1703–4, he did call on the Hungarians to rise for independence from Austria in 1809.

The internal situation in France was generally far more serious than that in its opponents, and notably so in the early 1790s. Indeed, the Revolution itself had started this process, forcing France to back down in the Nootka Sound Crisis of 1790 and thus to weaken its ally Spain in the confrontation with Britain over territorial claims on the Pacific coast of North America. In turn, the Revolutionaries were repeatedly affected by internal opposition.

Most notably, a large-scale Royalist rising in the Vendée region in 1793 was triggered by government attempts to enforce conscription. Initial Royalist success, which benefited from the advantages of fighting in wooded terrain and from the lack of troops in the region, led to brutal repression, including widespread atrocities against non-combatants, as well as the destruction of crops. More generally, the army served in France and abroad as a coercive agency of de-Christianisation, enforcing the Revolutionaries' ban on Christian practice. In contrast, underlining the ideological dimension, strong piety was linked to more explicitly anti-Revolutionary violence and to support for Royalism. The Vendéan rebels called themselves the Royal and Catholic Army. The coastal location made this particularly dangerous for the Parisian authorities as it provided the potential for maritime links with Britain. Geography, therefore, made a strategy possible. The Vendéan army was permanently about ten thousand strong, which was a small force, but it was significant both as the kernel of an episodically far larger force, and because a small number of determined troops was important in a civil war context. Furthermore, the war in the Vendée was a more serious challenge, as many of the commanders had served in the royal army.

This was a conflict of ambushes and massacres, but also of battles. The weakness of the government forces in 1792–93, a reflection of their commitment to war with Austria and Prussia, allowed the peasant insurgency to develop and spread, with major victories in late March 1793 and then again at Thouars on May 5, Saumur on June 9, Châtillon on July 5, and Vihiers on July 18. However, in turn, sixteen thousand government troops were sent to the region later in 1793: the Mainz garrison under Jean-Baptiste Kléber, which had surrendered to the Austrians and been allowed to serve again but not against other European powers. Having gained experience on campaign in Germany, they helped account for the major governmental victory at La Tremblaye near Cholet on October 15. A series of victories played the key role in defeating the insurgency, notably by hitting its morale and ending its sense of impetus and purpose, but also by reducing numbers through casualties.

The insurgents had sought to alter their axis of operation by crossing the river Loire into Brittany in October, thus making a link with the

British easier, but the latter idea was not really viable, in part due to the delays in communications, but also because deploying amphibious forces took time. Having crossed the Loire and advanced to Laval, where the government forces were defeated, the Vendéans unsuccessfully attacked Granville on November 13–14 in an attempt to gain control of a port. This failure owed much to the movement of regulars from the Cherbourg garrison. The Vendéans' soldiers rejected the decision to march to Caen, which would have established themselves in Normandy, but won a major victory at Dol on November 21 and another at La Flèche, only to be crushed at Savenay on December 23. In a reminder of the tension between urban and rural, the rebels also faced difficulties in capturing cities, especially Angers and Nantes, again a persistent problem for insurgencies: cities tended to be fortified and better defended. Atrocities by the government forces, including the execution of several thousand prisoners in Nantes in October, had spurred the rebels to activity, and if the switch by the government to a more conciliatory stance led some of the rebels to agree terms in January 1794, still, the government's emphasis in early 1794 was on a brutal repression by the "infernal columns." This repression helped crush the Vendée, and it remains a cause of bitter division to this day in France.[42]

The need for a political dimension to strategy as well as a military solution was captured in the instructions from Louis Lazare Hoche to the troops fighting the insurgents:

> Whilst swearing to wage a war to the death against those miscreants who have refused to profit from the National Convention's amnesty, the Republican troops will, however, respect the peaceful inhabitants of the region. This will enable them to distinguish between Republicans doing their duty and those detestable individuals who have chosen to follow the despicable career of robbers and murderers.[43]

Yet, this distinction proved difficult to make, not least because of the demonisation of opponents indicated by the last comment. The failure of British-backed intervention in the shape of the Quiberon expedition of June–July 1795 helped Hoche overcome the Royalists in western France in 1795–96. The expedition Royalists suffered from seriously divided command, which led to delays. Many of the Royalist prisoners were executed. A consideration of this failure alongside those of the French in Ireland in 1798 and the British in Holland in 1799 underlines the difficulties of such intervention.

Provincial opposition in France was not only mounted by Royalists. The division among the Revolutionaries that resulted in 1793 in the bloody purge of the Girondins by the rival and more radical Jacobins led, that year, to a series of revolts, especially in southern France, revolts termed "federalist" by the revolutionaries. Those in Bordeaux (and nearby), Caen and Marseille were swiftly repressed, but the opposition in Lyon and Toulon was fierce, although overcome. These revolts overlapped with counter-revolutionary activity, and much of western and southern France was in a state at least close to insurrection from 1792. Particular disturbances arose from a background of widespread instability, for radical governmental policies encouraged popular opposition. Only in 1794, with the Thermidor coup overthrowing the Jacobin government, was there a reaction at the centre against radicalism. Instead, the government became the force of propertied order, a key step on the way to stability, or at least to the lessening of opposition.

Among foreign powers, the British, as with the Toulon occupation in 1793 and the unsuccessful Quiberon expedition in 1795, put particular effort into exploiting discontent within France. This bridged peace and war because already, in 1790, when war had seemed likely during the Nootka Sound Crisis, the British had successfully intrigued with political opponents of the French government.[44] Although the governments were different, the same technique was used from the onset of conflict. This ultimately produced short-term successes for Britain, such as helping to finance the election of Royalist deputies in the French elections of 1797, but no long-term gains.[45] At the same time, such activity exacerbated divisions within France. Given the modern interest in strategies of hybrid warfare (warfare that incorporates political means), it is surprising that more attention is not devoted to the topic. Separately, the British government was divided over the wisdom of focusing on counter-revolution.

The part of European France that was regained last from rebels was Corsica, which had only been bought (from Genoa) in 1768 and conquered in 1769. Turning against France, the Corsicans requested British protection in 1793. A British fleet arrived the following year, and the French troops on the island were totally defeated, although Horatio Nelson lost an eye in the eventually successful siege of Calvi. A democratic constitution was established, with an elected Parliament and a British viceroy. There was talk of Britain being offered the crown of Corsica. However, in 1796, once Spain had joined France, the British withdrew from the Mediterranean, and the French reconquered Corsica at the end of the year.[46]

Yet again, this is a reminder of the multiplicity of players, and thus strategies, in the warfare of the period. In Corsica, the British strategy of intervention in France was most successful, albeit only in the short term, because it could use the navy to full effect and thus operate in the traditional British strategic culture of amphibious expeditionary warfare. The fate of Corsica was an instance of the way in which the Mediterranean was understood not only with reference to competing local identities, but also in terms of geopolitical axes envisaged by foreign commentators and devised by strategists in distant capitals, and with its resources, notably naval bases, used to support their strategies.

By the end of the decade, despite insurgency in 1799, notably in Brittany, France was under greater central control, and although violence continued, Napoleon's seizure of power on November 9, 1799, was not followed by the regional risings seen in 1793. Napoleon's concordat with Pope Pius VII on July 15, 1801, eased tensions with the Catholic population and thus lessened the risk of rebellion.

Nevertheless, opposition remained an issue in France, although the other powers placed far less of an emphasis on it than in the 1790s, and correctly so. Disaffection certainly continued to be significant throughout the Napoleonic regime. Conspiracy was in the background and, on October 23, 1812, Napoleon's control faced an attempted small-scale coup by Claude-François Malet, a former general, who spread the report that Napoleon had died in Russia. The misjudged coup rapidly failed, leading to the execution of the conspirators. There are comparisons (as well as contrasts) with the mishandled July 1944 bomb plot against Hitler.

More seriously, the troop numbers available to Napoleon for the Waterloo campaign in 1815 were lessened by the need to send over six thousand men, in the Army of the West, to overcome opposition in the Vendée. On June 20, two days after Waterloo, the disorganised and disunited rebels were heavily defeated at Rocheservière, which led the Royalists to agree to the Treaty of Cholet, but news of Waterloo then resulted in a new situation. The strategic implications of such commitments are apt to be underplayed, but there was a need to consider the possibility of risings even when they did not occur, for example, that a rising in the Vendée would be matched by one in Brittany.

In addition, the case of rebellion was far more acute for France due to the range of its conquests. This was the situation in parts of Italy, Spain and Germany. In Pavia in 1796, Napoleon used summary executions and the burning of villages. Such insurgencies were not new, but they became more important in 1792–1815, in part because the French Revolutionaries and Napoleon transformed, destroyed, or took over existing power structures, and also because they accelerated processes of change that much of the population already found inimical. In particular, attacks on the Church and Christian practices, let alone full-scale atheistical de-Christianisation, were far from popular, challenging as they did both established beliefs and interests and senses of order, continuity, identity and legality. So also with the pressure of meeting onerous French demands for supplies and conscripts for their army, and with seizures of goods and money. These were not made more acceptable by the incorporation of conquered areas into France nor by the establishment of client regimes.

The net effect was widespread opposition and lawlessness, with, in addition, insurgencies of various types seen across larger areas of Europe as French forces advanced, for example into Naples. The French responded, as they had done in the Vendée, with troops, which were referred to as flying columns; with the use of the *gendarmerie* (mobile armed police); and by recruiting local allies.[47] In 1798, despite what Napoleon saw as the introduction of Enlightenment policies into Malta after he seized it, the island rapidly rebelled, in large part resulting from both an insensitive treatment of the Church, which, stemming from political convictions, was always a poor strategy, and also higher taxation. Besieged in Valetta, the French garrison was unable to regain control. Responding to rebellion against the French-allied Roman Republic, one French general observed, "It is absolutely the Vendée over again,"[48] which was an instance of the more general pattern of using one campaign as a frame of reference for another.

The success of insurgencies, not least in posing a formidable challenge, could owe something to the receipt or prospect of foreign help, which made Britain the key power for aiding insurgency, as its naval readiness and wealth made such activity possible, as did its geographical position. Austria and Prussia lacked this capability, and, although Russia had a background of such support, notably in the Turkish empire and in Finland, it was less impressive than that of Britain. Indeed, the failure of Britain in this respect in 1793 was one of the most significant strategic outcomes of that decade. The British failed adequately to coordinate with French opponents of the regime, beginning what was to be a pattern. In part, this reflected British deficiencies, notably in amphibious capability, but it was also due to a prioritisation on the war in the Low Countries and the West Indies. Arguing that "feeding Toulon with troops and at the same time attempting large operations in the West Indies is quite impossible," George III and the Cabinet chose a focus on the Caribbean, even though George understood that "all attacks on France if postponed must be more difficult of execution" as the republic consolidated its power.[49] Eighty-nine thousand British and European troops in British pay were sent to the Caribbean in 1793–1801.

Separately, coastal attacks were not seen as the basis for inland operations, and the priority in Europe, as in the 1690s and 1700s, was on the main army commitment, George writing of Toulon in 1793: "I entirely agree with Major-General Abercromby that the keeping possession of that port and any others on that coast is all that ought to be attempted, no one can conceive to what an expense any inland motion will arise."[50] In 1794, George only favoured an invasion of France to aid the Royalists if it could be achieved without reducing the forces in Flanders,[51] and he became more enthusiastic about such an invasion only as a consequence of failure in the Low Countries.[52]

In part, however, rivalries among the French opposition to the republic, combined with the opposition's unreliability and habit of exaggerating its support, helped handicap the strategy. There was also a division between two areas of operation, France's Mediterranean and Atlantic coasts. In the first case, troops were sent to the major naval base of Toulon in 1793 when Royalists seized control of the city, thus thwarting French naval plans for the Mediterranean. However, aside from problems in cooperation, not least with a Spanish force, the Revolutionaries deployed significant numbers, including Napoleon, who proved a highly effective artillery commander.[53] The British intervention in Corsica in 1794 was another instance of the same strategy, but one made vulnerable by Britain's deteriorating naval position in the Mediterranean.

On the Atlantic coast, the British landing of Royalists at Quiberon Bay in 1795 was an example of a more general problem with the amphibious strategy, namely that, once landed, the mobile strike capability it offered was lost and the advantage generally switched to the defenders. So also with the British expedition against the Belgian port of Ostend in 1798: a strong wind prevented the ships from coming in to allow the troops to re-embark, French reinforcements arrived and the British were forced to surrender. Evacuation was not only a tactical and operational matter in amphibious warfare, but also a strategic one, as any failure to withdraw troops and their resulting capture reduced the numbers available for this method of attack. There was no comparison with campaigning on land.

So also in 1799 when, in concert with a Russian force, an attack was launched at the northern coast of Holland, after the islands at the mouth of the Meuse (which were to be attacked unsuccessfully in the Walcheren expedition of 1809) and the Ems estuary were both dismissed as alternatives. As launched, the 1799 attack was designed to seize the Dutch fleet, part of the strategy of naval seizure that was so significant to Britain, as with the attack on Denmark in 1807. It was also hoped to encourage an uprising against the pro-French Batavian Republic and in favour of the exiled Orangists. The warships were seized, but in other respects the expedition failed, not least in the face of the depth of defence enjoyed by the French. As in 1798 and 1809, they had the ability to bring up reinforcements.

The opportunity to do serious damage by such means was less than it had been in 1793 when the Revolution was precarious. Looked at differently, the attack on Holland in 1799, although it failed in terms of a strategy of inciting counter-revolution, nevertheless also operated as part of the coalition strategy of cumulative pressure. Indeed, as a result of the latter, the ability to maintain more than one strategy at a time was significant and can make judgement of individual aspects somewhat flawed. Moreover, the British and Russians were able to evacuate their forces successfully.

RELATIVE CAPABILITIES

The range of practice in conflict contributes to the need to consider the complexity of war-making in the 1790s, as well as, separately, the limitations of French Revolutionary forces and the extent to which they could be defeated. This scholarship is not simply a case of the revenge of the particular on the general, of detail on theory, but also raises profound questions about the way in which the image of military change frequently serves as a substitute for reality. This is a point that is also pertinent for views held in the past. Thus, alongside the oft-repeated argument of a radical break occurring with the Revolution[54] comes the extent to which the French army was already changing considerably prior to that, notably in doctrine but also in organisation, artillery and tactics. Separately, there is the extent to which Revolutionary forces often reprised earlier situations, as in the advances across southern Germany in league with Bavaria in 1704 and 1741. Moreover, having rapidly conquered Nice and Savoy (on the French side of the Alps) in 1792, the French failed, as in 1747 during the War of the Austrian Succession, to break through the Alps in the face of Sardinian and Austrian opposition. In 1796, in contrast, the French exploited the same route used in 1745 when they entered Piedmont from the south via Genoa, which was then an ally. As so often happens, elements of continuity emerge, and an understanding of the *ancien régime* military as able to deliver results is an appropriate background to an assessment of the 1790s.

In terms of transition, the indecisive War of the Bavarian Succession (1778–79) was a far shorter struggle than those involving the French Revolutionaries and Napoleon, and it only found Frederick the Great at war with one power (Austria). As a result, the implications of the decline in relative Prussian effectiveness seen in this war were not developed prior to the French Revolution. These implications serve, however, as a reminder of the difficulties of model building. French success over Prussia in 1792–95 and 1806, in contrast to its earlier failure in 1757, is frequently seen as evidence of the passing of the *ancien régime*'s system, and of its replacement by French Revolutionary warfare and its Napoleonic successor. However, this pattern of ready transference of leading position and fitness for purpose,[55] a kind of baton passing, can be queried. Thus, Austria's ability to hold off Prussian attack in 1778–79, to succeed against the Turks in 1789, and to end rebellions in Belgium and Hungary in 1790 indicates that the situation prior to the French Revolutionary Wars was much more complex.

Moreover, this situation also looks towards Austrian successes against the French in the 1790s, notably in Belgium in 1793 and in Germany in 1795 and 1796, including battles such as Wetzlar (June 15), Amberg (August 24) and Würzburg (September 3) in 1796. Furthermore, the French success in crossing the Rhine in June 1796 at Kehl, a past centre of French pressure, as with the successful siege of 1733, was not sustained. Instead, the French were pushed back to the Rhine in 1796, although putting up a good rearguard stand on the Lahn in mid-September.

Like the Russians, the Austrians displayed an impressive multiple capability, including significant numbers of troops and, in the Austrian case, plentiful logistical support. Against the French, the Austrians proved to be tough opponents, while the Russians were also repeatedly to show impressive staying power and fighting quality. For example, in 1799, the French under Jourdan were defeated by the Austrians at Ostrach (March 20–21) and, even more, Stockach (March 25) and driven back across the Rhine, as well as being initially beaten in Switzerland by the Russians, and by the Russians and Austrians at Trebbia and Novi in Italy.[56]

Separately, Napoleon's impressive victories in Egypt in 1798, which attracted attention, did not match the major Russian achievement of defeating the Turks in 1787–92 and 1806–12. The Russians, moreover, also conquered much of Poland in the early 1790s and defeated a badly prepared Sweden in 1808–9, annexing Finland as a result. Russian success in Poland indicates the degree to which revolutionaries could be defeated by *ancien régime* regulars, and provides a contrast with Brunswick's failure during his advance into France in 1792. The Polish rising in the spring of 1794 led to the driving out of Russian garrisons from Warsaw and Vilnius. However, Russian, Prussian and Austrian forces were soon able to defeat their opponents and capture all the cities. The Russian advance under Alexander Suvorov (1730–1800) proved particularly effective. Victories at Krupczyce, Terespol, Maciejowice and Kobilka in September–October 1794 were followed by the bloody capture of Warsaw in November.[57] Polish failure reflected the superior military resources of the partitioning powers, as well as the geographical vulnerability of Poland, also seen in 1939, to attack from a number of directions. Furthermore, the first two partitions, in 1772 and 1793, had already removed much of the Polish room for manoeuvre that had been enjoyed in previous years. Each war is always specific to its particular circumstances, and the same point can be made about the British defeat of an Irish rebellion in 1798, a rebellion belatedly supported by a French force that was defeated.[58] Nevertheless, the failure of Poland, which received no comparable foreign support to that in Ireland, helps contextualise French success from 1792. The contrast underlines the significance of particular political alignments and developments, notably international relations and alliance possibilities, in affecting the fate of revolutionary forces. The Poles

faced formidable opponents who could agree on ending Polish independence.

The range of the Russian military was demonstrated against the
French, albeit within the technological constraints of the period. Thus,
Alexander Korsakov's army crossed the Russian frontier on May 15,
1799, and reached Prague two months later.[59] Its average speed, at less
than fifteen miles a day, would have been cut had the troops been marching not in the summer but during spring thaw and flooding, autumn rain,
or winter snow, and in the face of opposition. The Russians had earlier
displayed a similar capability, advancing into Germany in 1716, 1735 and
1748.

In 1799, Russia entered the War of the Second Coalition against
France, and Suvorov advanced into northern Italy, the first time the Russians had operated there. His victories, especially Cassano d'Adda, Trebbia and Novi, were brutal battles in which repeated attacks finally found
weaknesses in the French position. Like Napoleon, whom he never faced
in battle, Suvorov was a believer in the tactics of attack and in campaigning through taking the initiative, and he had little time for sieges. This
provided, and reflected, a temperament and tone of warfare that was as
significant in strategy as more abstract ideas. Just as Wellington, in
1808–13, was to repeat against the French in Portugal and Spain methods
he had developed and used in India, notably against the Marathas in
1803, so Suvorov employed against the French techniques developed earlier in successful conflict with the Turks in 1773–74 and 1787–91. Willing
and able to accept a high rate of casualties and to mount costly frontal
attacks, Suvorov relied on bayonet attacks, not defensive volley firepower, and showed that an emphasis on aggression, attack and risk was not
restricted to the French. Rather than the wastage of ammunition seen
with unaimed volley fire, Suvorov preferred aimed firepower.[60]

Tactical proficiency and command skill, therefore, were far from limited to the French. The Russians were also capable of devising aggressive
tactical and operational methods. A force of marked institutional continuity, the British navy abundantly demonstrated the value of professionalism and the extent to which success was not dependent on radicalism,
in politics or in war. Furthermore, Britain showed novelty, from the introduction of an income tax to raise revenue and reduce dependence on
borrowing, to the use of slave soldiers in the Caribbean.

THE DIRECTORY

On July 27, 1794, the prospect, held out by Robespierre in a speech on July 26, of fresh purges led to the coup of Thermidor 9, named after the month in the Revolutionary calendar. Denounced in the National Convention as a tyrant, Robespierre and his close allies, including Saint-Just, were arrested at once. Declared outlaws, they were executed the following evening in the *Place de la Révolution*, with no rising mounted to save them. In the "Thermidorian Reaction," a less radical regime took their place, leading in turn, in 1795, to the creation of the Directory government. Ironically, the Thermidorians and Directory can be seen as another form of extremism, that of an extreme ideological centre. The Jacobin Clubs were closed in 1794–95, while the National Guard, which had been radical from the summer of 1792, became the force of propertied order and helped defeat uprisings in 1795, notably the insurrection of Germinal 12 (April 1), a rising of the poor in Paris, and, even more, that of Prairial 1 (May 20). Also in 1795, a "White Terror," particularly in the South, took revenge on the Jacobins. Alongside political reaction, there was a cultural turning towards elitism and against the arbitrary violence, expropriation, compulsory virtue and sobre uniformity of the Terror. There was also a return to fashions in clothes, while, in 1795, the *Place de la Révolution* was renamed the *Place de la Concorde*.

The National Convention dissolved itself in November 1795 to make way for a new constitution and regime, that of the Directory. Although a bicameral legislature and a system of checks and balances were created, real power rested among the five directors who composed the Directory, and particularly with Paul Barras.

France's success and the continuation of the war resulted in a growing intensity in the debate among her opponents about war goals. The restoration of Bourbon control in France as the key strategic goal and means was pushed hard by counter-revolutionaries such as the British commentator Edmund Burke, including in his *Letters on a Regicide Peace* (1796), but others argued that this was unrealistic and that it was necessary to become reconciled with the Revolution. The idea that domestic change within France could be accepted so long as she renounced foreign gains was not, however, credible, because not enough French politicians were willing to accept it and fight for it. Instead, war brought them benefit and ensured their power. In general, French policy did not reveal a consistent

willingness to accept limits that were acceptable to others. Indeed, the
continuation of the war encouraged fresh ambitions on the part of France,
as well as, from her opponents, a fearful desire for her defeat and for
revenge and security.

Although the Directory, which governed until November 1799, saw
both the operation of armies and the larger strategic context shifted back
towards more traditional great power politics, the directors believed,
with reason, that war was necessary in order to support the army, to
please its generals, and, for these and other reasons, to control discontent
in France. War did this in part by providing occupation for the volatile
commanders, the views and ambitions of many of whom were not limited to the conduct of war, while their strength was increased by the consequences of the *levée en masse*. Yet, victories led to pressure for further
conquests in order to satisfy political and military ambitions and exigencies, and the Directory had to support the war. It also had to deal with the
massive deficit inherited from the monarchy, as the issue of *assignats*—
paper money—had not solved the problem, because the Revolutionary
regime could not control its debts, and the *assignats* lost value in the face
of serious inflation.

The political "centre," the base of the Directory, was divided and, in
very difficult circumstances, was under challenge from both Left and
Right, and instability was accentuated by both elections and conspiracies.
In the coup of Fructidor 18 (September 4, 1797), the two moderate directors were removed by their more assertive colleagues, the Chamber was
purged of many Royalist deputies and a more Jacobin style of politics
was adopted. This "Second Directory" denied the constitutional Royalists
gains made in the elections of that March.

The different prospects offered by a Royalist France had already been
thwarted by the failure of attempts to overthrow the government in 1795,
notably with fighting in Paris on Vendémiaire 13 (October 5) in which
Napoleon employed government forces, particularly artillery, to great
effect. Far more than the reputed "whiff of grapeshot" was used to crush
the Royalists, about 1,400 of whom were killed. Napoleon benefited by
being promoted to *général de division* and soon after given command of
the French army in Italy.

Interest in peace was not pursued with great energy, but the directors
were divided over the strategy for war. In 1797, there was also division
over whether to accept the peace terms with Britain provisionally nego-

tiated by Charles Maurice de Talleyrand, the foreign minister from 1797 to 1807. Particular directors, furthermore, argued for concentration on Continental or oceanic goals, and there was also a debate over where France's German frontiers should be.

The Alsatian Jean-François Reubell, who was the most influential in foreign policy of the five directors, and an ally of Barras, sought a peace that would guarantee what were presented as natural, and therefore rational, frontiers: the Rhine and the Alps, to add to the Pyrenees which, from 1796, marked a border with an ally. Natural frontiers appeared a counterpart to the redrawing of boundaries within France, as long-lasting provinces were replaced by the new *départements* and their supposedly more rational boundaries. This rationalisation, however, also entailed a significant expansion of French power into Germany and the Low Countries. Reubell saw this as a reasonable compensation for the gains made by Austria, Prussia and Russia through the Partitions of Poland.

In northern Italy, initial French victories led to pressure for further conquest in order to satisfy political and military ambitions and exigencies. Napoleon rose to further prominence through his successful operations as commander of the French Army of Italy in 1796–97.[61] His successes contrasted with the failed French invasions across the Rhine in 1795 and 1796, and Napoleon made what was intended to be a secondary theatre, the primary one for fame, albeit in part by repeatedly defying the Directory's instructions. In a situation where military victory was a political necessity, a victorious general could seek to challenge political control. Italian rulers responded to French success, with Ferdinand III of Tuscany recognising the French Republic in 1796, and Piedmont, the pope and Naples accepting an armistice, while Venice kept neutral because the French let it think there was no risk.

With both Germany and Italy, there was no equivalent to Napoleon's successful advance into central Europe in 1805–6, nor to the defeat of the main Prussian and Russian armies. However, to judge the Revolutionaries by pointing out that Napoleon later achieved more far-flung and rapid triumphs is, in part, harsh. The situation facing the French was far more difficult in the 1790s than it was in the 1800s, and, separately, Napoleon's military position was a creation of the 1790s, indeed, a (not *the*) solution to the problems it posed.

It proved difficult for the Revolutionaries to fix success, not least because lesser powers could be swayed by intimidation by others, as in

1796–97 when Austria put successful pressure on Baden, Bavaria and Württemberg. Moreover, French occupation policy lost popular support. Nevertheless, in Italy, Napoleon managed to regain the initiative, a characteristic feature of his imaginative generalship and opportunistic approach to international politics. Marching to within seventy miles of Vienna, he forced Austria to accept the Truce of Leoben on April 18, 1797. Napoleon benefited from having defeated Piedmont in 1796, and then obliged it into providing support, including troops.

Napoleon's victories and insubordination had already destroyed the Directory's initiative, earlier in 1797, of peace on the basis of the French gain of Belgium, with the conquests of Austrian possessions in Italy returned. His victories instead ensured that the Directory, which was primarily interested in the annexation of the left bank of the Rhine (from which France was vulnerable), and which saw Italian gains as negotiable in return for Austrian consent, had to accept the Leoben terms and the accompanying French commitment to Italy. Austria agreed to cede Belgium to France, and the Milanese (Lombardy) to a newly formed French satellite republic, the Cisalpine Republic. Typically, the constitution issued for the latter in 1797 declared that sovereignty resided in the adult male population as a whole, but the vote was limited, while the legislators of the two councils, and the directors who administered the republic, were all named by Napoleon, a use of politics to forward military strategy. This was a major extension of French power, one that accorded with French policies in Italy from the late fifteenth century. The Cisalpine Republic also provided France with an allied army.

Austria, the previous ruler of the Milanese, was to receive the Veneto (Venice's possessions on the Italian mainland) in return. Venice would be compensated with Bologna, Ferrara and Romagna, territories seized by France from the Papal States in the Treaty of Tolentino of February 19, 1797. The principle of compensating victims at the expense of others, a principle established in *ancien régime* international thought but less so in practice, was now being applied with both ruthlessness and energy. Napoleon was to become a master of the technique.

The Directory, angered by Napoleon's failure to secure the left bank of the Rhine, hoped for additional gains in the Rhineland, gains that in practice cut across any idea of real compromise with Austria in Germany. French goals in Germany and Italy now represented a major shift from her recent policy. In June 1797, Napoleon remodelled much of northern

Italy into the Cisalpine and Ligurian Republics, the latter based on Genoa where the previous republican system had been far more grounded socially and culturally. This proactive position was increased by the coup of Fructidor 18 (September 4) in Paris, when, using troops, the Royalists, who had done well in the recent elections, alongside two moderate directors, Barthélemy and Carnot, were removed as their more assertive colleagues, Barras, Reubell and La Révellière, grasped control. The struggle between the directors was matched by that between the generals, and to an extent that the concept of French strategy at this point is problematic. Pichegru, Hoche and Napoleon played roles in the 1797 Fructidor coup, Pichegru being one of those arrested. This role was an aspect of a more widespread collapse of discipline that Napoleon in particular exemplified in the late 1790s. Unlike, however, generals such as Dumouriez, Napoleon kept just outside the bounds of treason, although, in part, that reflected the combination of luck and circumstances.

To avoid the resumption of war, Austria was obliged to accept the Treaty of Campo Formio on October 18, 1797. The location of the treaty's signing, at a village near Udine, in what is now northeast Italy, from which an advance could be launched on Vienna, was a testimony to the range of Napoleon's advance. France's gain of the Ionian Islands, Venetian Albania, the major north Italian military base of Mantua, and the prospect of most of the left bank of the Rhine, as well as Austrian recognition for the Cisalpine Republic, exceeded the hopes of Louis XIV and Louis XV. France was left the dominant power in Italy and Germany, although Austria, in turn, received Venice, the Veneto, Salzburg, and the likelihood that it would benefit from the congress that would be held to negotiate peace between France and the Holy Roman Empire. The cession of the Republic of Venice to Austria was condemned by the Jacobins as a betrayal of revolutionary ideals. In strategic terms, this cession was not to prevent later French expansion, but, in practice, a measure of strategic depth was provided for Austria. As with the earlier unfulfilled plan for the exchange of Belgium for Bavaria, Austria gained a closer area at the cost of one that was more difficult to defend, but, due to the loss of Lombardy, the front line of any defence against French advance in and via Italy was now closer to Austria.

The congress, held at Rastatt, agreed to the cession of the left bank of the Rhine to France, with the secular rulers compensated at the expense of the ecclesiastical states, the terms outlined by Napoleon when he visited Rastatt in November 1797. As the ecclesiastical states had been great supporters of the imperial system, these terms augured the end of the Holy Roman Empire and thus helped to create a vacuum beyond the Rhine. The terms also exemplified the process of seeking the support of the defeated at the expense of others, the technique of divide and rule that the French, and notably Napoleon, were to employ so successfully.

Although there was a popular desire for peace within France, this was not the end of French expansion. Military convenience, lust for loot, the practice of expropriation,[62] ideological conviction, the political advantages of a successful campaign and strategic opportunism all encouraged aggressive action, both before and after Campo Formio. Key instances were with the occupations of Venice in 1797, the Papal States in February 1798, Malta in June 1798 and Piedmont in December 1798 and the invasion of Switzerland in February 1798.

NAVAL STRATEGY

The major expansion in Europe's navies in the 1780s was a background to the naval conflicts that began in 1793, but by then politics was already affecting the equations of naval strength. France had permanently handicapped itself in the naval war by the self-inflicted injuries of the Revolution. Half of its 1789 naval officer corps fled abroad, and many joined the Royalist forces, some being executed when captured after the failure of the Quiberon Bay expedition in 1795.

Moreover, thirteen ships of the line and eight frigates were lost when Toulon, France's naval base on the Mediterranean, sought British protection in 1793. In addition, twelve more ships of the line were disabled during the evacuation, and their repairs were delayed by the destruction of the arsenal's naval stores. So also with the Atlantic fleet based in Brest. It mutinied in 1793 and order was restored by terror. This did not bring victory. In the battle of the Glorious First of June 1794, although the merchantmen bringing American grain to France were able to complete their voyage, the French lost seven ships of the line, while three more were badly damaged. In contrast, no British vessel was lost, and the British also suffered fewer than one hundred casualties compared to over five thousand French ones. This was serious, as experienced sailors and navies were harder to replace than troops. In just over a year, France had lost much of its fleet. Moreover, thanks to the Revolution, professional disagreements in the French navy were given debilitating ideological significance.[63]

France's ability thereafter to drive opponents out of the war, however, had major consequences for fleet strength and the strategic context of naval warfare. This was in part a motivation of the policy, although it is important to be cautious about assuming a cohesion and clear pattern in French strategy. For Britain, the naval situation markedly deteriorated as France overran the Netherlands (1795) and forced Spain into alliance (1796). There was now a threat that Britain's opponents would combine their naval power to cover an invasion: combined, they enjoyed numerical superiority over the British. So also at the level of individual ports. Thus, Napoleon's occupation of Livorno, the major Tuscan port, closed it to the British. Cooperation with Spain also eased France's position in Italy, although the key element for the Italian Bourbon Duke Ferdinand of Parma was the proximity of French forces, which indeed occupied part of his territory from 1796. The Bourbon branch in Naples proved more difficult, as there were then no French forces in Naples, which also felt protected by the buffer of the Papal States.

The British strategic response to France's expanding alliance system, and notably cooperation with the Dutch and Spanish navies, was that of a refocus. There was a withdrawal of the navy from the Mediterranean in 1796, instead using Lisbon as a base. As a result, in 1797, Britain could not mount a response when France invaded Venice, seizing its navy and its bases in the Ionian Isles, such as Corfu. Moreover, the British garrison on the island of Elba was evacuated.

Separately, but as a reminder of the significance of domestic factors in absolute (and therefore also relative) strategic capability, the strategic possibilities for the French were greatly accentuated by the British naval mutinies of April–June 1797 in the Channel and North Sea fleets. Dissatisfaction over conditions, especially pay, provided a fertile basis for political discontent, which led to a blockade of the Thames, but also to an erosion of support within the navy as the mutiny became more extreme. Ultimately, the mutinies were brought to an end, and did not prevent a British naval victory at Camperdown over the Dutch on October 11, when, without losing any ships, the British captured eleven Dutch ships, nine of which were ships of the line. However, in the meanwhile, the situation had appeared highly uncertain. The dominance of Britain at sea appeared precarious, and with that, Europe's current oceanic situation. This was the most serious crisis for Britain during the entire period.

The British meanwhile prepared a strategy of total war as the response to any invasion. The flavour of attitudes can be seen from a 1796 memorandum from Major General David Dundas, later commander-in-chief of the army:

> When an enemy lands, all the difficulties of civil government and the restraint of forms cease; every thing must give way to the supplying and strengthening [of] the army, repelling the enemy . . . the strongest and most effectual measures are necessary. . . . The great object must be constantly to harass, alarm and fire on an enemy, and to impede his progress till a sufficient force assembles to attack him. . . . Every inch of ground, every field may to a degree be disputed, even by inferior numbers. . . . The country must be driven, and every thing useful within his reach destroyed without mercy.[64]

The French mishandled their strategic possibilities. In part, there was the problem of coordination with allies, which was always difficult, as France and Spain had demonstrated against Britain both in 1744 and 1779. Even for France alone, there was the problem, seen in 1759, of the coordination between her Atlantic and Mediterranean fleets, one that was to be fully demonstrated in the 1805 Trafalgar campaign. In 1797, separate defeats were imposed on Spanish and Dutch fleets, at Cape St. Vincent (February 14) and Camperdown (October 11), the former ending a Spanish attempt to join a Cadiz fleet to France's Brest one and thus acquire a key mass. That September, British peace negotiations with the French at Lille failed, but a sense of public joy was shown that December when a Naval Thanksgiving was held in St. Paul's Cathedral, with naval flags paraded through the streets by sailors. This was strategy as performance.[65] In 1798, a French fleet was crushed in the Mediterranean in Aboukir Bay in the Battle of the Nile (August 1–2), and a French squadron was to be heavily defeated off Ireland in the Battle of Tory Island (October 12). Moreover, in the 1790s, the French navy persistently suffered from major shortages of construction, materials, money and sailors.

The effectiveness of British naval power is usually discussed with reference to France, but was more significant for Spain, and thus for France's ability to run an alliance system accordingly. The battle of Cape St. Vincent was matched by Britain capturing Trinidad from Spain, while the blockade of transatlantic trade hit Spanish government finances hard, leading to increased debt and borrowing. Camperdown left the British dominant in the North Sea and affected French strategic possibilities in British home waters as well as the possibility of gaining support from the Baltic naval powers.

Mass and coordination were common elements on land and sea, but also operated differently. British squadrons also were not united into just one fleet, but they handled the resulting need to operate across a number of seas more successfully than their opponents. In part, this was a matter of superior fighting quality, but a key element was the strategic experience enjoyed by the Admiralty. This was the most sophisticated strategic powerhouse in the world at this point, one with institutional cohesion, an effective interaction of direction and delegation, a first-rate intelligence system and global range. The British also benefited greatly from their experience and understanding of the constraints and frictions of naval warfare; from an effective naval infrastructure, notably in logistics;[66] from the ability to raise most of their large naval manpower without impressment (conscription); and from the lack of allies at sea with whom it was necessary to combine. This was a continuation of the situation for Britain in the Seven Years' War (1756–63) and the War of American Independence (1775–83), one that underlined continuities in strategic context and means.

In work on this period, the naval dimensions of strategy are apt to be treated as secondary to those of land warfare; but that is questionable, not least if the significance of the maritime sphere is considered, in particular its global resonance and its integrative power. In the short, medium and long terms, naval supremacy allowed Britain not only to capture the bases of other colonial powers, but also both to develop new colonies in areas with low population density, such as Australia, and to wage war with native rulers in India with only limited interference from France. Naval strength and colonial power were the basis of Britain's ability to sustain its own war effort and to provide support to allies. Indeed, Britain devoted a formidable effort to retaining its Caribbean colonies and to capturing, or at least neutering and containing, those of France and, later, its allies.[67] George III responded in 1793 to the capture of Tobago: "Now is the hour to humble France, for nothing but her being disabled from disturbing other countries whatever government may be established there will keep her quiet."[68]

CONCLUSION

As an ironic counterpoint to French problems, one that also throws light on the broad range of strategy, the Revolution sought to impose a new pattern of knowledge, one that conquered time and space. A republican calendar was introduced in 1793. Dating the year retrospectively from the start of the republic in September 1792, with each year commencing at the autumn equinox, the new calendar also changed the weeks and months of the year and decimalised the hours and minutes of the day, linking the reform to the adoption of new decimal weights and measures.[69]

Meanwhile, in 1790, the National Assembly had adopted a report proposing uniform weights and measures based on an invariable model taken from nature, with the proposed basic unit as a universal measure being the length of a pendulum with a half period of one second at latitude 45 degrees, midway between the equator and the North Pole. The following March, there was a move from global to French data: the metre was chosen as one ten-millionth of the distance from the North Pole to the equator, as determined from the measurement of an arc of the meridian of Paris between Dunkirk and Barcelona. A survey was accordingly conducted in 1792–98 by Jean-Baptiste Delambre and Pierre Méchain, two eminent astronomers. They set off in opposite directions from Paris in order, by means of triangulation, to measure the distance of the arc. Political instability and war, notably with Spain, led the mission to take much longer than the anticipated year. Its attempt to implement a French schema was also revealed to be seriously flawed. The Malaspina expedition sent round the world by Charles IV of Spain in 1789–94 had made observations of gravity that confirmed that the earth was not symmetrical, as a pendulum revealed a stronger gravitational pull in the Southern Hemisphere, which corroborated the observations of Nicolas-Louis de la Caille at the Cape of Good Hope in 1750–52. The expedition revealed a different strength of gravity, length of pendulum, and curvature of the earth for every location at which observations were taken.

Thus, the French premise that the Meridian of Paris was the same as every other was misguided, and indeed the 1792–98 survey confirmed the irregularity. Because the world is not a perfect sphere, meridians vary in detail. The standard metre, adopted in 1799 by an international body convened in Paris, was not strictly accurate. Napoleon made the metre compulsory in 1801, but the 1799 metre was to be replaced by another that left out any reference to the shape of the earth.[70] Somehow, the revenge of its irregularity was all too apposite as an image for French strategy.

NOTES

1. Tim Blanning, *The Origins of the French Revolutionary Wars* (Harlow: Longman, 1986).

2. *AP.* 37, 491–93.

3. Robert Jenkinson, later 2nd Earl of Liverpool, to his father, Charles, Lord Hawkesbury, July 25, 1792, Oxford, Bodleian Library, Bland Burges papers, 37 fol. 62.

4. Auckland to Thomas, 7th Earl of Elgin, August 18, 1792, Broomhall, Fife, Elgin papers, 60/1/106.

5. Auckland to Alexander Straton, October 9, 1792, Ipswich, East Suffolk, CRO. 239/2/283.

6. Grenville to Ostervald, British envoy in Lisbon, January 9, 1793, NA. FO. 63/16.

7. Walpole to Francis, 5th Duke of Leeds, Foreign Secretary, September 19, 1789, April 13, 1791, Walpole to Grenville, July 23, August 29, September 24, 1791, May 23, June 9, 20, 1792, NA. FO. 63/12, 14–15.

8. Walpole to Leeds, November 25, 1780, NA. FO. 63/12.

9. Walpole to Leeds, December, 5, 10, 24, 1789, April 28, 1790, NA. FO. 63/12–13.

10. AE. CP. Ang. 583 fol. 26.

11. AE. CP. Ang. 583 fols 171–72.

12. *AP* 53, 472–74; Marc Bouloiseau, "L'Organisation de l'Europe selon Brissot et les Girondins, à la fin de 1792," *Annales historiques de la révolution française* 57 (1985): 290–94.

13. Pitt to Grenville, November 11, 1792, BL. Add. 58906 fols 144–45; Townshend to John Blofeld, November 11, 1792, Bod. Ms. Eng. Lett. C.144 fol. 274; Clive Emsley, "The London 'Insurrection' of December 1792: Fact, Fiction, or Fantasy," *Journal of British Studies* 17 (1978): 66–86.

14. George to Dundas, July 1, 7, September 13, October 6, 1794, BL. Add. 40100 fols 131, 133, 137, 141; George to Grenville, November 11, 19, 1794, BL. Add. 58858 fols 100, 107.

15. George to Grenville, April 17, 1795, BL. Add. 58859 fol. 11.

16. AE. CP. Espagne 629 fols 283, 296–97, 355, 376.

17. Bradford Perkins, *The First Rapprochement: England and the United States, 1795–1805* (Philadelphia, PA: University of Pennsylvania Press, 1955).

18. George to Dundas, October 11, 1795, BL. Add. 40100 fol. 157.

19. George to Grenville, June 7, 1795, BL. Add. 58859 fol. 18.

20. George to Grenville, November 30, 1795, BL. Add. 58859 fol. 42.

21. Heathcote to Grenville, August 9, 1796, NA. FO. 154/1.

22. James Riley, *The Seven Years' War and the Old Regime in France: The Economic and Financial Toll* (Princeton, NJ: Princeton University Press, 1987), 78–79, 103.

23. Ute Planert, "Innovation or Evolution? The French Wars in Military History," in *War in an Age of Revolution, 1775–1815*, ed. Roger Chickering and Stig Förster (Cambridge: Cambridge University Press, 2010), 84.

24. John Olsen and Martin van Creveld, eds., *The Evolution of Operational Art from Napoleon to the Present* (Oxford: Oxford University Press, 2011).

25. Karl Roider, *Baron Thugut and Austria's Response to the French Revolution* (Princeton, NJ: Princeton University Press, 1987), 153–54.

26. Graham to Grenville, January 16, 1797, NA. FO. 43/2.

27. Rory Muir, *Salamanca 1812* (New Haven, CT: Yale University Press, 2001), xi, 141.

28. Ian Robertson, *An Atlas of the Peninsular War* (New Haven, CT: Yale University Press, 2010).

29. Eman Vovsi, "'Brevet to the Scaffold or to Glory': The High Command of the French Army and Revolutionary Government, 1792–94," *Napoleonic Scholarship*, no. 4 (November 2011): 142–53.

30. Roger Blaufarb, *The French Army, 1750–1820: Careers, Talent, Merit* (Manchester: Manchester University Press, 2003).

31. Ken Alder, *Engineering the Revolution: Arms and Enlightenment in France, 1763–1815* (Princeton, NJ: Princeton University Press, 1997).

32. Notes of conversation with Carnot by M. Bornes, March 1798, Historical Manuscripts Commission, *Dropmore Papers*, 4:150.

33. Peter Wetzler, *War and Subsistence: The Sambre and Meuse Army in 1794* (New York: Peter Lang, 1985); Alan Forrest, "The Logistics of Revolutionary War in France," in *War in an Age of Revolution, 1775–1815*, ed. Roger Chickering and Stig Förster, 177–96 (Cambridge: Cambridge University Press, 2010); Jordan Hayworth, *Revolutionary France's War of Conquest in the Rhineland* (Cambridge: Cambridge University Press, 2019).

34. Tim Blanning, *The French Revolution in Germany: Occupation and Resistance in the Rhineland, 1792–1802* (Oxford: Oxford University Press, 1983), and *The French Revolutionary Wars, 1787–1802* (London: Longman, 1996), 158–69.

35. Alexander Grab, "The Politics of Finance in Napoleonic Italy, 1802–1814," *Journal of Modern Italian Studies* 3, no. 2 (1998): 127–43.

36. NAM. 1975-09-62-1.

37. William Cobbett, ed., *Parliamentary History of England* 33 (London, 1818), cols 226–27.

38. A. J. Reinermann, "The Papacy, Austria, and the Anti-French Struggle in Italy, 1792–1797," in *Austria in the Age of the French Revolution, 1789–1815*, ed. Kinley Brauer and William Wright, 47–68 (Minneapolis: Center for Austrian Studies, University of Minnesota, 1990).

39. Paddy Griffith, *The Art of War of Revolutionary France, 1789–1802* (London: Greenhill, 1998).

40. David Bell, *The Cult of the Nation in France: Inventing Nationalism, 1680–1800* (Cambridge, MA: Harvard University Press, 2001).

41. Alan Forrest, *The Soldiers of the French Revolution* (Durham, NC: Duke University Press, 1990), and *Napoleon's Men: The Soldiers of the Revolution and Empire* (London: Hambledon Continuum, 2002).

42. Rob Harper, *Fighting the French Revolution: The Great Vendée Rising of 1793* (Philadelphia, PA: Pen and Sword, 2019).

43. Jonathan North, "General Hoche and Counterinsurgency," *Journal of Military History* 67 (2003): 532.

44. Charles Miles, ed., *The Correspondence of William Augustus Miles on the French Revolution, 1789–1817*, 2 vols. (London: Longmans, Green, 1890), 1:150–71.

45. Harvey Mitchell, *The Underground War against Revolutionary France: The Missions of William Wickham, 1794–1800* (Oxford: Oxford University Press, 1965); Maurice Hutt, *Chouannerie and Counter-Revolution: Puisaye, the Princes and the British Government* (Cambridge: Cambridge University Press, 1983).

46. Desmond Gregory, *The Ungovernable Rock: A History of the Anglo-Corsican Kingdom and Its Role in Britain's Mediterranean Strategy during the Revolutionary War, 1793–1797* (Toronto: Associated University Presses, 1985).

47. Michael Broers, *Napoleon's Other War: Bandits, Rebels and Their Pursuers in the Age of Revolutions* (Witney: Peter Lang, 2010).

48. Ricky Parrish, "Jacques Étienne Macdonald: Military Administration in the Roman Republic, 1798," *Consortium, 1996,* 201.

49. George to Dundas, November 16, 1793, George to Grenville, December 1, 1794, BL. Add. 40100 fol. 103, 58858 fol. 114; Michael Duffy, *Soldiers, Sugar and Seapower. The British Expeditions to the West Indies and the War against Revolutionary France* (Oxford: Oxford University Press, 1987), 320.

50. George to Dundas, November 16, 1793, BL. Add. 40100 fol. 105.

51. George to Grenville, September 13, 1794, BL. Add. 58858 fol. 83.

52. Memorandum by George of November 30, enclosed with George to Grenville, December 1, 1794, BL. Add. 58858 fol. 113.

53. Bernard Ireland, *The Fall of Toulon: The Last Opportunity to Defeat the French Revolution* (London: Weidenfeld and Nicolson, 2005).

54. David Bell, *The First Total War: Napoleon's Europe and the Birth of War as We Know It* (Boston: Houghton Mifflin, 2007).

55. John Lynn, "The Evolution of Army Style of the Eighteenth Century," *War and Society* 2 (1984): 23–41, and "The Evolution of Army Style in the Modern West, 800–2000," *International History Review* 18 (1996): 505–45.

56. Gunther Rothenberg, *Napoleon's Great Adversaries: The Archduke Charles and the Austrian Army, 1792–1814* (Bloomington: Indiana University Press, 1982); Lee Eysturlid, *The Formative Influences, Theories, and Campaigns of the Archduke Carl of Austria* (Westport, CT: Greenwood, 2000).

57. Jerzy Lukowski, *The Partitions of Poland, 1772, 1793, 1795* (Harlow: Longman, 1999), 163–74; Richard Butterwick, *The Polish-Lithuanian Commonwealth, 1733–1795: Light and Flame* (New Haven, CT: Yale University Press, 2020), 361–62.

58. Dáire Keogh and Nicholas Furlong, eds., *The Mighty Wave: The 1798 Rebellion in Wexford* (Dublin: Four Courts Press, 1996).

59. Lieutenant Colonel John Ramsay, British Commissary with Korsakov, to Grenville, July 14, 1799, BL. Add. 63819 fol. 2.

60. Bruce Menning, "The Imperial Russian Army, 1725–1796," in *The Military History of Tsarist Russia,* ed. Frederick Kagan and Robin Higham (Basingstoke: Palgrave, 2002), 73.

61. Virgilio Ilari, Piero Crociani, and Ciro Paoletti, *La Guerra delle Alpi, 1792–1796* (Rome: Ufficio storico dello Stato maggiore dell'Esercito, 2000).

62. Cynthia Saltzman, *Plunder: Napoleon's Theft of Veronese's Feast* (New York: Farrar, Straus and Giroux, 2021).

63. William Cormack, *Revolution and Political Conflict in the French Navy, 1789–1794* (Cambridge: Cambridge University Press, 1995).

64. Dundas, memorandum, October–, 1796, BL. Add. 59280 fols 189–92.

65. Gillian Russell, *The Theatres of War: Performance, Politics and Society, 1793–1815* (Oxford: Oxford University Press, 1995).

66. James Davey, *The Transformation of British Naval Strategy: Seapower and Supply in Northern Europe, 1808–1812* (Woodbridge: Boydell and Brewer, 2012).

67. Duffy, *Soldiers, Sugar and Seapower*.

68. George to Dundas, June 1, 1793, BL. Add. 40100 fol. 79.

69. Matthew Shaw, *Time and the French Revolution: The Republican Calendar, 1789–Year XIV* (Woodbridge: Boydell and Brewer, 2011).

70. Ken Alder, *The Measure of Things: The Seven-Year Odyssey That Transformed the World* (New York: Simon and Schuster, 2002); Robert King, "Finding the Figure of the Earth: The Malaspina Expedition (1789–1794)," *Hydrographic Journal* 119 (January 2006): 25–29.

FOUR

To Global Strategies, 1798–1803

Our navy keeps every one of our enemies bound in chains upon their own coasts.

—Geoffrey Mowbray, 1798[1]

Once in command of the invasion of Egypt in 1798, Napoleon revealed the full extent of the militarisation of French strategy and diplomacy, notably an absence of the sense of mutual understanding that is crucial to the successful operation of an international system. The end of the War of the First Coalition in 1797, with Britain left in isolation, had not been followed by France seeking to stabilise a new order, internationally or domestically. In part, the problem, as for the English Parliament in the late 1640s after the Civil War, was that an army had been created that could not be demobilised. In functional terms, it had to be found new tasks, but taking that view means downplaying the undoubted significance of the ethos of violence which continued important to the Revolutionary identity. Moreover, the Fructidor coup of September 4, 1797, was a move for continued militarisation and violence. Unstable domestically, France could scarcely create a stable international order.

In 1798, the French proved particularly expansionist in Italy, where the Army of Rome was formed to suppress an anti-French rising, but also at the expense of the Swiss Confederation. This aggressiveness sought to sustain the Revolution by creating a series of friendly buffers, notably in the form of "sister republics," the Parthenopean, Roman, Cisalpine, Helvetian and Batavian. The new order in the Papal States permitted France to control the major Adriatic port of Ancona, which provided a port,

71

accessible from France via Lombardy and Emilia-Romagna, from which pressure could be exerted in the eastern Mediterranean.

Napoleon erroneously assumed that the Turks, the imperial overlords of effectively autonomous Egypt, could be readily intimidated or bribed into accepting French action, in short that they could be treated like Austria in Italy. Furthermore, Napoleon's sense of grandiloquence and autonomy, and his belief that both French policy and the Orient were designed to serve his views, emerged from his recollection:

> In Egypt, I found myself freed from the obstacles of an irksome civilization. I was full of dreams. . . . I saw myself founding a religion, marching into Asia, riding an elephant, a turban on my head and in my hand the new Koran that I would have composed to suit my needs.[2]

Seeking a strategic continuity with Alexander the Great, Napoleon had also imbibed the Jacobin ideology towards religion, that of creating a new, supposedly rational, one.

Reality, as so often with Napoleon, was to prove otherwise. Napoleon's cultural supposition of superiority, his arrogance of power[3] and a total absence of situational awareness[4] that prefigured his failure in Russia in 1812, led to a lack of sensitivity that caused Sultan Selim III to declare war. Indeed, Napoleon's large-scale expedition to Egypt proved a major strategic gamble. In July 1797, the month in which he became foreign minister, Talleyrand, had told the *Institut de France* that the Egyptian expedition would lead to a conquest of India, a possibility that had attracted particular interest from the early 1780s, although one that was quite beyond French capability. Nevertheless, Napoleon asked Piveron de Morlat, who had served as French agent in Mysore in 1778–86, to join his staff in Egypt. Napoleon's secretary, Louis Antoine Fauvelet de Bourrienne, thought that the general wished to repeat the triumphs of Alexander the Great by marching overland against India.

Napoleon's expedition was the first successful amphibious invasion of Egypt since that of the Romans and contrasted with the total French failure against Egypt under Louis IX, St. Louis, in 1249–50, as well as with recent Spanish failures against Algiers in 1775 and 1784. Napoleon's victories in Egypt and his capture of Alexandria and Cairo, all in 1798, certainly underlined the vulnerability of powerful centres of the Islamic world, one to which Constantinople was nearly exposed by the British fleet in 1807. Whether this capability contributed to a coherent French strategy was far less clear; but the expedition certainly revealed a volatility in power politics that suggested new opportunities and needs for strategic insight and planning.

The conflicts at the same time in southern and northern India and in Persia indicated the broader scope of the volatility in power politics, as well as providing a way to contextualise Napoleon's strategies. In particular, although apt in his arrogance to see himself as the prime mover, Napoleon in 1798–99 was not the only dynamic force in the Islamic world. The activities of Agha Muhammad of Persia (r. 1779–97) and of Zaman Shah of Afghanistan (r. 1793–1800) demonstrate the extent to which the personal and family strategies they pursued, and the tribal contexts in which they operated, were not residual features. In Persia, the late 1780s and early 1790s saw the Qajar tribe under Agha Muhammad take over, destroying the previously dominant Zand. In a fashion similar to disunity among the anti-French powers, this process was helped by Zand disunity, which in turn was accentuated by failure. The capital, Isfahan, was captured in 1785, the cities of Shiraz and Kirman following in 1792 and 1794. Agha Muhammad also sought to reconquer former Persian territories and to assert sovereignty, which he did in Georgia in 1795 and Khurusan (in northeast Persia) in 1796. His threat to Afghanistan in 1799, including backing Zaman's rebellious brothers, a threat encouraged by Britain but not dependent on it, ended the possibility that Zaman Shah would advance across northern India defeating Britain's protégés.[5] Thus, albeit to a highly autonomous degree, Persia became part of the world of British power politics, not in order to affect Turkey, as in past Western strategic planning, but as part of a wider policy of security for India, one frequently discussed by the British in terms of the confrontation with Russia in the "Great Game." France proved less successful in affecting, still more determining, the power politics of the region than Britain.

To take another ruler of the period who was more successful than Napoleon, Nguyen Anh, from a base around the Mekong delta, conquered all of Vietnam by 1802 and proclaimed himself Emperor Gia-Long, holding the position until his death in 1820 and creating a dynasty that continued until the monarchy came to an end in the mid-twentieth century. Ironically, he had benefited from French help following a treaty in 1787, and, however modest, this assistance outlasted the *ancien régime*. In Siam, Chakri, a general, staged a successful coup in 1782 and became ruler as Rama I, ruling until 1809 and successfully thwarting major attacks by Myanmar. He also established a new dynasty, one that has lasted to the present.

Longevity is not the sole measure of strategic success, although it is a good one. The question whether there was any strategic purpose to Napoleon's invasion of Egypt in 1798, one of the most dramatic episodes in his career, emphasises the issue of "whose strategy?" He had been thinking of Egypt while in Italy in 1797, and this led to his interest then in France acquiring the Ionian Islands (from Venice) and Malta, which seemed the stepping stones to Egypt. Napoleon was later to write about Julius Caesar, who clearly interested him as a republican general of would-be destiny.[6] For Napoleon, rather like Caesar when invading England in 55 and 54 BCE, concerned with keeping his army together as a means of personal power, and not interested in the Directory's risky idea of an invasion of Britain, the expedition fulfilled a key purpose while also enabling him to evade the unwelcome control of the Directory and providing him with the excitement of combat, the apparent prospect of success, the opportunity to win fame and the means to further a domestic political angle.

In practice, however, the expedition exposed a portion of the French military to the strength of the British navy, and such that the army, with the supporting French fleet annihilated at the Battle of the Nile, was left vulnerable. Unwelcome both militarily and politically, this was poor practice for an amphibious assault on Britain and a permanent loss of strength for the French navy, one that was not worth it. The loss helped make the Egyptian expedition a strategic folly, and to an extraordinary extent. Even had there been no naval defeat for France, Egypt was not a promising environment for an army without any experience of operating there, militarily or politically. Aside from disease, the logistical task was formidable, and the defenders considerable. There was also the question of how best to anchor any success politically.

There was no viable route by land from Egypt to India, or really for the French by sea to India, and not least because in 1795, in a key strategic blow, the British seized the Dutch base at Cape Town. The following year, a Dutch fleet of three ships of the line and four frigates, en route to the Indian Ocean, was forced to surrender at Saldanha Bay in Cape Colony, and the warships and most of the crew were taken into British service. A French frigate squadron was able to sail to Mauritius in 1796, but it achieved little and its remnants were destroyed there by the British in December 1799.

Napoleon's notion of beginning a partition of the Turkish empire, while less unviable than that of reaching India, was seriously flawed. There was little reason to anticipate Turkey yielding or Russia accepting such a course. Moreover, his rapid success in battle did not end resistance in Egypt in 1798–99 or the Near East.

The focus on Napoleon is ironic, as a more impressive strategic achievement in 1798–99 was that of countering him. This was a matter in part of the British naval movements in 1798 and the successful British-backed resistance to Napoleon's siege of Acre in March–May 1799. Napoleon had earlier failed to win the alliance of Ahmad Pasha al-Jazzar, the Acre-based governor of the provinces of Sidon and Damascus, and he proved a resolute defender of Acre.

The British had sent a fleet back into the Mediterranean in 1798, in part thanks to their naval victories in 1797, which, indicating the cumulative nature of strategic possibilities, expanded their naval possibilities. The dispatch of the fleet served a variety of strategic goals, both commercial and political, not least trying to persuade Austria to rejoin the war. The fleet was not only hugely important to the conflict in Egypt and the Near East. The British fleet also gained another strategic front, one that challenged the French in Italian waters and Italy. French successes there on land, however, helped offset this situation.

On the part of others, there was no sense that France had found limits, which helped impel the formation of the Second Coalition in 1798. By January 1799, it included Austria, Britain, Naples, Russia and Turkey. This was a membership very different to the First Coalition, as Prussia, Spain and the Netherlands were not involved. In a major continuance of *ancien régime* practice, British subsidies greatly encouraged the process of coalition formation, for the funding of the larger armies made necessary by international competition was a strategic requirement of the period.[7] Indeed, this brings to the fore an issue in assessment, that of the relationship between strategic means and goals. The provision of funds was an aspect of both, but the emphasis varies depending on the degree to which the very maintenance of an army is seen as the goal as well as a means. For France, this was more so than some of the strategic discussion might suggest.

As always, the political context was central, but in a variety of ways. Crucially, it led to a resumption of the large-scale warfare that made stabilisation impossible. To a degree, this was due to the failure to extend the peacemaking of 1797 to include Britain, which helped ensure that British strategy came to the fore, in this case the need for a new coalition against France.[8] At the same time, the circumstances characteristically displayed a situation of multiple agency, with the new coalition divided and uncertain, while Prussia refused to join either side. Given the significance of the Prussian army and Prussia's exposure to Russian pressure, this was particularly important to any coalition directed against France and, indeed, remained a major weakness until 1813; as in 1806 (and exemplifying the problem of creating a cohesive opposition to France), Prussia only joined in against France after Austria was defeated, which contributed greatly to the sequential character of French war-making. The other powers used the war to pursue their own strategic objectives, and this repeatedly provided France with opportunities, but cooperation between Russia and Turkey, leading to and following an alliance signed on January 3, 1799, was a real strategic discontinuity.

The Second Coalition against France did very well initially in 1799. The French were repeatedly hit hard in southern Germany, Switzerland and, in particular, Italy, while Napoleon's army was isolated in the Middle East. Rulers that might have turned to France were brought into line by the Second Coalition, notably Bavaria and Württemberg by the Austrian advance. Moreover, the maritime challenge to the British navy had already been heavily defeated in 1797–98. Each of these were individually impressive, but the collective achievement was important, both in creating a sense of failure within France and in taking away the advantages, particularly logistical, gained by advancing into opposing territory.

A range of military means was used by the Allies. For example, the Royal Navy played a major role in forcing the French out of southern Italy. Encouraged by the British, Ferdinand IV of Naples had joined the anti-French camp in 1798, invading the Roman Republic on November 23, his forces, in a strategy of forward defence, briefly driving the French from Rome. However, the Neapolitans had attacked before Austria was ready and willing to fight. As a result, the French were able to concentrate on Naples. That December, the poorly supplied Neapolitans were defeated at Civita Castellana on December 6 and pushed back. Ferdinand fled to Palermo on Nelson's flagship, while Anglo-Neapolitan forces burned the Neapolitan fleet to prevent the French from seizing it.

The fate of monarchs was of major consequence because of the significance of monarchical legitimacy to the identity of states and thus to their capacity for continued struggle. This point is a reminder that functional or realist interpretations of strategy have to allow for the values and practice of the age. So also, for example, for Napoleon's subsequent control of the papacy and his resulting ability to use it both to help consolidate his position in France and to play a greater role in Italian politics in the early 1800s.

In a reminder of the very different types of conflict involved in the warfare of the period, Naples was left in 1798 with a four-way struggle between the Royalists, the advancing French, the *giacobini* (Italian Jacobins) and the *lazzaroni* (the poor who were in favour of revolutionary ideas, but not of French troops). The *giacobini* and *lazzaroni* fought each other in January 1799 in street fighting that cost over four thousand lives, before the French and *giacobini* enforced control.

The political and the military were intertwined in the subsequent strategy of the Parthenopean Republic, the satellite regime established in Naples by the French on January 26, 1799. It introduced republican and atheistic celebrations as well as freedom of religion, a programme which won few allies in markedly Catholic Naples; refused to employ anyone who had served the king; and could not cope with shortages of bread and firewood. In Naples, France had a forward Mediterranean base alongside, and in support of, Napoleon's forces in Egypt, but the base was insecure. Cardinal Fabrizio Dionigi Ruffo formed the *Santa Fede* (Holy Faith) Army in Sicily in January 1799; landed in Calabria, the southernmost part of the mainland, on February 8; and started reconquering the kingdom of Naples, marching on the capital. In addition, in an unprecedented step that reflected the degree to which the war was creating new alliances, a thirty-two-thousand-man Russo-Turkish expeditionary force with forty men of war captured Corfu on March 3. The Russians then arrived on the Adriatic coast of Italy, landed in lower Apulia, and marched north, capturing the cities of Taranto and Foggia, before moving west and capturing Ariano, Avellino and Nola. At the same time, an Anglo-Sicilian force threatened Naples. On April 15, five hundred Sicilian loyalists were landed from British ships, together with British forces, seizing Castellammare di Stabia and its naval arsenal. A second Anglo-

Sicilian force landed south of Naples at Salerno (where the Allies were to land in 1943) and approached Naples, seizing en route the towns of Vietri, Cava, Citara, Pagani and Nocera. Although the French troops reacted well against the attackers, subsequent Anglo-Sicilian seizures of the islands of Ischia and Procida in early May completed the blockade, and Naples was captured on June 13. The *giacobini* in the city suffered from a *lazzaroni* uprising, and many were murdered. The monarchy was restored.

Benefiting from Austro-Russian pressure on the French in northern Italy and Switzerland, this was one of the most impressive campaigns of the entire period. It produced a verdict that lasted until 1805, a period greater than those that tend to attract attention. If that outcome was only due to Naples making terms with France in 1801, this outcome in part was because the 1799 verdict indicated a need for French caution, something that Napoleon would have done well to consider with Spain in 1808. Subsequently, in 1799, Allied forces, including a British naval blockade of Genoa, had cleared much of Italy of the French, a process eased by anti-French risings, including in Piedmont and Tuscany. In terms of winning success, the creation of the sister republics had been counterproductive.[9]

As discussed in the last chapter, Britain and Russia also cooperated from August 27, 1799, in an invasion of the North Holland peninsula in support of the exiled Prince of Orange. Initially successful on land, there was also the capture on August 30 of eight ships of the line and three frigates, a significant portion of the Dutch fleet, much of which had mutinied. However, there was no pro-Orangist revolution, and the French and Dutch forces were able to block the Anglo-Russian advance, leading to the retreat and then evacuation of these units under an agreement signed on October 18, the Convention of Alkmar. The contrast in anti-French popular activism to the situation in Italy, especially Naples, was in part a consequence of a weaker international intervention, but differences in society and religious commitment also played a part. Ideological fervour did not only continue to play a role in the fighting in Naples. In August 1799, Grenville wrote to Sir Charles Whitworth, the ambassador in St. Petersburg, about the need for Anglo-Russian cooperation, "for the cause of religion and morality, and for the maintenance of civilized society."[10]

The range of the War of the Second Coalition put considerable pressure on the French, a process that was not helped by Napoleon taking an army to the Near East in 1798, experienced troops that could have made a significant difference to the campaigning in Europe, and notably in northern Italy, an area with which he was familiar. The Allies, however, also found that their dispersal of effort, while important politically and, to a degree, necessary logistically, hindered the concentration of forces. Thus, a lack of Austrian support, caused, in particular, by a focus on Germany, helped lead to a Russian defeat by the French in Switzerland in late September 1799.

Divisions within the Second Coalition had gravely weakened it, and they assisted the French in regaining the initiative. In a vital running together of political and military factors, the Austrians were concerned about Russia's determination to restore the king of Sardinia to his dominions in Piedmont, which clashed with Austrian goals in northern Italy. At the same time, there were clashes over command factors, notably disagreements over Suvorov's plans and his failure to give due weight to logistics, and, in particular, differences over the respective Austrian and Russian troop losses that in part arose from tactical factors. The Austro-Russian army in Italy separated into its component parts, leaving Suvorov to advance over the Alps to join another Russian army in Switzerland. Outnumbered and short of supplies, Suvorov then had to abandon Switzerland, a defeat that encouraged the unpredictable Tsar Paul to withdraw Russia from the war. He ended his alliance with Austria in October 1799.

Although Russian relations with Britain did not collapse until late 1800, this withdrawal seriously undermined the Second Coalition in both military and political terms. Indeed, in terms of the geopolitics of strategy, participation by Russia was, of all the powers, the most crucial after that of Britain. Those two powers were on the edge of Europe and, like all the edge powers, had an imperial hinterland. In the case of Russia, this hinterland stretched to the Pacific, whereas those of Britain, France, Spain, Portugal, the Dutch and the Danes all went beyond the Atlantic. Because of the dependence of the latter category on naval power, Britain took the key role in transoceanic power politics, although that role had to be maintained by naval victories and blockades.

There was no similar encumbrance for the deployment of Russian power, which, in 1799, extended to Holland and Switzerland, whereas

France could bring no comparable pressure on Russia. This posed a fundamental challenge to France, one that was different to that during the War of the First Coalition, in which Russia had not participated. Indeed, in terms of the geopolitics of strategy, or what has been termed "grand strategy," the wars saw the bringing to full fruition of the rise of both Russia and Britain.

At the same time as the Second Coalition was under pressure, France was under great strain, and the Directory unpopular and discredited by division. The electoral franchise remained very broad, and the level of participation was reasonably high. The elections of 1798 had produced a large group of radical deputies, only for the Directory to annul many of the results, because the ethos and practice of participatory politics threatened the stability of elite power and helped make the Directory appear unsettled. This situation encouraged its overthrow in 1799. Abandoning his army on August 24 so as to flee back to France by sea, which he did successfully, Napoleon himself evaded responsibility for the debacle in Egypt, which underlines the point about relevant strategic perspective. Napoleon was helped in this evasion by his own propagandist skills, the problems affecting the Directory and his rapid seizure of power.

The unpopular Directory swiftly succumbed to the coup mounted by Napoleon and others on November 9 (Brumaire 18, according to the Revolutionary calendar), and he became First Consul and general-in-chief. That sounds very easy and as if the outcome was seamless and a necessary product of strategy and circumstances. However, this was far from being the case. Instead, there was bungling on the part of both conspirators and opponents, and a loss of nerve by Napoleon. Moreover, it was far from inevitable that the Directory would fall, rather than be able to overcome a challenge, as it had done in 1797.

So also with the aftermath. The divisions that were deepened by the Terror, plus the continuation of the war, had made it virtually impossible to establish successfully any sort of stable liberal regime after 1795. As a consequence, the outcome of 1799 was always likely, although it might have been a stronger form of civilian rule rather than that of Napoleon. The bourgeois then turned to Napoleon because he safeguarded, if not political freedom, at least the status and power that were challenged by elections and electioneering.

Although the time frame was very different, the fall of the Directory in part exemplified the issues of war-caused fiscal strain and failure in international relations that had been seen with *ancien régime* France, first due to the cost of its intervention in 1778–83 in the War of American Independence and secondly as a result of postwar diplomatic failures.[11] Yet, the Directory had fallen far more rapidly than the *ancien régime* monarchy. This rapidity was the pattern of republican political change, and one that posed serious problems for Napoleon. It was unclear whether he would be part of a pattern of failure.

Combined with the change in Russian policy, Napoleon's seizure of power posed issues of policy and strategy for the other powers. In part, these issues were a matter of taking forward already existing divisions. Thus, in Britain, there were disagreements over strategy within the ministry. Henry Dundas supported amphibious operations, and William Grenville backed interventionism in Europe.[12] Convinced that Napoleon would speedily fall,[13] George III was against peace until France showed both stability and restraint.[14] As a crucial aspect of coalition strategy, he also believed that negotiations with Napoleon would discourage allies.[15]

When Napoleon seized power, it was far from clear that he would manage to profit from the new weakness of the Second Coalition and prove able to defeat Austria in 1800, as he was to do at Marengo in northern Italy that June, nor, more conclusively, to dominate Europe through repeated successes in 1805–9. It is very important not to read back from these successes to the change of government in 1799 or to the Revolutionary armies of the 1790s. It is also necessary to note the repeated failures of Napoleonic war-making in 1812–15. The eventual triumph of the *ancien régime* armies over Napoleon then certainly does not demonstrate their earlier superiority in the 1790s, not least due to their development in the meantime. Nor, however, does this eventual triumph prove that success in 1812–15 against France was due either to copying French systems or to matching them, or, indeed, to both. Instead, the issue indicates the folly of drawing clear lessons about respective effectiveness or about the nature of military proficiency and progress across the period or in any particular part in it. Despite this caveat, professionalism, the key merit of *ancien régime* militaries, was to emerge as the vital principle of military organisation throughout.[16]

Focusing, as is usual with authors, on the apparent significance of his subject, 1800 was chosen by Antoine-Henri Jomini as the year in which "the system of modern strategy was fully developed."[17] This bold, not to say bombastic, description of the Marengo campaign was ironic in light of the more recent stress on improvisation in explaining Napoleon's success, in that battle, that year, and more generally, and, linked to this, on him as an opportunist.

Napoleon's opening campaign as First Consul in 1800 was a surprise invasion of northern Italy, boldly begun with a crossing of the Great St. Bernard Pass, so that he arrived in the Austrian rear and threatened their line of supply, undercutting the Austrian advance on Lyon. This prefigured his outmanoeuvring of the Austrians in the 1805 Ulm campaign. In 1800, at the subsequent Battle of Marengo, however, on June 14, Napoleon had failed to understand the development of what he had set in motion. In this, he prefigured his own problems against the Prussians at Jena in 1806, as well as those of Helmuth von Moltke the Younger, the chief of the German General Staff, when invading France in 1914. At Marengo, Napoleon found the Austrians to be a formidable and unpredictable rival. The Austrians gained the initial advantage by a counter-intelligence coup, bribing Napoleon's chief scout to report that the Austrian army was retreating, which led him to split up his army in order to cut it off. The Austrians then surprise-attacked the reduced force left with Napoleon. Napoleon's enforced retreat for much of the battle was only reversed because of a successful counter-attack mounted by French reinforcements.

Rather than a brilliant victory, Napoleon was driven by the desire to engage and win. By forcing a battle whose shape was unclear, he, like the British admiral Horatio Nelson, placed great reliance on the subsequent mêlée, which rewarded the fighting qualities of individual units, the initiative and skill of subordinates and, in Napoleon's case, the ability luckily to get back the forces he had sent to cut off the Austrians, who returned to the sound of the fighting. There was no comparable rescue for Napoleon at Waterloo. At Marengo, as elsewhere, Napoleon also was able to dominate the news agenda and present a positive spin on his generalship.[18] This was an important aspect of his *modus operandi*, and one that his rivals also sought to achieve, but less effectively so, notably in Britain, where there was a strong opposition press.

The relationship between battle and campaign in evaluating strategic skill is thus complex. Had Marengo gone differently, the strategic wisdom of the campaign could have been re-examined. Moreover, the exploitation did not work, as it had against the Austrians in northern Italy in 1797, because Napoleon was now responsible for French strategy as a whole. Indeed, the Austrians after Marengo advanced in Germany at the expense of Bavaria, France's ally, and were only defeated by the French (and not by Napoleon) at Hohenlinden six months later.

A re-examination of Napoleon's relative strategic skill in this period might also have occurred had due attention been devoted to the strategy that allowed an impressive British concentration of strength to provide and support an attack on the French forces in Egypt, as well as British successes in battle with the French in Egypt in 1801. This was one of the most decisive campaigns of the war, a situation that was eased by being against an opponent that had no room for manoeuvre. Such a lack of depth was a particular issue in conflict in some areas outside Europe, although not in the Americas, where there were European settlement colonies.

This British concentration involved operations in the Mediterranean and in the Red Sea, both of which had multiple permutations or knock-on consequences depending on the process one envisages. The combination of "home waters" and the Mediterranean was long established for the British navy, but that with the Indian Ocean was not, and Britain had never sought the degree of coordination and planning attempted in 1798–1801. The successful attack on Mysore in 1799 was an aspect of the British strategy. Plans for an expedition from India to Batavia (Jakarta), which was ruled by France's Dutch ally, were abandoned, and British forces did not capture it until 1811. Instead, Britain moved first ships, and then troops from India, to the Red Sea in order to support the main attack from the Mediterranean. Already, in 1795, the British had carried out a reconnaissance of this sea where they had never previously operated, a sea that had difficult winds, in order to gain necessary information. A base was established in 1799 on the island of Perim in the Straits of Bab-el-Mandab at the mouth of the Red Sea, but, as the island was waterless, it was evacuated. The British plans included seeking to extend influence into the Hijaz in order to thwart any French use of the Red Sea to advance into the Indian Ocean.[19] In the event, British troops, some from India and some from Cape Town, where the Dutch had been defeated in 1795, marched from the Red Sea to the Nile.[20] Given such achievements, it remains surprising that so much attention is devoted to Napoleon.

There was no substitute for power in defining strategic possibilities. Major British successes in 1798–99, over the French navy at the Battle of the Nile and over Tipu Sultan of Mysore at Seringapatam, respectively, followed by their victories over the French army in Egypt in 1801, made it clear that France would not be able to project her power successfully along the Egypt–India axis. Indeed, France was less successful in the Indian Ocean than had been the case in 1780–83, and less than in the Caribbean during the American War of Independence.

The alternative idea of Franco-Russian cooperation against British India was advanced by Tsar Paul I in 1801.[21] This threat fired up George III and the British government, which had come close to war with Russia as recently as the Ochakov Crisis of 1791, but a crisis was avoided in 1801. Tensions in the Franco-Russian agreement played a role in this avoidance as Napoleon was unwilling to heed Paul's views on Italy, Malta and Turkey. They could agree on Paul putting pressure on Britain through a League of Armed Neutrality—of Russia, Denmark, Sweden and Prussia, formed in 1800—that opposed the British searching of neutral shipping, but that was only a short-term basis for an agreement in a situation that was becoming more volatile as peace neared. The overthrow and assassination of Paul on March 24, 1801, and his succession by his less quixotic son, Alexander I (r. 1801–25), was crucial, as it ensured a dramatic break with an already problematic agreement.[22] Relations were mended with Britain that April.

In a running theme, Napoleon proposed joint Franco-Russian action anew against British India in 1808 in order to harm Britain's economy and benefit France in wealth and prestige. Aside from serious political differences between France and Russia, this strategy was not credible. Russia could deploy force into the eastern Mediterranean if Britain was supportive, but lacked the naval strength to make a significant impact on British India. Overland, the distances, support problems and likely opposition were too great.

Failure in Egypt in 1801 did not end Napoleon's Asian strategy. In 1803, General Charles Decean sailed from the French Indian Ocean base of Mauritius to try to reoccupy Pondicherry. His squadron carried some 1,250 men, many young officers intended to continue France's earlier policy of raising and training forces for native rulers. They could not land at Pondicherry, however, because it was occupied by the British. Moreover, that year, General Gerard Lake, the British commander-in-chief in India, destroyed the French-trained native forces in northern India, notably at Laswari on November 1, while General Arthur Wellesley, later

Duke of Wellington, himself defeated the Marathas at Assaye (September 23) and Argaon (November 29).[23]

French strategy also involved trying to win the backing of Persia. Sent from Paris in the spring of 1805, Pierre-Amédée Jaubert arrived in Teheran in 1806. His instructions included an offer of military help, and his embassy was followed in 1807 both by the arrival of a Persian envoy to France and by the dispatch of a French military mission charged with reorganising the Persian army. The two powers signed the Treaty of Finckenstein of May 7, 1807, but, as so often with the strategic underpinnings of alliances, their priorities were different. Looking back to an issue created by Russian expansion from the 1780s, the Persians wanted help in driving the Russians out of Georgia in the Caucasus. Napoleon, in contrast, wished to see Persia exclude British influence and hoped that it could be a base against British India, which was a misreading of the situation in South Asia.

Transoceanic power projection, in terms of both capability and plans, whether plausible or wilder, was not only restricted to Britain. In terms of capability, in 1796, a Spanish squadron reached Manila, the first major Spanish fleet sent there. In 1800, a naval station in Manila was founded, and in 1802 a shipyard in Cavite was established in order to build and support warships against pirates.

French victories in 1800, that of Marengo, and, even more, Jean Moreau's at Hohenlinden east of Munich on December 3,[24] led Austria to agree to peace with France on February 9, 1801, by the Treaty of Lunéville. That, however, did not mean that the Austrians were unable to fight well, as Johann Klenau had demonstrated in Swabia earlier in 1800. Nevertheless, having been defeated at Hohenlinden, Archduke John retreated, losing a series of actions and many prisoners to the French pursuit. When the French neared Vienna, the Austrians sought an armistice, which they were granted on December 25. Close to Royalists and critics of Napoleon, Moreau was to be banished in 1804, returning from America to Europe in 1813 to advise Tsar Alexander, only to be mortally wounded fighting the French at the Battle of Dresden. He was a classic instance of the talent lost by the authoritarian Napoleon, rather like Charles Lee in the American War of Independence after he fell out with the far less authoritarian George Washington.

By the Treaty of Lunéville, Austria essentially confirmed the 1797 Treaty of Campo Formio. In addition, the Grand Duchy of Tuscany was

removed from Ferdinand III, who was to be compensated with a secular-
ised Salzburg, of which he became ruler in 1802, in turn, in its place,
gaining Würzburg, a new duchy, in 1805. Tuscany was transformed into
the kingdom of Etruria, a new buffer state for the French-dominated
section of Italy. This was granted to Louis I, son of Ferdinand, Duke of
Parma, which had been occupied by the French since 1796. Naples made
peace with Napoleon. With this settlement, the French dominance of
western Europe seemed assured, although Napoleon was swiftly to compromise it.

Britain followed Austria into a peace agreement with France, although
this proved politically divisive in Britain. The peace preliminaries with
France signed in London on October 1, 1801, led Grenville to go into
opposition. The Treaty of Amiens followed on March 17, 1802, Cornwallis, a marquess from 1792, signing for Britain. Its restoration of colonial
gains to France and its allies, including Cape Town to the Dutch, was
bitterly unpopular in Britain, not least because of the realist factor that
there was a conviction that they would have to be conquered anew,
which indeed proved accurate when war resumed.

Napoleon, meanwhile, pursued, or at least toyed with, a range of
ambitious strategies. In 1802, he was interested in Joseph Bonaparte's
implausible idea of conquering the Barbary States in North Africa as part
of a coalition including the United States and Naples, and using them to
grow products currently obtained from further afield, including cotton.
More credibly, Napoleon sought to benefit from peace with Britain by
pursuing a "Western Design," seeking to create a major empire that
would include Louisiana, Florida, Cayenne, Martinique, Guadeloupe and
Saint-Domingue. This plan focused on the dispatch of twenty thousand
troops to the last in 1802 in order to re-establish French control. Amphibious forces landed at numerous points, including Fort Dauphin, Cap-
Français, Port-de-Paix and Port-au-Prince, and, combined with rapid subsequent advances by land, this ensured that the defenders, under Toussaint L'Ouverture, lacked any strategic depth. Indeed, French forces converged on the Crête-à-Pierrot area, forcing battle on Toussaint, who was
seized and deported to France. Most of his generals defected to Charles
Leclerc. However, resistance continued, and the resumption of war with
Britain on May 18, 1803, led to a blockade of Saint-Domingue's ports.
Their food supplies cut, the French lost the initiative and were pushed
back. Finally driven back to Le Cap, the French force agreed a truce with

the Haitian army under Toussaint's successor, Jean-Jacques Dessalines, and in November 1803 was transported by British warships to Jamaica. Proclaimed on January 1, 1804, the independence of Haiti represented the total failure of France's Caribbean strategy, an outcome that was never to be reversed.

This failure arose in large part from an absence of any political grasp of possibilities. This absence arose not only from a lack of the "situational awareness" crucial to strategic formulation and implementation, but also from the values, notably racism, involved. Napoleon does not come out of the episode well. In addition, repeating his failure in the Near East, France's Caribbean strategy fell short of military practicalities. These entailed not only local opposition and the British role, but also the devastating impact of disease, particularly yellow fever, which killed Leclerc, the commander.

To an extent, the 1802 Caribbean expedition showed Napoleonic strategy as a coalition enterprise. Thus, the French force included five thousand Polish troops who had fought for the French in Italy in the 1790s. Most of those sent to Haiti died of yellow fever. Like the later use of Irish troops in central Europe, rather than against the British, the deployment of Poles reflected the degree to which the national interests of France's allies were totally subsumed to Napoleonic imperialism.[25]

Napoleon, moreover, was not able to win regional support in the Caribbean for his struggle against Britain. Indeed, the French mishandled the strategic opportunities offered by both Spain and the United States. The collapse in 1791–93 of relations with Spain had encouraged ideas that France could benefit from the overthrow of Spanish colonial rule in the New World, either directly or by using the possibility of winning better relations with Britain[26] or the United States.[27] Subsequently, France's war with Spain from 1793 was followed, after peace in 1795, by the strength of intimidation within an alliance, the latter leading to France regaining Louisiana from Spain in 1800, although, in return, a Spanish Bourbon, the Duke of Parma, gained Tuscany from a branch of the Habsburgs. Louisiana, which meant much of the American West, was then sold to the United States for sixty million *louis*, or fifteen million dollars, in 1803, thus probably thwarting the eventual capture of New Orleans by a British amphibious operation, which would have faced fewer obstacles than that defeated there in 1815 by the Americans under Andrew Jackson. An aftermath of the loss of Saint-Domingue, this sale provided useful funds, but the sale did not become the basis for a Franco-American military alliance against the British.

The different possibility that Louisiana would be the basis of an independent state captured the sense of uncertainty focused by Aaron Burr, a former American vice president and now freewheeling adventurer. Burr approached Anthony Merry, the British envoy, telling him that Louisiana wanted independence but needed the protection of a foreign power and a link to Trans-Appalachia, for which he also sought independence. Putting on pressure, Burr said that if British protection was refused, he would turn to France. Telling Merry that an independent Louisiana would provide Britain with commercial advantages, as it was a growing market, Burr initially sought two or three British frigates and the same number of smaller vessels off the mouth of the Mississippi in order to stop the Americans blockading the river. Burr also sought a loan of £100,000 and the support of a British consul at New Orleans.[28]

By the end of 1805, Burr had increased both his needs, to two or three ships of the line as well as the other ships already asked for, and also the opportunities apparently on offer. He told Merry that West and East Florida would also make themselves independent from Spain, and that he thought that parts of Latin America would follow. As a result, Burr argued, France would win greater benefits if Britain turned down the opportunity to intervene. He claimed that conflict between America and Britain was likely anyway, as Thomas Jefferson, the president from 1801 to 1809, was determined to resist the British blockade of France. Merry saw the possibility of a very different geopolitics: he thought that if the West of the United States split off, the East would separate from the southern states, and "thus the immense power which is now risen up with so much rapidity in the western hemisphere" would be wrecked by division.[29] Burr, however, complained about a lack of British response, and Merry feared, instead, that intervention by France and Spain was becoming a possibility and that Burr's plans had expanded to include a filibustering invasion of Mexico.[30]

In the event, Burr failed, because he exaggerated his strength, was unable to maintain secrecy, and lacked the opportunities enjoyed by Napoleon in 1799. Burr's scheme was but one of the very many of the period that reflect the multiplicity of would-be strategic players and a general sense of uncertainty that encouraged a strategy of scheming. This was not only so by these players, but also by the major powers willing to consider using them.

The American gain of Louisiana in 1803, including the crucial port of New Orleans, ensured that the Spanish stranglehold on the Gulf of Mexico was broken, challenging the Spanish position to east and west: in West Florida and Texas. Arguing that France had not complied with the conditions under which it had obtained Louisiana from Spain in 1800, the Spaniards delivered a memorial against the Louisiana Purchase, but it had no effect. The Spanish hope that Louisiana in French hands would serve as a barrier against American expansion towards Spain's other colonies by committing French support to their retention had been cruelly exposed, instead vindicating Spanish concern in the late 1770s that an independent United States would be destabilising for the Spanish empire. Indeed, in 1803, Jefferson told Edward Thornton, the British envoy, that he would press for Louisiana's eastern limits before it had been ceded to Spain in 1763 when Britain gained Florida, namely to include part of what had become British West Florida in 1763. Jefferson regarded the Rio Perdido east of Mobile Bay (now the western border of Florida) as the appropriate frontier, a challenge to the Spanish position in West Florida as a whole.[31]

Two years later, Jefferson told Merry that Spain was hostile to America and that, if there was war, he would invade first Florida and then Cuba, the last, as the key to the Gulf of Mexico, necessary, he argued, for the defence of Louisiana and Florida.[32] Jefferson indeed attempted to gain Florida in 1806; his successor, James Madison, president from 1809 to 1817, pursued the same objective; and, in 1811, while thwarting a poorly conceived American attempt to seize East Florida, Spain failed to win British help against successful American expansion into West Florida.[33] They were allies against France, but Britain was unwilling to provide deterrence against America.

More generally, Jefferson pressed to define and claim Louisiana as hugely as possible, despite historical evidence, and Madison followed suit. The dispatch in 1804 of the Corps of Discovery, an expedition under Meriwether Lewis and William Clark that had been planned before the Louisiana Purchase, asserted American interests across the new possessions to the Pacific. Lewis and Clark also sought to establish an overland route there, a goal for which it was important to discover the headwaters of the Columbia and then follow it to the Pacific, which they reached at the close of 1805. The expedition, on which the British envoy reported,[34] was also seen by Jefferson as a way to thwart the possibility that the British would develop the potential for transcontinental routes shown by Alexander Mackenzie, who had crossed the continent in Canada in 1793,[35] and it helped focus attention on the Pacific Northwest as a key area of American interest. National assertion through cultural competition was displayed in the instructions to find proof to discredit Buffon's theory of New World degeneracy. Further south, the Red River Expedition of 1806 provided valuable information, including a map of the river, information that was to help subsequent American expansion.

Napoleon's failure to gain strategic advantage from the Caribbean prefigured the later, and larger, disaster of the loss to Napoleon's system of Spain's overseas empire when his takeover of Spain in 1808 did not extend further. Indeed, throughout, the exploitative and insensitive treatment of Spain, which was far worse under Napoleon than it had been under the Revolutionaries, lessened and eventually destroyed its value as an ally. This destruction gravely compromised France's opportunities as a global power. This French failure was as significant as the more narrow military dimension focused on British sea power: that sea power would probably have been less effective if the Spanish empire had backed Napoleon from 1808. The French, for example, had obtained much greater value in 1779–83 from their alliance with Spain during the War of American Independence. This contrast further underlines serious doubts about the credibility of Napoleonic strategic understanding even before the military and political debacle of 1812–13, on which attention tends to concentrate.

Replacing the standard focus on Napoleon by the world sweep[36] is necessary. Yet, like the earlier approach, such a focus risks suggesting anew the salience of a central narrative. That emphasis was certainly Napoleon's view, with his attention to himself, but, however, it does not allow for the multifaceted character of strategies in a period of umbrella warfare: of a number of conflicts under a central title.

On the edge of Europe, but the director of an overseas empire from Brazil to Timor, Portugal is a good instance of this situation. Thus, once in power, Napoleon pressed Spain to force Portugal to break with Britain, which, in another instance of the continuance of geopolitical goals and strategic means, was a device already used, albeit without success, in 1762 in order in part for France to take advantage of having Spain as an ally under the Third Family Compact of 1761. Such a break would expose the Portuguese empire to British pressure, along the lines of that on the Dutch, French and Spaniards. Portugal again refused, and in 1801 France and Spain invaded.

This led to the sort of war that is largely neglected for this period, namely a brief one without battle. Yet, these wars, and their strategies, could be of consequence, indeed major consequence, and also certainly contributed to the overall character of conflict in the period, as well as helping to explain the particular distinctiveness of some of the campaigning in the wars that gather attention. In 1801, the key effort was made by Spain, but it focused on a border conflict. It captured poorly defended Portuguese posts, notably Olivenza, but, when the Spaniards attacked the formidable fortress of Elvas, the assault was repulsed. The Spanish first minister, Manuel de Godoy, did not advance further into Portugal, despite picking oranges near Elvas and sending them to the Queen of Spain with the message that he would move on to Lisbon, which he had the campaigning time to do.

Begun on May 20, 1801, the "War of the Oranges," however, ended on June 6. Godoy was content with minor gains that were winnable rather than a strategy of speculation. By the Treaty of Badajoz, Portugal ceded Olivenza to Spain; paid a heavy indemnity, which the Spanish government needed; and agreed to close its ports to British ships. In response, the British occupied Madeira in order to thwart a possible French or Spanish occupation of an island on key trade routes. This demonstrated the wider oceanic significance of European power politics. Despite the Vienna Peace Treaty stipulating its return, Olivenza was to be a permanent gain, unlike those made by Napoleon. This contrast in outcome is interesting, even instructive, both in the short and in the long term.

NOTES

1. Geoffrey Mowbray, *Remarks on the Conduct of Opposition during the Present Parliament* (London: J. Wright, 1798), 115.

2. Claire-Elizabeth de Rémusat, *Mémoires de Madame de Rémusat, 1802–1808*, ed. Paul de Rémusat (Paris, 1884), 1:274.

3. These two elements were not unique to France.

4. This was seen with the British handling of its North American colonies prior to the revolution of 1775.

5. Hasan Fas'i, *History of Persia under Qajar Rule* (New York: Columbia University Press, 1972), 52–54.

6. Robin Maguire, ed., *Napoleon's Commentaries on the Wars of Julius Caesar* (Barnsley: Pen and Sword, 2018).

7. John Sherwig, *Guineas and Gunpowder: British Foreign Aid in the Wars with France, 1793–1815* (Cambridge, MA: Harvard University Press, 1969).

8. John Sherwig, "Grenville's Plan for a Concert of Europe, 1797–1799," *Journal of Modern History* 34 (1962): 284–93.

9. Massimo Viglione, *Rivolte dimenticate: Le insorgenze degli italini dalle origini al 1815* (Rome: Città Nuova, 1999).

10. Grenville to Whitworth, August 6, 1799, NA. FO. 65/27.

11. Munro Price, "The Dutch Affair and the Fall of the *Ancien Régime*, 1784–1787," *Historical Journal* 38, no. 4 (1995): 875–905.

12. Piers Mackesy, *War without Victory: The Downfall of Pitt, 1799–1802* (Oxford: Oxford University Press, 1984); Michael Duffy, "Pitt, Grenville and the Control of British Foreign Policy in the 1790s," in *Knights Errant and True Englishmen: British Foreign Policy, 1660–1800,* ed. Jeremy Black, 151–77 (Edinburgh: John Donald, 1989).

13. George to Grenville, November 20, 1799, BL. Add. 58861 fol. 61.

14. George to Pitt, June 28, 1800, NA. PRO. 30/8/104 fol. 287.

15. George to Grenville, January 1, 1800, BL. Add. 58861 fol. 81.

16. Dennis Showalter, "Tactics and Recruitment in Eighteenth Century Prussia," *Studies in History and Politics* 3 (1983–84): 36.

17. Antoine-Henri Jomini, *Summary of the Art of War* (Philadelphia, PA: Lippincott, 1862), 137.

18. Owen Connelly, *Blundering to Glory: Napoleon's Military Campaigns,* 2nd ed. (Wilmington, DE: Scholarly Resources, 1999); Charles Esdaile, "De-Constructing the French Wars: Napoleon as Anti-Strategist," *Journal of Strategic Studies* 31 (2008): 515–52.

19. Malcolm Yapp, *Strategies of British India: Britain, Iran and Afghanistan, 1798–1850* (Oxford: Oxford University Press, 1980); Edward Ingram, *Commitment to Empire: Prophecies of the Great Game in Asia, 1797–1800* (Oxford: Oxford University Press, 1981), and *The British Empire as a World Power* (London: Frank Cass, 2001), 178–83; R. W. Beachey, *A History of East Africa, 1592–1902* (London: I. B. Tauris, 1996), 14–15.

20. Piers Mackesy, *British Victory in Egypt, 1801* (London: Routledge, 1995).

21. John Strong, "Russia's Plans for an Invasion of India in 1801," *Canadian Slavonic Papers* 7 (1965): 114–26.

22. Hugh Ragsdale, *Détente in the Napoleonic Era: Bonaparte and the Russians* (Lawrence: Regents Press of Kansas, 1980).

23. André Palluel-Guillard, "Napoléon et les Indes," in *L'Inde, La France, la Savoie. Le Général de Boigne* (Chambéry: ADUS, 1996), 87–108.

24. James Arnold, *Marengo and Hohenlinden: Napoleon's Rise to Power* (London: Pen and Sword, 2005).

25. Jan Pachoński and Reuel Wilson, *Poland's Caribbean Tragedy: A Study of Polish Legions in the Haitian War of Independence, 1802–1803* (New York: East European Monographs, 1986).

26. AE. CP. Ang. 582 fols 137, 167, 222.

27. AE. CP. Ang. 582 fol. 225, 583 fol. 49.

28. Merry to Henry, Lord Mulgrave, March 29, April 29, August 4, 1805, NA. FO. 5/45 fols 128–32, 192–93, 259.

29. Merry to Mulgrave, November 25, 1805, NA. FO. 5/45 fols 322–31.

30. Merry to Charles James Fox, Foreign Secretary, November 2, 1806, NA. FO. 5/49, fols 218–24.

31. Thornton to Robert, Lord Hawkesbury, Foreign Secretary, October 28, 1803, NA. FO. 5/38 fols 307–8.

32. Merry to Mulgrave, November 3, 1805, NA. FO. 5/45 fol. 314.

33. James Cusick, *The Other War of 1812: The Patriot War and the American Invasion of Spanish East Florida* (Athens: University of Georgia Press, 2003); John Stagg, *Borderlines in Borderlands: James Madison and the Spanish-American Frontier, 1776–1821* (New Haven, CT: Yale University Press, 2009).

34. Merry to Mulgrave, August 4, 1805, NA. FO. 5/45 fol. 254.

35. David Nicandri, *River of Promise: Lewis and Clark on the Columbia* (Bismarck, ND: Dakota Institute Press, 2010).

36. See Jeremy Black, "The Napoleonic Wars in Global Perspective," in *The Projection and Limitations of Imperial Powers, 1618–1850*, ed. Frederick Schneid, 149–69 (Leiden: Brill, 2012), and, on a far greater scale, Alexander Mikaberidze, *The Napoleonic Wars: A Global Scale* (Oxford: Oxford University Press, 2020).

FIVE

Central Europe at Stake, 1804–9

General Jean-Baptiste Bernadotte was appointed envoy to the United States in January 1803, but, due to British naval power, he was unable to assume that duty. Instead, he commanded I Corps of the *Grande Armée* in the Ulm-Austerlitz campaign of 1805, a change in duty that captured a transition towards a period of large-scale conflict. Napoleon had certainly been planning for a resumption of war. He founded the *Ecole Spéciale Militaire de Saint-Cyr* in 1802 to train officers and devoted much time to its syllabus. Some four thousand officers were trained there between 1805 and 1815. Napoleon also reorganised the *Ecole Polytechnique* in 1804, and the role of mathematics in French military education increased.

For all his egocentric ambition and posturing, Napoleon was genuinely interested in a kind of rational modern administration, and found it appropriate to present himself accordingly. Alongside his emotional commitment to what would be termed Romanticism, there was a statist Enlightenment drive to his governance. He introduced some worthwhile features of government, notably issuing a new civil law code, the *Code Napoléon* (1804), and also reorganised financial, local and judicial administration. More generally, the cult and practice of self-conscious modernisation was advanced as explaining the logic and value of the Revolutionary and Napoleonic systems. Both cult and practice drew on the rejection of the past seen with the radicals of the Revolution, but also reflected a deliberate engagement with an ideology of efficiency under Napoleon. A greater use of modernisation was an aspect of the latter, and, for example, Jean-Antoine Chaptal, minister of the interior from 1800 to 1804, sought to use useful information in order to encourage industrial innovation.

Napoleon's ideas of rational modernity, however, were often crude, for example his views on economic and financial matters, while he repeatedly undermined his efforts by his rapacity, militarism and neo-feudalism, the last very much seen with the new imperial nobility. Napoleon was also an opportunist who operated by jettisoning the unpopular aspects of the Revolution, such as the abolition of slavery and the breach with Catholicism. Slavery was restored in 1802, and the entry to France of West Indian black and mixed-race people was prohibited; although, in 1802–3, Napoleon's attempt to crush black independence in Saint-Domingue failed, and Haiti, as a result, became independent in 1804. The decimal calendar was discarded by Napoleon in 1805–6 for commercial and scientific reasons, but also as part of his wider reaction against the Revolution and of his reconciliation with Catholicism, albeit both processes being very much on his own terms. At an instructive personal level, Napoleon reversed the Revolution's measures against hunting, which he greatly enjoyed at the château of Fontainebleau, which he restored.[1]

These aspects of his rule tend to be forgotten in today's public discussion of Napoleon, especially by those who praise him, take the face impression of achievement, and fail to notice the underlying reality. Indeed, the ambivalent nature of enlightened despotism, not least the degree to which support for reform was a matter of enhancing preparedness for conflict, is captured by Napoleon's policies, not least his repeated preference for war. Although we should not be surprised by the fact that Napoleon made both good and bad decisions, he certainly did not really understand compromise, and his system and psyche required force and success, and repeatedly so, while he also relished a warrior cult, as in the celebration of the mythical Celtic poet Ossian in the decoration of his wife, the Empress Joséphine's, palace at Malmaison.

Indeed, Napoleon reconceptualised military honour: in place of dynasticism, his military dictatorship emphasised the honour of dedication and professionalism, both of which were focused on Napoleon and defined by him. The army represented this process and was the vital means to disseminate the relevant values. Aside from offering energy and talent, Napoleon skilfully promoted an image of successful heroism and masculine militarism,[2] indicating the continuity of *gloire* from the *ancien régime*, but also its new idiom in a more populist age.[3] His opponents, both international and French, were to find this idiom difficult to match. Awards were freely distributed in order to reward service in the *Grande Armée*, on the morale of which Napoleon spent much time, a practice to be seen as late as his solicitude for his troops in the aftermath of the battle of Ligny in 1815. In 1804, eighty thousand troops witnessed Napoleon handing out medals to almost two thousand others in an elaborate spectacle staged on the cliffs at Boulogne, in which he encouraged soldiers to defend their reputation and the honour of the French name. This is a presence commemorated by the *Column of the Grande Armée* at Wimille, near Boulogne, with Napoleon wearing Roman clothes, albeit the column was not finished until 1841. Although French propaganda presented Napoleon as always in favour of peace, the regime, in practice, endlessly celebrated power, not least that of victory, in its activities, iconography and commemoration. Other states celebrated victories, but their legitimacy rested as well on dynastic legitimacy. Moreover, Napoleon was claiming to be different and better.

The move from a universal message contained within the promise and initial stages of the Revolution was taken further under Napoleon, in part because of the focus on his personal position. Like the Revolutionaries, but with a different conclusion, Napoleon looked back to antiquity, fashioning, in his own iconography and that of the regime, a self-image in terms of the achievements, glamour and status of the ancient world, especially Rome. In following this neoclassicism, there was a clear counterpointing to the alleged decadence of the Bourbon *ancien régime*. The despoiling of European artworks for the glorification of Paris reflected another instance of the Napoleonic appropriation of the past. In addition, celebratory works were produced, notably by Jacques-Louis David, including *Bonaparte Crossing the Great St Bernard Pass* (1800), *The Consecration of the Emperor Napoleon* (1805–7), and *The Distribution of the Eagle Standards* (1810). Particular victories were extolled in paintings, especially by Antoine-Jean Gros, and in the titles awarded to his generals.

The imperial ambitions of Napoleon are aptly displayed by the tacky lavishness of the palace at Compiègne. In turn, Bourbon palaces he did not favour were demolished, in part for building materials. Meanwhile, France's past continued to be despoiled by the destruction of much of its ecclesiastical heritage. This was particularly the case with the monasteries, as at the Abbey of Saint Jean des Vignes at Soissons, while the Basilica of St. Martin was destroyed in Tours. Others survived only by being used for non-clerical purposes, such as the Abbey of Fontevraud as a prison, and that of Fontenay as a paper mill.

Returning to 1802–3, the training of the French army benefited greatly from peacetime preparation. The stability of French control after the end of the Second Coalition also consolidated the raising of troops from occupied areas. Thus, the Austrian Netherlands (Belgium) provided nearly one hundred thousand men between 1798 and 1809. The French supported their presence in Italy by the conscription introduced in 1798.[4] As later in the case of Hitler, the costs of such cooperation discredited alliance with Napoleon, just as it had earlier weakened the satellite republics. The burdens of war also helped to cripple reform initiatives in the territories of German allies, such as Bavaria. The army of the kingdom of Italy grew from twenty-three thousand in 1805 to ninety thousand in 1813. The majority of those sent from it to fight in Spain, Russia and Germany died. The Grand Duchy of Warsaw had to man a thirty-thousand-strong army, much of which died in Russia in 1812. French economic control was disruptive and could also be harsh. In France and allied areas, soldiers displayed very varied responses to conscription, ranging from patriotic enthusiasm (the minority) to professional cohesion, although homesickness was a widespread problem, and one that encouraged desertion.[5]

Consideration of future conflict and what it might entail was widespread. In particular, the strategy of naval bases was important to the resumption of war with Britain, with the latter determined to retain Malta as a Mediterranean naval base,[6] despite being obliged to return it by the Peace of Amiens of March 25, 1802. The British did not evacuate Egypt, as required, until the winter of 1802–3, but Malta was strategically more important. Furthermore, in part due to the strategic assumptions bound up in a Mediterranean fleet, both as a force enabler on the route to India and as a facilitator of alliances, the British deployed a large force to the Mediterranean in 1803 when war resumed on May 18. Nevertheless, prefiguring British strategy in 1940–41 between the fall of France and Hitler's invasion of the Soviet Union, the fleet's commander, Horatio Nelson, felt that the underlying British strategy had to be political: the hope that Napoleon's government would be "upset by French men," which, indeed, by working on continued French political instability, appeared to be the only means to remove his power. In the meanwhile,

Nelson had to resume the long hours of blockade and cast around the Mediterranean for bases from that perspective, finding Sardinia "an invaluable possession in every respect. It is the Ceylon [Sri Lanka] of the Mediterranean,"[7] an interesting example of the degree to which European strategic suppositions could be refracted through the lens of the transoceanic world. Keeping Malta out of French hands was as important as using it for Britain.

The significance of naval bases was further shown once war resumed, with Napoleon promptly ordering the seizure of the Neapolitan port of Taranto. This angered Alexander I of Russia, already cross about the French annexation of Piedmont in September 1802. He saw the seizure of Taranto as a revival of Napoleon's forward policy in the Mediterranean, and thus a threat to Russia's interests in the Balkans. Elba had been annexed that summer. Parma had also been taken over in 1801. Alexander's concern is a reminder of the many might-have-been strategies of the period, not least Napoleon's growing interest in an invasion of Britain.

In peace as well as war, Napoleon devoted much energy to improving France's military position. Occupied areas; satellite states, such as Switzerland and the Ligurian Republic; allies, such as Spain; and neutrals were all expected to provide troops, ships or resources to help his goals. Once war had been renewed with Britain in 1803, Napoleon brought the Batavian and Italian Republics and Switzerland into the conflict on his side.

The strategies of the Wars of the Third (1805–7) and Fourth (1809) Coalitions were very much to be set by the anxieties and ambitions surrounding the failures of peace. Alexander's peace plan of 1803, a plan produced in response to Napoleon's request for mediation of his differences with Britain, was curtly rejected by Napoleon because it would have required France to evacuate Hanover, Italy, Switzerland and the United Provinces: in May 1803, a French force from Holland had marched into Hanover, which surrendered on June 3.

In turn, Alexander and his ministers were offended by the contemptuous way in which they were continually treated, and concerned by the onward march of French policy. They were anxious about France's views for the Ionian Islands and worried about French intentions in the Balkans. The kidnapping from Baden of Louis Antoine, Duke of Enghien, an *émigré* Bourbon prince believed to be conspiring against Napoleon, and his show trial and execution in March 1804 on charges of fighting the

French and aiding Britain, led to a marked deterioration in relations. Such symbolic acts were important. France rudely rejected the Russian protest, and relations were broken in August 1804.

The Russians then stepped up their efforts to persuade Austria to take a prominent role in an alliance against France, efforts that had already led to refusals in December 1803 and April 1804. Napoleon meanwhile wooed Prussia, which, in May 1804, allied with Russia to maintain north German neutrality. Responding to the failures of 1792–95, Frederick William III was keen to keep Prussia at peace, which he also saw as the way to preserve its expansionist gains in Germany and Poland in 1740–95, and to make fresh ones as Germany was remodelled. This role, as a second-rank carnivorous bottom feeder, was to be protected by maintaining a neutrality that prevented attack by France or Russia, and thus avoided earlier geopolitical strategic dilemmas.[8]

The Russians allied with Britain in the spring of 1805, but Alexander sent a peace mission to Paris, only to abandon it when Napoleon annexed vulnerable Genoa to France in June, turning it into three *départements*. This annexation both demonstrated French power in Italy and asserted it over a major Mediterranean port.

In the early 1800s, in the aftermath of serious defeat, with its armies in need of replenishment, a very heavy debt, revenues under pressure and a lack of allies, the Austrian government sought to accommodate itself to French power. It adopted a conciliatory approach towards extensions of Napoleon's power in Germany and, in particular, Italy, where Napoleon annexed Elba and Piedmont in 1802, and had himself elected president of the Italian Republic, as the Cisalpine Republic was now called. These and other steps were unwelcome to Austria, which wished to regain its position, and increasingly looked to do so in mid-1805 as it responded to a sense that concerted action against France was possible.

Characteristically driving matters to a point, Napoleon, that August, demanded that Austria demobilise and formally declare its neutrality, in other words, surrender its capacity for independent action, which was what Germany was to demand of France in 1914, again in order to divide possible opponents and lessen Russian options. This step helped lead Austria to cooperate with Britain and Russia. Austria declared war on France and, in September, invaded her ally Bavaria. That might appear an aggressive step, but it was crucial to a strategy of active defence, as Bavaria in the past had served as a hostile base from which French forces could invade vulnerable Austria, notably so in 1741. Austria also wished to pre-empt the arrival of allied Russian forces in southern Germany. To do so would lessen the possibility that Russia would seek, not least under the guarantee of the German constitution it had gained by the Peace of Teschen of 1779, to direct or at least influence its politics,[9] rather as the Russians had sought to do in the Mediterranean.

Britain had tried to win over Spain, but the latter remained part of the French system, and highly important to its ability to confront Britain. Its financial significance to France led to a British attack on Spanish treasure ships off Ferrol on October 5, 1804, and, that December, to a Spanish declaration of war. While helpful, this did not, however, enable Napoleon to win his naval struggle with Britain, a struggle that had to be won if Britain was to be invaded and the Mediterranean left free for the projection of French power.

Britain's determination to fight hard was shown not only with the attack on the treasure ships without a declaration of war, but also with the surprise declaration of war on France in 1803. This caught many French merchantmen at sea where they were plucked off by the navy. Moreover, in 1807, without a declaration of war, and pursuing a strategy of preclusion, Britain attacked neutral Denmark in order to seize its fleet.

Napoleon's invasion plan for Britain showed the limitation of his strategy, as, lacking a political dimension, it was totally dependent on victory, and with the latter very high risk. To Napoleon, who had a paranoid dimension to his reasoning, Britain, an "eternal enemy," as he declared in a proclamation to the army of October 26, 1806, its gold and its intrigues, was the centre of all opposition to France's position on the Continent. This denied due agency to other powers and exaggerated the consequences of Britain's approaches. Nevertheless, however flawed and unsophisticated, the reason to bring down Britain could appear crucial to French strategy across Europe.

As earlier for the French when allied with Spain in 1733–35, 1743–48, 1762–63, 1779–83 and 1796–1802, the naval situation had now improved. Napoleon's desire for naval superiority appeared a prospect thanks to Spanish support, but his resulting plan in 1805 was highly complex, and far more so than the Dutch invasion of England in 1688; French invasion plans in 1692, 1744 and 1759; or the Franco-Spanish plan in 1779. Napoleon planned for French and Spanish squadrons to escape British blockaders, join together and, as a united force, defeat the British. As with the

Spanish Armada in 1588, its counterparts just mentioned, or the German plan in 1940, superiority in the Channel was required for an invasion to be mounted. In 1805, it was sought for four days in order for his troops to cross from Boulogne, and, having landed in Kent, they were to overrun London within a week before dictating peace.

The British correspondingly had a defensive strategy on land, notably using both the Weald and the Thames as defensive positions. However, their prime reliance was on the navy, and this, indeed, thwarted the French plan for coordination, both by maintaining a successful close blockade of Brest and by blocking a larger Franco-Spanish fleet in an inconclusive battle off Cape Finisterre on July 22, capturing two Spanish warships. Against instructions from Napoleon to sail to the Channel to cover an invasion, the Franco-Spanish fleet under Pierre-Charles Villeneuve fell back to Cadiz, much to the fury of Napoleon. Napoleon, in response, cancelled his invasion plans and turned against Austria on August 27.

When the Franco-Spanish fleet finally set sail on October 19–20, it was for Italian waters, designed to prevent the British intervention in Naples. At Trafalgar, however, on October 21, Nelson destroyed the Franco-Spanish fleet. This fleet possibly could better have achieved Napoleon's goals by remaining a powerful fleet-in-being in Cadiz instead of leaving port. Had it done so, the British could have been fixed as blockaders on a difficult station. Villeneuve was found dead in April 1806, his death attributed to suicide or to murder on Napoleon's orders.

WAR WITH AUSTRIA, RUSSIA AND PRUSSIA, 1805–7

The French had benefited from the years of peace on the Continent from 1801 in order to train their infantry, increase their artillery and cavalry and produce better-balanced corps. The earlier years of war had provided experienced troops and, crucially, an officer corps and non-commissioned officers sifted by merit. Under Napoleon, there was more systematisation in the organisation of the French army, notably by the ministers of war Louis-Alexandre Berthier and his successor, from 1807 to 1813, Henri Clarke. However, the corps system required talented subordinates capable of independent command, but also of coordination with other corps commanders in pursuit of the overall plan. This goal was far more difficult to fulfil than some of the discussion in general works on the value of the corps system might suggest. The organisational structure, in the shape of independently operating corps, to an extent drew on the earlier pattern of separate French armies, as with those of Jourdan and Pichegru in the Rhineland in 1795.

This system provided a mobility that Napoleon used to strategic effect, with his search for a single-campaign end to the conflict. However, the pressure for a rapid close, one obtained in large part as a consequence of operational surprise, also reflected Napoleon's opportunism[10] and the character of his logistical planning, in particular his emphasis on improvisation. This was seen with the successful attack on Austria in 1805, for which there were weaknesses in the logistical structure and preparations, notably insufficient forage.[11] Improvisation meant heavy pressure on France's allies and occupied territory to produce resources, and an emphasis on troops living on the country. In western Europe, where living off the land on the march was easy and could assuage the wait for supply trains to catch up with a fast-moving army, things, nevertheless, more or less worked.

The War of the Third Coalition that began in 1805 opposed Austria, Britain, Naples and Russia to Napoleon, but, as in the War of the Second Coalition, not Prussia, Spain or the Dutch. Having invaded Bavaria, which, as with French attacks in 1704, 1741 and 1809, was aligned with France, the Austrians halted and were successfully counter-attacked by the French. Decisive victories at Ulm (October 20) and Austerlitz (December 2) completely changed the situation. Napoleon moved the *Grande Armée*, originally deployed at Boulogne in preparation for an invasion of England, into Germany by rapid marches, with supplies crucially provided by German rulers whom Napoleon both wooed and intimidated, Württemberg allying with Napoleon on October 5.[12] Eased by a lack of resistance, but requiring successful delegation and coordination, the advance of separate corps across a broad front lessened the logistical strain and considerably increased the speed of advance.

Napoleon outmanoeuvred the Austrian army under Karl Mack von Leiberich. The Austrians were preparing for a French attack from the west through the Black Forest, but they were outmanoeuvred by the rapid advance of the French from the Middle Rhine to the Danube in their rear, an advance that in part matched the successful Anglo-Dutch advance to the Danube under John, Duke of Marlborough, in 1704. The overly cautious Austrian response, one that displayed both confusion and incompetence, left an army bottled up in Ulm. The forward position of the Austrians, at a considerable distance from the advancing Russians, left them vulnerable to attack without support. This forward strategy might appear foolish, but it was politically understandable as a way to ensure South German support, and it was essentially what Wellington and Blücher did in 1815 when they did not fall back to wait for the Austrian and Russian forces closing on eastern France.

In contrast to Napoleon's repeated failure in 1815, Prussian neutrality in 1805 was, for France and Prussia, a form of strategic outflanking of Austria, while Napoleon managed the operational outflanking of the Austrians at Ulm, and a tactical equivalent at Austerlitz. The Austrians appear woefully negligent because they allowed themselves to be outflanked, but their strategy of a forward defence had a point. If they had handled it well operationally, they would have avoided being outflanked and, instead, if defeated, would have been in the same position as the Russians were at Borodino in 1812 and Wellington at Waterloo in 1815: able to retreat back on their axis of advance, having used the defensive to inflict casualties on the attacking French—in short, a fallback in, and to strengthen, their position. To have not tried to adopt a forward defence would have entailed abandoning southern Germany to the French, exposing both Austria to attack and the emperor to the loss of his position in the empire. In strategic terms, the Austrian decision therefore was wise. The problem, as also in 1809, was the very poor operational execution and more general command problems in terms, in particular, of communications and logistics, as well as, crucially, French moves.

After the Ulm surrender, Napoleon, with nearly two hundred thousand troops, faced by an outnumbered Austrian army in Bavaria, overran southern Germany and Austria, occupying Vienna as an open city on November 12. This advance undercut Austrian operations in Italy, where, indicating a determination to regain position, their largest army was deployed under Archduke Charles, but to little effect. The evaluation and prioritisation of risk is a key element of strategy, and the Austrians mishandled that in 1805, as they were to do in 1866 when opposed to both Prussia and Italy. In 1805, they estimated the French field army in Italy as 108,000, rather than the more accurate figure of 42,000. This helped ensure that the 92,000-strong Austrian army did not attack. It was outfought by Masséna and never able to influence the campaign north of the Alps. If Masséna could not join with Napoleon, that was a far lesser possibility anyway, and of less consequence. The Austrians had failed to shake the equanimity of French strategy, a key goal, or to create a situation of interior lines.[13]

The advance to Vienna brought Napoleon closer to the advancing Russians, whom he wished to force into battle in order to prevent the attrition of a long war. At Austerlitz, in the modern Czech Republic, on December 2, Tsar Alexander I and an eighty-five-thousand-strong Austro-Russian army, attacked the seventy-five-thousand-strong French. A powerful assault on Napoleon's right was held and, in a surprise attack, the French turned the weak flank of this Russian attack in order to win. The French were better able than their Russian counterparts to win and employ the initiative, and to use numerical superiority at the particular point of contact they had sought. Aside from Napoleon's superior generalship, the French command system proved better able to integrate the different arms effectively. Alexander was humiliated.

These successes prefigured the rapid Prussian victories over France, under Napoleon's nephew, Napoleon III, in 1870. The Prussians, however, were helped then in fighting a successful limited war by the absence of any other enemies, a key strategic context, and by a determination to try to bring the war to an end swiftly. In practice, the war went on until 1871, but Napoleon I lacked a comparable restraint as far as limited war was concerned.

Soon after Austerlitz, Austria left the war by the Treaty of Pressburg of December 26, 1805. This won her back Vienna but cost her Venetia, Istria, Dalmatia, the Vorarlberg and the Tyrol, which reduced her revenues and manpower. A massive indemnity of forty million francs was also imposed. These terms, however, subsequently made it difficult to support Napoleon in Vienna other than on the basis of expediency. Indeed, Napoleon's strategy throughout was highly transactional. Germany seemed securely under French leadership. However, the attitudes he inculcated, fear and resentment, looked towards the later problems he faced, including the Austrian resumption of the war with France in both 1809 and 1813.

Napoleon had also benefited from the balance of insurrection. For most of the period, it stood against the French Revolutionaries and Napoleon, but, in 1805, there was no such rebellion within or outside France. Indeed, the French benefited from the degree to which there was the possibility of disaffection in Hungary, as, most recently, in the early 1700s and late 1780s.

Napoleon's movement of the army designed to invade Britain into central Europe, combined with the result of Trafalgar, encouraged plans for the dispatch of a British army to North Germany. Twenty-five thousand men were deployed by late January 1806, and the North Sea port of Bremen was occupied, rather as British forces had been successfully sent to Emden to help Prussia in 1758 during the Seven Years' War, operating thereafter in Germany until campaigning stopped in 1762. However, this strategic option, a way to demonstrate support for the Third Coalition in an area of British dynastic interest due to the Electorate of Hanover, was undermined by the mixture of strategic and operational factors that always deserve consideration when assessing not so much friction but the more active countering to which strategies are subject. In this case, the slow pace of British preparations, and the delays caused by North Sea winter storms, were significant, but more so was Napoleon's ability to reset the system by his victory at Austerlitz. The strategic situation collapsed before the British could contribute, and they speedily evacuated northern Germany in February 1806. Thus, in this case, a very secondary theatre did not determine events, nor dictate Napoleon's priorities.

So also in southern Italy. Seeking to display strength and to attract Russian backing for the Third Coalition, the British had landed a force in the Bay of Naples on November 21, 1805, in order, in cooperation with a Russian expeditionary force, to protect southern Italy from French attack, and thereby provide security in depth for the Russians in the Ionian Islands and the British in the Mediterranean, notably Malta. There was a potential threat from this force to the French in northern Italy, but Masséna was neither fixed nor even distracted. Thus, certainly in this case, the Mediterranean maritime strategy did not impose on the Continental strategic environment. After Austerlitz, the French, having defeated their primary foe, the Austro-Russian army in central Europe, advanced in strength, forty-four thousand troops invading Naples on February 8, 1806. The city of Naples was occupied on February 14 and the Neapolitan army heavily defeated at Campo Tenese in northern Calabria on March 9. That army then collapsed. Lacking strength and cohesion, the British and Russian forces withdrew, while Ferdinand IV fled to Palermo. The British occupied Sicily in order to protect it from French invasion.[14]

Conflicts and campaigns frequently drew together different types of warfare, which can make their analysis more difficult.[15] Thus, the rising in Calabria in 1806 against French control, a form of irregular warfare, benefited from seaborne help from the nearby British bases in Sicily and Malta, including, that year, the dispatch of regular troops to Calabria, who were victorious at Maida on July 4, but the British force soon after withdrew. Instead of the success of British-supported Neapolitan action in 1799, there was in 1806 a lack of effective rebel leadership. This lack was combined with the French deployment of forty-eight thousand troops (there had been far fewer troops available for the French in Naples in 1799), use of flying columns, brutality, murderous control of food supplies and ability to exploit local vendettas. Employed frequently by the French, this combination proved crucial, although the struggle in Calabria lasted several years and cost the French twenty thousand dead and many resources. The French failed to learn from Calabria the lessons that could have been drawn for the case of Spain.[16]

At the same time as the French conquest of southern Italy, Trafalgar was of great strategic benefit as it destroyed the Franco-Spanish fleet that could have taken advantage of the conquest of Naples, a fleet far larger than that destroyed by Nelson at the Battle of the Nile in 1798. Naples would have had more strategic point for France had there been no Trafalgar. Sicily and Malta would have been clearly vulnerable, and any French agreement with Russia would have posed an even greater threat to Britain than that eventually posed from 1807.

Moreover, France would have been in a stronger position to put pressure on the Turkish empire. Indeed, in 1803, General Horace Sebastiani, having visited Egypt, reported to Napoleon that six thousand French troops could recapture it. British failure there in 1807 suggests, however, that the possible impact of such intervention should not be exaggerated. In the event, Selim III, who had renewed the Russo-Turkish treaty in September 1805, responded to Napoleon's stronger position in 1806 by recognising his title as emperor; agreeing to close the Bosporus and the Dardanelles to Russian warships, which affected the possibility of Russian naval deployment into the eastern Mediterranean; and replacing pro-Russian *hospodars* (governors) in Moldavia and Wallachia. Russia and Turkey moved closer to war.

Exploiting the tensions within German states and his own victory, Napoleon meanwhile had totally reorganised Germany. The creation of the kingdom of Bavaria on January 1, 1806, violated the principle that there could only be one king in the empire. That July, Napoleon established an institutional basis for French intervention, the *Rheinbund*, or Confederation of the Rhine, a strategic asset which linked France and sixteen south and west German states, including Bavaria, Württemberg and Baden. Territorial gains helped make these rulers allies, with Württemberg doubled in size. Designed to limit Austrian and Prussian influence, the *Rheinbund* also represented a rejection of the Russian intervention in German politics under the Peace of Teschen of 1779 that Russia had mediated in order to end the War of the Bavarian Succession.

With its capital at Frankfurt, the *Rheinbund* was also intended to give Napoleon, who became its protector, control over the forces and resources of the confederation members, and it backed him against Prussia later in 1806. There was no attempt to create an alternative to French direction: the Diet of the confederation never met, although that was in part because several of the key states, especially Bavaria and Württemberg, strongly opposed the convening of the Diet or other institutions that might have any power whatsoever over their internal affairs. Napoleon did not much care as long as the military contingents marched with him when called upon. As a consequence, he saw no reason to push the imposition of these other aspects of the alliance. Nevertheless, this was an authoritarian system, and different from the federalism of the Second Reich (1871–1918), let alone the First.

Napoleon also had the emperor, Francis, dissolve the empire (the First Reich), so that he now became only emperor of Austria, a title he had assumed in October 1804. This dissolution occurred on August 6 when Francis II abdicated his title (becoming only Francis I of Austria) and released all imperial states and officials from their oaths. The German territories thereby became fully sovereign. The Austrians were forced to accept Napoleon's reorganisation of Germany when Napoleon moved the entire *Grande Armée* into Upper Austria. They even handed over the imperial crown, part of the totemism of rule and pre-eminence, and a coronation crown probably from the tenth century. In 1806, Napoleon also made Württemberg and Saxony kingdoms, the latter part of his strategy of building up an ally in east-central Europe capable of opposing Russia and offsetting Austria and Prussia.

Frederick William III of Prussia had refused to support the Third Coalition and, instead, in a classic example of divide and rule, secured Napoleon's recognition of his occupation of Hanover after the French withdrew. Bavaria gained Ansbach from Prussia in exchange for this recognition, and yielded Berg to Napoleon, who made his brother-in-law Joachim Murat its ruler. However, Napoleon's dishonesty over the fate of Hanover, his creation of the *Rheinbund* without consulting Prussia and his exploitative treatment of Prussia, together with French bullying, threats and infringements of the Prussian neutrality zone, on the one hand, and Prussian opportunism, on the other, led to conflict in October 1806. Earlier, Prussia had tried to mediate as a prelude to intervention, which was what Chancellor Metternich of Austria was to do in 1813 (see chapter 6). However, this Prussian attempt was undercut by Napoleon's success at Austerlitz.

The outbreak of war with Prussia was late in the year and appeared to give little time for the French to inflict any defeat before the Russians and British could provide support. Indeed, to a degree, Prussia appeared far better off than in 1756–62 when fighting France, Austria and Russia. However, the strategic situation had been transformed by improvements to the French military system from 1792, notably the combination of large-scale recruitment and the acquisition of experience,[17] and Napoleon had determined to act fast, attack, and destroy the cohesion of the Prussian army.

With all the *Rheinbund* backing Napoleon, French forces were successful against Prussian divisions at Schleiz (October 9) and Saalfeld (October 10), before the poorly commanded and outmanoeuvred Prussians were defeated at Jena and Auerstädt on October 14 by French forces that ably used the opportunities of the battlefields. At Jena, massed artillery, the fighting quality of French troops and substantial numbers of skirmishers inflicted heavy losses on the Prussian lines. Napoleon crushed what he thought was the main Prussian army at Jena, but, at Auerstädt, Louis-Nicolas Davout, with the twenty-seven thousand men of III Corps, held off and finally defeated the main Prussian army of at least fifty thousand troops.[18] Subsequent battles, notably at Halle (October 17), Prenzlau (October 28) and Lübeck (November 6), saw further Prussian forces defeated, while the French occupied Berlin on October 27, Napoleon visiting the tomb of Frederick the Great as Hitler was to do that of Napoleon after his defeat of France in 1940.

Jena persuaded the Danes that Napoleon could not be resisted, as did the French advance to nearby Lübeck. The French position in the Baltic was further strengthened when Western Pomerania, the Swedish German possessions of Stralsund and Rügen, were seized in 1807.

Jena also led Selim III of Turkey to gain confidence in response to the Russian intimidation underlined in November by the occupation of Moldavia. Selim declared war on Russia on December 24, 1806. In response, the British sent a squadron to press for the expulsion of the French envoy. The Turks procrastinated while adverse winds affected the British in late February 1807. French experts advised the Turks on deploying their artillery, and the British squadron withdrew. However, soon after, the *janissary* corps, opposed to Selim's reforms, rebelled, leading to a change of sultan.

In a politics of trickery and bullying, meanwhile, neutral powers were exploited and attacked by Napoleon. Peace became war by other means. Hanover was occupied in 1803 and anew in 1806; the Hanseatic cities and much of the Papal States following in 1806. The kingdom of Etruria (Tuscany) was dissolved in December 1807, before being turned into three French *départements* when annexed by France in May 1808.

After Rome was occupied in February 1808, some of the Papal States were annexed to Napoleon's kingdom of Italy that March, the rest following in May 1809. This was the culmination of a process of incessant bullying that led to Napoleon's excommunication by Pius VII, a step that did not trouble Napoleon and that was countered by the arrest of the pope. Whereas medieval rulers had put up antipopes, Napoleon took over the Papal States. Moreover, by increasing French control of Central Italy, this step accentuated the impact of conquering Naples and also helped strengthen Italy as a basis for French power projection in the Mediterranean, an option enhanced by French shipbuilding. Pius remained confined in Savona and then France. He was not able to return to Rome until May 1814.

In 1810, Switzerland lost the Valais, while the Canton of Ticino was occupied. The kingdom of Holland was annexed to France in 1810, as were Hamburg, Lübeck, Bremen and Oldenburg. This served to increase France's ability to enforce the Continental System, the assault on British trade. Having intervened in Spain in 1808, Napoleon allocated Spain north of the Ebro to four military governorships as a stage towards annexation. Opposition within Napoleonic Europe was repressed, forty-eight thousand troops being committed to suppress the rebellion that began in Calabria in 1806.

At the same time, the expansion of Napoleonic Europe saw an intensification in the shape of conscription. Conscription was introduced by Napoleon's ally Bavaria in 1804–5, and extended there in 1809 and 1812, helping to lead to the Tyrolean rebellion of 1809, while 31,400 of the 36,000 Bavarians sent to Russia in 1812 became casualties. In 1809, Joachim Murat, the new French ruler of Naples, introduced French-level conscription. Some soldiers were motivated by ideological factors, but there was also opposition to conscription, as in the Netherlands where it was introduced with annexation to France in 1810, and in Italy. This opposition was an instance of the politically counterproductive nature of conscription, and its dependence therefore on success.

Napoleon did not demand that his allies introduce conscription, but he did require troops based on their treaty commitments. It was their choice how to raise them, but it was common at the time to see conscription as a French imposition, and in every German state it was one of the most hated aspects of the alliance with France. In turn, the Allies demanded military support in 1813–14, and conscription did not disappear with Napoleon's fall. French control over allied forces was direct, being consistent at the corps level and usually lower, the exception being for the Bavarians in 1813. Thus, in 1809, the Saxon army was put under the command of Bernadotte and designated the IX Corps of the *Grande Armée*. This system caused all manner of irritations, but also simplified command and control.

Although it had fought on Prussia's side, Saxony was not treated as a defeated country. Indeed, Elector Frederick Augustus III, who became King Frederick Augustus I in 1806, also became Duke of Warsaw in 1807, in a short-lived remake of the Saxon-Polish union. This strategy serves as a reminder that alongside long-stable frontiers, there were others of very recent standing, which provided Napoleon with an opportunity to reorder areas as but one aspect of a process of such reorderings. Less positively from his point of view, that process over the previous fifty years had been seen in eastern Europe, more specifically in Poland and the lands near the Black Sea, rather than western, where such significant change had largely only begun in the previous half-century in 1792. Partly as a result, change in western Europe linked to French imperialism appeared more disruptive, while in eastern Europe it required not only keeping Austria and Prussia down but, even more clearly, confronting Russia. Reversing the relative Saxon decline at the expense of Prussia in the eighteenth century was not a major issue for Russia, but giving a strengthened Saxony a role in Poland very much was so. Moreover, in 1809, the Duchy of Warsaw was further expanded at the expense of what Austria had gained from Poland in 1795, thus increasing the duchy's frontier with Russia. Like the creation of the Duchy of Warsaw in 1807, this also demonstrated to the partitioning powers that Napoleon could, and would, unmake the Partitions of Poland, which, in particular, was a threat to Russia.[19] Napoleon's strategy reflected his view of the exigencies of the moment, but also looked back to *ancien régime* support for Poland against Sweden, Austria and Russia.

Control over Germany was a crucial prelude to the continued prosecution of the war with Russia. In 1807, the Russians were engaged at Eylau in East Prussia (February 7–8), where repeated French attacks failed to break the Russians, who withdrew during the night. French casualties were heavy (more than Austerlitz, Jena and Auerstädt combined), and, although Napoleon had gained possession of the battlefield, and Russian losses were heavier, he had won neither tactically nor operationally. Indeed, the possibility of defeating him had been demonstrated.[20] At nearby Friedland, however, on June 14, the Russians attacked with their back to the Alle River, losing heavily. The location of these battles showed how East Prussia was a buffer for Russia but also for France's new empire.

This conflict, brought to an end by the Treaty of Tilsit of July 7, 1807, was punishing, but it further vindicated the resilience of the French military machine. The fighting of 1805–7 had demonstrated the superiority of the French corps and divisional structure over the less coherent and less coordinated opposing forces. French staff work, at army and corps levels, was superior to that of both Austria and Russia, and this helped to vitiate the numbers France's opponents put into the field. The quality of French staff work enabled Napoleon to translate his wide-ranging strategic vision into practice, and to force what might have been a segmented war into essentially a struggle in one major theatre of operations where he could use the *Grande Armée* effectively. The concentration of strength was designed to provide victory in what was seen as the primary military theatre. Tilsit made redundant the dispatch in July of British forces to Swedish Pomerania, from where they could have campaigned into northern Germany, and they were withdrawn.

At the same time, the 1807 campaign in Poland demonstrated serious, indeed very serious, weaknesses in the French system and in Napoleon's generalship, the two being linked and interacting to a damaging extent. This was to be far more apparent in 1812 when Russia was invaded. Already, in 1807, the French logistical ethos and process did not work well in eastern Europe, the French did not cope with the impact of weather and the nature of communications, and they proved unable to master the Russian response.

WAR WITH BRITAIN, 1806–9

Despite negotiations in 1806, no serious effort was made to settle differences with Britain, foolishly so, as the resources of worldwide British trade financed opposition to France. These negotiations were designed by Napoleon only to isolate Britain, preparatory to an eventual new French attack. The British were prepared to accept French hegemony in Europe west of a Russian sphere, but Napoleon was not ready to make such hegemony even vaguely palatable. While peace was not on offer, war was to be total. The failure of invasion plans led to a turn to economic blockade, which was seen as a way to force compliance through bankruptcy and thus also end Britain's ability to finance European opposition to France. This was a strategy to complete the harrying of Britain's trade through privateering, the latter made difficult by British naval action, especially the blockade of French ports. However, such a strategy required compliance, including on the part of a number of ostensibly independent actors, and thus a degree of control over the European continent that was to prove elusive.

This was an aspect of a clear politico-economic strategy. The entire Continent was to subordinate its policymaking to France and to become a captive market for French industry, a strategy later attempted by Germany in World War II. The expenditure formerly devoted to transoceanic products, notably sugar, coffee, tea and chocolate, was to end because only Britain was now able to provide them. Instead, the money would be spent to the benefit of France. It would also benefit from the extent to which Britain would be unable to purchase exports from the Continent, notably Baltic grain and timber, which would therefore become less expensive in the French-dominated empire, although less valuable to the exporters, especially Russia and Sweden. Thus, others would suffer to the benefit of France, which would have an empire far larger than its pre-Revolutionary one. The preference for a political reading on economics suffered, however, from a lack of understanding of both politics and economics. In a would-be triumph of the will, Napoleon did not care about the political or economic cost to others, and he understood neither economic theory nor the economics of the moment. Napoleon sought also to engage with the wider global dimensions, particularly by exacerbating differences between Britain and the United States, but his levers for the wider world were weakened greatly when he took over Portugal and Spain in 1807 and 1808 respectively, only totally to lose the chance of influence over their empires. Moreover, Napoleon's assumption that he could provoke revolution in Britain was deeply flawed. Again this was to be matched by Britain's twentieth-century opponents when they hoped for revolution or at least a more pliable government.

Launching Napoleon's Continental System, the Berlin Decree of November 21, 1806—its place of issue under French occupation—stipulated a blockade of Britain, the confiscation of all British goods and the arrest of all Britons. The decree was for France's allies as much as France. The former were pressed to develop their navies for use against Britain. The assault on British trade, which was expanded by the Edict of Fontainebleau (1807) and the two Decrees of Milan (1807), was a unilateral policy formulated and executed without consultation with client states, allies or neutrals. The Continental System hit long-established trades, infringed sovereign rights, and created enormous hostility. As a result, an economic policy centred on French interests meant that Napoleon's effort to anchor his new dynasty in Europe found no popular roots. Indeed, in 1810, he bluntly noted in so far as Italy's was concerned, *"la France avant tout."*[21] Building on the unpopularity of conscription at the behest of France, alliance with France was revealed as costly and humiliating, whereas action against Britain might have been rendered more popular if Napoleon had been willing to abandon some of his hegemonic goals.

Napoleon's grand logistical strategy of the Continental System, a blockade by means of trade denial, turned out to be more damaging to France's allies than it was to Britain, and also made it far harder both to achieve consensus in continental Europe[22] and to negotiate any agreement with Britain. The regulations overlapped with the logistical pressure to provide for Napoleonic warfare, helping to broaden the rejection of both. Moreover, fraud was an aspect of a more general non-compliance with Napoleonic requirements. Even in already conquered areas, such as Italy, the demands of military support, whether direct, as in the requisitioning of mules, or indirect, as in higher taxation, encouraged obstruction, if not resistance. Opposition to conscription was an aspect of this wider reaction.[23] Separately, the strategy of the Continental System also helped lead to the expansion of French military activity, thus requiring more conscripts and taxes.

The viability of this economic strategy, anyway, was greatly changed by the aftereffects of British victory at Trafalgar. In November 1807, Britain issued Orders in Council prohibiting the indirect trade which neutral ships (mostly American) had been carrying between enemy countries and their colonies. The direct trade via neutrals had been banned that January. Now it was no longer permissible to call at some neutral port en route. In April 1809, a new set of British Orders in Council declared a firm blockade. This was totally unacceptable to America.

The British enjoyed a clear superiority over France in ships of the line and, although Napoleon subsequently sought, with some success, to build up his fleet and develop dockyards, his naval strength had been badly battered by losses of sailors in successive defeats. Moreover, his attempt to translate his far-flung territorial control into naval power was unsuccessful, and to an extent far greater than the situation on land. This was already apparent in 1807, when the Portuguese and Danish fleets were kept out of French hands, the former by British persuasion and intimidation, the latter by British attack.[24]

Furthermore, a series of British victories, while each less impressive than Trafalgar, nevertheless inflicted considerable damage on the French system. On February 6, 1806, a squadron of five of the line that had escaped from Rochefort was destroyed off Saint-Domingue, while on March 13, 1806, two warships sailing back from the Indian Ocean were captured as they neared France, and in December 1811, a British attack on Griessie (now Gresik) in Java destroyed three ships of the line, the last Dutch warships in the region.

Meanwhile, believing that everything was possible for him, Napoleon pushed the limits. Yet again, he made the fundamental mistake of not shutting down one conflict before embarking upon another. Portugal was invaded in November 1807, despite its attempts to appease Napoleon, because he insisted on closing it to British trade and saw its conquest as a way to increase the French military presence in Iberia. In addition, Napoleon hoped to close Latin America to Britain's trade, which would greatly hinder its commercial position and ensure that the Continental System spanned the Atlantic.

As an instance both of his strategy of divide and rule and of his willingness to create totally new political entities, the secret Treaty of Fontainebleau of October 27, 1807, between Napoleon and Charles IV of Spain proposed a partition of Portugal. The kingdom of Northern Lusitania, based on Oporto, was to go to Louis II of Etruria, in return for his loss to France of Etruria (Tuscany). This would be a way of pleasing Spain, as Louis, an infant, was under the regency of his mother, Maria Louisa, a daughter of Charles IV. Much of the south would go to Charles's favourite minister, Godoy, and become the principality of the Algarve, with its capital at Évora. The remainder would be under French control, with their capital at Lisbon. The treaty, however, was never implemented.

Once rapidly conquered, with Lisbon entered by the French under Junot on November 30, there was no attempt to conciliate the Portuguese. Napoleon, instead, launched a smash-and-grab, instructing Junot, whom he had made governor of Portugal as well as Duke of Abrantes, to requisition the property of the fifteen thousand people who had left for Brazil and also ordering a one-hundred-million-franc fine. Heavy taxes were followed by executions of those who did not cooperate. Increasingly imperious and unwilling to listen to critical advice, Napoleon dismissed his experienced, independent-minded foreign minister, Talleyrand, in August 1807. Napoleon was also to turn out his brother Louis in July 1810 because, as king of the Netherlands, he was insufficiently compliant over the Continental System. The notion of Napoleon as defensive minded scarcely matched his treatment of the views of those close to him. Moreover, he found it very difficult to take advice, which was not the basis for strategic understanding.

RELATIONS WITH RUSSIA, 1807–9

By the Treaty of Tilsit of July 7, 1807, Alexander I had reached an agreement that left Napoleon dominant in western and central Europe. This was an acceptance of French hegemony that previous tsars had refused to signal. Indeed, in 1735 and 1748, Russian armies had moved into Germany in order to put pressure on France. Such an acknowledgement was especially important given the rise of Russian power in the closing decades of the eighteenth century with the partition of Poland and the defeat of the Turks. The signature at Tilsit, on the Russo-Prussian frontier, was a testimony to the range of Napoleon's power, while the treaty applied the principle of the partition of Poland to the whole of Europe. Handing over the Ionian Islands and the port of Cattaro (Kotor, in modern Montenegro) to France, Russia lost little territory (and gained some of Prussian Poland), but her policy was now intertwined with that of Napoleon, while Austria was totally isolated.

Alexander agreed not only to deliver his Mediterranean base, the Ionian Isles, to France, but also to join with her in offering Britain peace terms. If these were rejected, Alexander was obliged to go to war with Britain and to coerce Austria, Denmark, Portugal and Sweden into doing the same. In return, France agreed to fight Turkey if she rejected the peace with Russia that Napoleon was to seek to obtain. If so, the Turks were to lose most of the Balkans, thus creating the need for a Franco-Russian entente over the fate of what would be a fatally weakened Turkish empire. Thus, the interconnectedness of struggles was demonstrated in a strategy designed to move them in France's favour. Instability in Turkey, which he had pressed to fight Russia, but where Selim III was deposed in May 1807 and Mustafa IV was to be in July 1808, had encouraged Napoleon to feel that it was a broken reed and therefore to consider a new situation after Tilsit. The alignment with Turkey was abandoned, and, instead, mediation between Russia and Turkey was offered. In practice, Napoleon decided it was in his interest not to let Russia become too powerful. This entailed his deciding between keeping most of the Turkish empire under Constantinople, letting Austria get a significant tranche, and ensuring that France received Constantinople, all of which were options that angered Alexander. Meanwhile, Britain called the Russian bluff, rejecting Russia's terms without leading to war, and then seeking to benefit from Alexander's growing suspicions of Napoleon. In turn, this effort increased Napoleon's concerns about Alexander.

More immediately, Frederick William III was abandoned at Tilsit by his Russian ally. Under the Franco-Prussian treaty of July 9, Prussia was to lose her territory west of the Elbe to the kingdom of Westphalia, Cottbus to Saxony, much of Prussian Poland to the Duchy of Warsaw and a small part of Prussian Poland to Russia. In total, Prussia was reduced from 125 to 61 million square miles and from a population of 9.75 million to 4.5. The Prussian army was also reduced in size, being limited to forty-three thousand men, a size that made it impossible to protect even the territories that remained and one that ensured that Prussia would not be a major player in coalition warfare unless the situation changed. This made Russia more significant, although also launching a Prussian movement for reform and renewal that offered a range of political and ideological nostrums to ensure the strategy of renewed strength while also encouraging a Prussian impulse for German nationalism.[25]

Napoleon followed up Tilsit by continuing to occupy Prussia, which, in March 1808, was ordered to pay an indemnity of 154.5 million francs, and, also, by trying to make Russia invade Sweden; to accept a French gain of Silesia from Prussia, if Russia seized Moldavia and Wallachia from the Turks; and to grant French companies monopoly privileges in Russia. The Russian envoy in Paris from October 1807 to October 1808, Count Pyotr Tolstoi, a general, saw such demands as part of an inexorable aggrandisement driven by Napoleon's personality and his reliance on his large army. Tolstoi urged preparations to resist French attack.

Meanwhile, the Franco-Russian entente had transformed the situation in the Baltic, although the Russian naval challenge to the British fleet in the Baltic in 1808 proved inconclusive and short-lived as the Russians retreated to the safety of harbour, the strategy they were later to follow in the Crimean War (1854–56). The Baltic was strategically vital not so much due to the capacity it offered for amphibious operations, but, rather, as a consequence of its being the principal European source of naval stores, as well as a major source of grain.

In 1808, the Swedes rejected the offer of a British force sent to help them resist Russia. The British also sought to persuade Sweden to conquer Norway from France's ally Denmark, and thus affect another subordinate, but potentially significant, strategic sphere, the North Sea world. The last tends to be ignored, but it was of great concern to the British and led to their acquiring the island of Heligoland in the 1814–15 Vienna settlement. In the event, Swedish-ruled Finland fell to Russian attack in 1808–9 in a conflict that was kept separate from the main war, like the Winter War between Russia and Finland in 1939–40. The Swedes were to conquer Norway, but not until 1814.

WAR WITH SPAIN

In 1808, Napoleon used the disputes between Charles IV and Crown Prince Ferdinand—who succeeded Charles as Ferdinand VII on March 17 as a result of a coup—in order to replace the Bourbon monarchy in Spain by a Bonapartist one, that of his brother Joseph. That was not the original objective, the latter instead being rather a matter of increasing French control over Spain, its navy and its empire, which was what Ferdinand was actually offering. However, Napoleon's desire instead for total control became both goal and context. An alliance amounting to indirect control was not enough, and Charles and Ferdinand were tricked and bullied into handing over the kingdom to Napoleon. His dynastic aggrandisement in the person of Joseph matched, but in a totally different context, the establishment of a Bourbon branch on the Spanish throne in 1700. In part, Napoleon's policy reflected dynasticism as strategic goal and means, but there was also the strategy of keeping Spain under control. The comparison of Napoleon in 1808 and Louis XIV in 1700 is instructive, as Louis in part was motivated by a determination to keep the Austrian Habsburgs out of Spain, but there was no such danger in 1808. Instead, the context was one not of any threat to French interests but of the opportunity presented by Tilsit as well as anger about Britain's continued opposition.

Instead of consolidating his position, Napoleon forced a crisis. Anti-French risings in Spain (from May 2) and Portugal led to the Peninsular War, creating a military and political problem that was to challenge Napoleon for the remainder of his period of office, although rarely to dominate his concern. A surrounded French corps of twenty thousand troops surrendered at Bailén on July 21, and Joseph fled Madrid. In response, Napoleon was not interested in even considering compromise or restraint. Indeed, the tone of his strategy, the key element in strategy, was demonstrated in his determination to reimpose control, and, in doing so, to make an example. That was scarcely necessary, as his opponents in central Europe were quiescent or vulnerable. Moreover, any conflict in Spain would affect the situation in Portugal, and France was least well-placed to cope with British intervention or pressure in Iberia. In addition, any failure would compromise the attempt to derive benefit from the Spanish overseas empire. Napoleon totally misjudged the situation in Latin America.

Indeed, in so far as there was a strategy directed against British trade, rather than an aspiration to that end, such a strategy would be compromised by leaving the Spanish overseas world to turn to Britain. With his failure to take over this world or indeed Spain peacefully, Napoleon lost his opportunity to continue a major maritime and transoceanic struggle with Britain. The process by which other Western transoceanic empires came into the British orbit, through some, or all, of conquest, intimidation, alliance, protection or trade, was greatly pushed forward. It was also seen with the uninvited British occupation of the Portuguese colonies of Goa from 1799 to 1813, and Macao from 1808 to 1811.

The invasion of Spain also gave Napoleon a new war aim. Under the treaty with Alexander signed at Erfurt on October 12, 1808, which essentially confirmed Tilsit and underlined Austria's isolation, no agreement was to be made with Britain unless she recognised the Bonapartist position in Spain. These terms would have entailed French dominance of Latin America, and that underlines the extent to which, as in 1700, the Spanish succession was a struggle for Atlantic dominance. British troops were sent to Portugal in 1808 and, after several years campaigning, eventually overcame the French in Spain in 1813. In the meanwhile, France also had to fight Spanish regulars and guerrillas, operations that absorbed large numbers of troops. Spanish naval strength had also been lost from the French camp, greatly limiting Napoleon's post-Trafalgar attempt to rebuild his navy in order to challenge Britain anew. The French, moreover, lost the six ships of the line sheltering in Cadiz and Vigo as well as the use of the key Spanish naval bases. By 1810, Britain had 50 percent of the ships of the line in the world, up from 29 percent in 1790, in short still a leading position, but with that position now meaning far more in terms of both absolute and relative strength.

Napoleon's success in invading Spain in 1808, advancing via Vitoria and Burgos to Madrid, proved only operational because, greatly encouraged by French exactions and other aspects of French policy, resistance continued. This was abundantly the case in Catalonia, an important region because of its proximity to France; its industrial and mercantile significance; its major port, Barcelona; and its position athwart routes to other regions. By September 1808, the French only held two major positions in Catalonia, Figueres and Barcelona, both of which were in effect besieged, while Napoleon had had to send three additional divisions into the region in October. These besieged and captured Roses and, in December, relieved Barcelona, but the situation was difficult for the French.

More generally, French logistical demands placed a great strain on the Spanish economy and greatly exacerbated opposition, encouraging resistance.[26] Opportunistic banditry played a role in resistance, but the efforts of Spanish troops were more significant. Poorly armed, poorly supplied and poorly trained, Spanish armies and irregulars were repeatedly defeated by the French, who, helped by larger numbers of troops in 1810–11 and by improvements in counter-insurgency operations, conquered the regions of Andalusia (except for the besieged but sea-supplied city of Cadiz) in 1810, Estremadura in 1811 and Lower Catalonia and Valencia in 1811–12. Imposing serious blows, the French were present in most of Spain.

Nevertheless, the Spanish army was able to maintain its structure and continue fighting, which reduced the numbers of French troops available for counter-insurgency warfare. The burden, in terms of garrisons and casualties, on the French of operating against Spanish forces was considerable. The Spaniards were generally unsuccessful in formal conflict, and British generals could be highly critical of their organisation. However, as with the opposition to the Japanese in occupied areas of China in 1937–45, their regular and guerrilla operations denied the French control over the Spanish countryside and, in particular, greatly harmed their communications and logistics. Moreover, due to the need to confront the Spaniards, the French were unable to concentrate their larger forces against the British, who were based in Portugal, where they successfully held off the French in 1810–11 and from which they advanced into Spain, as in 1812. In 1813, the main French field army, which was heavily defeated by the British under Wellington, with significant Portuguese and Spanish support, at the Battle of Vitoria on June 21, one of the more decisive battles of the war, was weakened by the detachment of substantial forces to deal with guerrillas in Navarre and the Basque Country.

To a degree in the peninsula, the French were on interior lines compared to the British, but the wretched land communications gave Britain, with its control of the sea, an advantage over the French, albeit one that had to be protected by the blockade of the French Mediterranean naval base at Toulon. Moreover, France's interior lines were threatened by the resilience of Spanish opposition. By moving into Spain, Wellington also faced the challenge of communication links, but these were a matter of distance, supplies and vulnerability to French attack, not guerrilla opposition.

Thanks to its length, the Peninsula War was different from the other large-scale Napoleonic campaigns. This contrast had strategic, political and logistical contexts and implications, but also ensured that relations between civilians and occupying or allied forces played out over a longer time span. They were also of great significance due to the struggle to win Spanish support. Both British and French soldiers were apt to see Spaniards as somewhat uncivilised, and there was also a sense of sexual competition over Spanish women, with British soldiers inclined to present themselves as heroic liberators.[27] For Spaniards, more realistically, troops were apt to be a curse.

As with other states, the subsequent analysis of the struggle against Napoleon was affected by patriotic and nationalist interpretations, as well as by assumptions about the most effective nature of insurrectionary warfare. Because the struggle was seen as Spain's *Guerra de Independencia*, it had a particular resonance. As with America in 1775–83, the subsequent emphasis was on guerrilla campaigns rather than on the regular Spanish army, which was largely ignored. However, in practice, this army was important, and notably so in its ability to keep operating, while the guerrillas were more tied to the regular Spanish army, and thus the government opposing the French, than is sometimes implied. Much of the "little war" was waged by regular troops, while even those commands which originated outside the regular military structures of the state were in many instances sooner or later both militarised and incorporated into the army. In Spain, there is not much of a stress on British support, but it also was highly significant in the resistance to France.[28]

French observers, at the time and subsequently, commented on the guerrilla tactics of the Spaniards, which helped provide them with an explanation of failure. Thus, Jean-Frédéric-Auguste Lemière de Corvey, who had also served in the Vendée, emphasised, in his *Des Partisans et des corps irréguliers* (Paris, 1823), the ability of guerrillas to isolate regular troops, denying them mobility and defeating them without battle.

In practice, the combination of Spanish regular troops, guerrillas and British intervention no more forced a French failure than French invasion forced success. However, this combination did mean that any such French success required a strategy entailing more and many troops, large quantities of supplies, a search for local allies, a careful definition of what success could entail, opportunities forgone elsewhere, and risks incurred. Napoleon was simply incapable psychologically of such a prudent strategy. He needed success and, if not in one sphere, then elsewhere. This was a key background to his rash provocation of Alexander and his decision for war.

WAR WITH AUSTRIA, 1809

The Bonapartist coup in Spain in 1808 also gave an edge to Napoleon's pressure on Austria. During the spring and summer of 1808, Austrian fears led to a large-scale rearming and mobilisation, with Austrian princes making inflammatory statements that quickly came to Napoleon's attention. His pressure for Austrian disarmament was thereby founded on Austrian moves and on very good intelligence supplied by his embassy in Vienna. Napoleon's strategy was to dissuade Austria from action, including by means of diplomatic pressure exerted by Alexander I. In the wake of his meeting with Alexander at Erfurt, Napoleon felt confident that he could go to Spain, and deployed his forces accordingly, including dissolving the structure of the *Grande Armée* in October 1808. His confidence that Austria had been deterred was a miscalculation, while Alexander also erred in assessing Austrian intentions.[29]

The French treatment of Spain did not encourage Austria, where, on February 8, 1809, the government again decided on war: it both felt its safety threatened by French strategy, which included a demand for disarmament, and feared a recurrence of the coup method already staged against Spain. Moreover, Napoleon's entanglement in the Peninsular War appeared to present Austria with a major opportunity, and notably so if it could win additional support. Whereas in 1800 and 1805, Napoleon had not had to confront a two-front war on the Continent, now he did, and Spain, in addition, had been subtracted from his list of allies. Nevertheless, Napoleon was not going to be influenced by that, while, unlike in 1799 and 1805, Russia was not willing to act against France. Once armed, the Austrian finance minister warned that the armaments could not be long sustained, thus increasing the pressure for action. There was an understandable sense that there was no choice, that French policy anyway threatened to impose the consequences of defeat, and that war was the sole alternative.

Austria got both war and defeat in 1809. Francis declared war in April, invading Bavaria on the 9th, only for Napoleon, with his 170,000-strong *Armée d'Allemagne*, much of it German, to gain and use the initiative, rapidly beating the Austrians at Abensberg, Eggmühl and Regensburg, in a series of clashes rather than a major battle. The Austrians were handicapped by poorly conceived war aims, inadequate and divided central leadership and a foolish strategy. They had misjudged Prussia and seriously exaggerated the degree of support they would receive in Germany, and therefore the problem that would be created for Napoleon. This was a classic instance of wish fulfilment as strategy. Indeed, Bavaria, Saxony and Westphalia each provided Napoleon with a corps.

Having succeeded in South Germany, Napoleon then invaded Austria and was able to capture Vienna on May 13. Four days later, he ordered the annexation of those parts of the Papal States not seized the previous year. However, Napoleon found Austria a tougher opponent than in 1805. Furthermore, his bold advance, a hallmark of his style, proved a risky strategy, as it exposed him, at the end of a long supply line, to problems in a number of directions. With his style of command the substance, as so often, of his strategy, Napoleon sought to press on to a fresh victory that would overcome his opponent's will. It was entirely typical that, in the subsequent advance, Napoleon displayed an inadequate grasp of the need to secure sound reconnaissance, notably on the state of the Danube and the pontoon bridges that could be constructed. This failure was an aspect of a broader situational deficiency in Napoleonic strategy than in the early 1800s, that of assessing his opponents.

At Aspern-Essling (May 21–22, 1809), Napoleon's overly bold and inadequately reconnoitred attack on a superior Austrian force was repelled, in part because the Danube bridges were broken, and he had to abandon the battlefield in the face of a serious Austrian advance and better Austrian generalship. Thereafter, Archduke Charles rested on the defensive, while Napoleon ably prepared a fresh attack across the Danube. At Wagram on July 5–6, Napoleon proved the better general, and the French corps commanders were superior to their Austrian counterparts. Napoleon's counter-attack drove the Austrians from the field, but it was no Austerlitz. The French victory was essentially due to leadership, and to their overall superiority in troops and matériel, in what was a battle of attrition. There are no agreed casualty figures, but the French suffered maybe thirty-four to thirty-seven thousand casualties and the Austrians thirty to forty-one thousand. The Austrians did not then collapse, but withdrew and were able to fight again at Znaim on July 10–11.[30]

Austrian effectiveness in these battles has been seen as a stage in the emergence of modern war.[31] However, this analysis places too great a weight on one campaign, rather as with the weight placed on Napoleon's success in 1805. Nevertheless, the analysis reflects the extent to which Napoleon was facing more impressive opponents from 1807.

The Austrians had also invaded northern Italy in 1809, but that campaign did not make a material difference. Isolated diplomatically and militarily, the Austrians, moreover, received no help from Frederick William III of Prussia or the other German rulers. Prusso-Austrian rivalry and mistrust were important to Napoleon's success. The large diversionary British attack intended to destroy the threat from the dockyards at Antwerp to British naval supremacy was too late, unsuccessful and very costly in manpower. The rising in Bavarian-ruled Tyrol was initially successful, but, understandably due to the focus on the main challenge, it never received effective Austrian support, and Bavarian and French forces eventually reconquered the region. However, they only did so after a bitter conflict, including a number of serious checks for the Bavarians, which indicated the difficulty of counter-insurgency warfare. This difficulty led most troops to prefer conventional battle, even one as deadly as Wagram.[32] There were also revolts in Italy and Germany against Napoleon's system.

Now allied with France and pursuing its own interests, Russia offered no support to Austria. Instead, Russia attacked her with sixty thousand troops, occupying Galicia, Austrian Poland. Yet, this attack was not on the scale that Napoleon required and was also mounted in a way that angered his allied Polish forces from the Duchy of Warsaw. Napoleon, indeed, felt betrayed by Russia, and Alexander had certainly wanted France defeated. Russian conduct in the crisis demonstrated the unfixed nature of post-Tilsit international relations and the resulting context of strategic uncertainty in which the major powers sought to avoid isolation. Yet, there was also a fundamental difference. Alexander did not want Austria weakened, as that would strengthen Napoleon and leave no balance or restraint. Napoleon, however, had no such hesitation about weakening third parties, which exemplified the difficulties of trying to cooperate with him.

The Treaty of Schönbrunn of October 14, 1809, not only awarded Austrian territory to France and Bavaria, particularly the Illyrian Provinces to France and Salzburg for Bavaria, but also left the Duchy of Warsaw, a French client state in Poland, with significant gains from Austria. As a result of France acquiring the Illyrian Provinces, Austria was left landlocked, and France acquired a Balkan foothold, which could serve as a basis for further expansion. Humiliated, Austria was treated as Prussia had been in 1807–8: it had to pay a large indemnity, and its army was limited to 150,000 troops. Austria, moreover, had to recognise Joseph as king of Spain and join the Continental System.

In 1810, after Alexander I had not responded to Napoleon's wish to marry his sister, Anna Pavlovna, Napoleon married the Archduchess Marie Louise, a spoil of war designed to cement Austria's new relationship with France. Until the summer of 1813, the Austrians sought peaceful partnership with Napoleon, and to prevent France and Russia from allying against them. The rivalry and mutual distrust of Austria and Russia after 1805 was important to Napoleon's success, and the temporary resolution of this rivalry in 1813 hit Napoleon hard.

At the same time, the conflicts in 1807–9 had revealed deficiencies in the Napoleonic army, deficiencies that contrasted markedly with the successes in 1805–6. This was clear not only with overall battlefield achievement but also with those of particular branches, notably the artillery. Napoleon's experience of the devastating massed fire of the more heavily gunned Russians at Eylau in 1807 led him to press forward his own massing of artillery, greatly increasing the number of cannon in his massed batteries.[33] Already, the production of the heavier twelve-pounders had been pressed forward in 1805. The competitive context, however, has to be noted. At Aspern-Essling in 1809, as many as 190 Austrian guns had inflicted serious damage on the French, this a reflection of Austrian improvements from 1805. There are separate questions about whether French tactics, and indeed operational methods, degenerated later on during Napoleon's reign, and whether he devoted insufficient attention to tactical details and improvement.

Separately, in Poland in 1807, in Spain at any point and in Russia in 1812, the French logistical system fell apart, as roads were non-existent or poor, and the land was barren. By contrast, 1808–9 was, as part of an effective use of operational art, a logistical triumph. Major elements of the *Grande Armée* allocated to the new *Armée d'Espagne* were moved from central Germany to Spain in 1808 almost seamlessly, in the context of the time. In 1809, when the Guard had to shift from Spain to France and then became part of the new *Armée d'Allemagne*, which was a large force assembled to operate against Austria that was moved to the Upper Danube, this move was a major achievement. Napoleon complained a lot, but he did apologise to Clarke as a result of the redeployment working well. The European powers were taken unawares by this logistical capability, which contrasted with the difficulties Napoleon had encountered in Poland in 1807. Moreover, once arrived, the French operated with greater resolution and rashness than the Austrians, not least with the crossing of the Danube.[34]

Napoleon's logistical method (it was scarcely a system) encouraged a movement into fresh pastures. However, this was no solution where supplies were limited, as in Russia and Spain, or already exhausted by frequent campaigning, and was also of limited value when French forces rested on the defensive. In his chapter on "Maintenance and Supply" in *On War*, Clausewitz noted:

> How vast a difference there is between a supply line stretching from Vilna [Vilnius] to Moscow, where every wagon has to be procured by force, and a line from Cologne to Paris, via Liège, Louvain, Brussels, Mons, Valenciennes and Cambrai, where a commercial transaction, a bill of exchange, is enough to produce millions of rations![35]

Clausewitz thereby drew attention to the significance for the logistical landscape of pre-existing mercantile networks and agrarian wealth. In western Europe, there was a higher population and more resources, the roads were relatively good, and the distances from France were less than in eastern Europe. In Spain, as in Russia, moreover, resistance greatly harmed French communications and logistics, which, again contributed to the unstable character of the French hegemony.

Separately, corruption was always endemic in the War Ministry, although Napoleon sought to curb it until he was away for too long in Russia in 1812. Other problems included muddle at the local level behind the lines, notably crossed wires and disputes with local administrators. More generally, the rhetoric of Napoleonic reform did not generally match the reality of a new conservatism in the shape of a highly personalised imperial monarchy focused on operational military command, bringing forward an imperial aristocracy based primarily on military service.

THE NAVAL WAR

Meanwhile, Britain's naval strength and success remained necessary and vital. The general situation was more favourable for Britain than in 1795–1805, especially after the Spanish navy and crucial naval bases were denied France in 1808. Furthermore, the blockaded French navy was no longer a force that was combat ready and therefore a strategically valid tool. The longer it remained in harbour, the more its efficiency declined, as officers and crews had less operational experience. It remained difficult for the British to predict French moves when at sea, but the French were less able to gain the initiative than hitherto, and the risk to British security and commerce therefore decreased. The French and allied squadrons that did sail out were generally defeated, both reflecting and sustaining the major strategic asymmetry in Britain's favour. Blockade was an important part of this process, reducing the supplies to French squadrons and preventing them from sailing forth. In part to extend the ready range of naval activities, including blockade, the British accordingly developed naval bases and facilities, especially at Malta, Gibraltar and Lisbon.[36]

In 1805–7, aside from France's Atlantic base at Brest, the British focused their blockade on the Spanish Atlantic base of Cadiz, but, thereafter, they concentrated even more on the French Mediterranean base of Toulon, the blockade the first line of defence for British and allied interests, such as the protection of Sicily; the ability to mount offensive operations, including in eastern Spain; and moves to limit French operations in the eastern Mediterranean. Toulon had become more significant a threat because in early 1808 the French Rochefort squadron evaded blockaders and got there. That spring, Napoleon ordered the movement of the fleet to Taranto so as to be able to support operations in the eastern Mediterranean, although, in the event, there was no such move of operational activity.

British anxieties reflected the potential significance of naval strategy. Thus, in January 1811, the British feared that the Toulon squadron would be able to escape and attack Wellington's position at Lisbon, providing a second version of the Yorktown disaster of 1781. However, there was no sortie, and although in 1808 the French fleet was able to relieve their garrison on Corfu, French attempts at sorties from Toulon failed in 1809 and 1812.

Moreover, to Napoleon's absolute fury, the British had rapidly responded to Tilsit in September 1807 by attacking Copenhagen and seizing the Danish navy. This was a dramatic alteration in the naval balance of power in the Baltic and North Seas, and more generally of significance for Napoleon's ability to put pressure on both Sweden and Russia. Although Alexander was angered by the attack, it also demonstrated the weakness of the French system and of French strategy, and at the very moment that Napoleon was seeking to repurpose both after the difficulties he had encountered in fighting Russia. In what was a year crowded with incidents, the attack on Portugal in October was a response designed to demonstrate French power as well as to provide the opportunity to establish a military presence in Spain.

Naval strength was a vital resource in alliance diplomacy, in economic strategy and in providing support to British operations on the Continent, notably in the Peninsular War, particularly underwriting an impressive logistical system that was a major strategic asset.[37] Although there were differences between admirals and generals,[38] commitment to the Peninsular War was a promising strategy for a variety of reasons, not least taking advantage of opposition to Napoleon, providing a forward defence to the Portuguese and Spanish overseas empires and keeping key harbours out of French hands, particularly Cadiz and Lisbon. However, there were also problems, and, in comparative terms, it is worth noting the total British failure when coming to the support of Greece in 1941. Any deployment of troops risked leaving troops vulnerable and with their evacuation difficult. This was particularly so if these troops operated into the interior and became exposed to responses by superior opposing forces, as happened to Sir John Moore in Spain in 1808–9. Once the objective extended beyond a coastal purpose, then the entire risk element of the strategy was transformed.

Naval strength also made the strategy of capturing colonies possible. In 1807, Francisco de Miranda, a prominent Venezuelan revolutionary, warned the British government that France could move troops from Martinique to Venezuela, then part of Spanish America,[39] but British naval power made that unlikely. In the period covered by this chapter, there were British failures, notably against Spanish-ruled Buenos Aires in 1807, but the British continued the colonial conquests seen after war had resumed in 1803, in particular gaining Cape Town in 1806. The Danish West Indian islands and several of the Dutch ones followed in 1809, as did Fort Louis, on the Senegal River, the last French base in Africa, and Martinique. In 1810, Guadeloupe and Mauritius were captured, and, in 1811, Dutch Java. Moreover, in India, the British were able to bring the Second Maratha War (1803–6) to a successful conclusion without French intervention, a key advantage that had been lacking in the early 1780s. This indicated the marked deterioration in France's strategic position since the *ancien régime*.

Another measure of respective strategic capability was provided by the astonishing expansion of mercantile harbour facilities in Britain, one that was not matched in France even at the height of the Napoleonic empire. The excavations for the twenty-acre London Dock were begun at Wapping in 1801. It was furnished with a comprehensive range of warehouses, like the West India Docks opened in 1802. Further downstream came the East India Docks in 1805, and, on the southern bank of the Thames, work began on the Surrey Commercial Docks in 1807. In 1800, just before the development of enclosed docks, some 1,800 vessels were being moored in the river at London.

This was a wealth France could not match, however much it tried, both by economic policies in French-dominated Europe and by the anti-British Continental System. Moreover, to Napoleon, British wealth was serious, as he blamed Britain for his problems elsewhere, for example for stirring up Austria against him in 1809. This almost paranoid tendency to blame the actions of others on Britain's undoubted efforts to stir up opposition was an aspect of Napoleon's bullying, each part of the psychological context for his strategy. That he had a second-rate navy with poor naval commanders exacerbated the problem, continually undermining his strategic plans and options unless narrowly focused on land operations. Napoleon's strategic response, that of rebuilding his navy through conquest, failed at almost every turn, in part due to the success of the British response, but also because the emperor really did not understand his options and constraints. This was an aspect of a major feature of strategic purpose, tone and mood.

NOTES

1. Ruth Scurr, *Napoleon: A Life Told in Gardens and Shadows* (London: Chatto and Windus, 2021).
2. Philip Dwyer, *Napoleon: The Path to Power* (New Haven, CT: Yale University Press, 2008); Michael Hughes, *Forging Napoleon's Grande Armée: Motivation, Military*

Culture, and Masculinity in the French Army, 1800–1808 (New York: New York University Press, 2012).

3. Peter Paret, *The Cognitive Challenge of War: Prussia 1806* (Princeton, NJ: Princeton University Press, 2009).

4. Phillip Cuccia, "'Giornale Della Libertà': The French Occupation and Administration of Mantua, 1797–99," *Consortium, 2001*, 182; Frederick Schneid, *Soldiers of Napoleon's Kingdom of Italy: Army, State and Society, 1800–1814* (Boulder, CO: Westview, 1995).

5. Alan Forrest, *Napoleon's Men: The Soldiers of the Revolution and Empire* (London: Hambledon Continuum, 2002).

6. Dundas to General Sir Ralph Abercromby, May 5, 1800, NA. WO. 6/21, p. 28.

7. Nelson to Addington, March 19, 1804, Exeter, Devon CRO. 152M C 1804 ON33.

8. Brendan Simms, *The Impact of Napoleon: Prussian High Politics, Foreign Policy and the Crisis of the Executive, 1797–1806* (Cambridge: Cambridge University Press, 1997); P. G. Dwyer, "Two Definitions of Neutrality: Prussia, the European States-System, and the French Invasion of Hanover in 1803," *International History Review* 19 (197): 522–40.

9. Frederick Schneid, "The Grand Strategy of the Habsburg Monarchy during the War of the Third Coalition," *Consortium, 2007*, 313–21.

10. Charles Esdaile, "De-constructing the French Wars: Napoleon as Anti-strategist," *Journal of Strategic Studies* 31 (2008): 515–52.

11. Martin van Creveld, *Supplying War: Logistics from Wallenstein to Patton* (Cambridge: Cambridge University Press, 1977), 40–74; A. Starrepoulos, "General Talleyrand, I Presume? The 'Reorganisation' of the Logistics of the *Grande Armée* in 1807," *Consortium, 2007*, 269–78.

12. Frederick Schneid, *Napoleon's Conquest of Europe: The War of the Third Coalition* (Westport, CT: Greenwood, 2005), 106–10.

13. Frederick Schneid, *Napoleon's Italian Campaigns, 1805–1815* (Westport, CT: Greenwood, 2002).

14. William Flayhart III, *Counterpoint to Trafalgar: The Anglo-Russian Invasion of Naples, 1805–1806* (Columbia: University of South Carolina Press, 1992).

15. Michael Broers, *Napoleon's Other War: Bandits, Rebels and Their Pursuers in the Age of Revolutions* (Witney: Peter Lang, 2010).

16. Milton Finley, *The Most Monstrous of Wars: Napoleonic Guerrilla War in Southern Italy, 1806–11* (Columbia: University of South Carolina Press, 1994).

17. Dennis Showalter, "Reform and Stability: Prussia's Military Dialectic from Hubertusberg to Waterloo," in *The Projection and Limitations of Imperial Powers, 1618–1850*, ed. Frederick Schneid (Leiden: Brill, 2012), 93.

18. David Chandler, *Jena 1806: Napoleon Destroys Prussia* (London: Osprey, 1993).

19. Jaroslaw Czubaty, *The Duchy of Warsaw, 1807–1815: A Napoleonic Outpost in Central Europe* (London: Bloomsbury, 2016).

20. James Arnold and Ralph Reinertsen, *Crisis in the Snows: Russia Confronts Napoleon; The Eylau Campaign, 1806–1807* (Lexington, VA: Napoleon Books, 2007).

21. Napoleon to Eugène, Viceroy of Italy, August 23, 1810, *Napoléon*, 21:60–61.

22. Katherine Aalestad and Johan Joor, eds., *Revisiting Napoleon's Continental System: Local, Regional, and European Experiences* (Basingstoke: Palgrave, 2015).

23. Michael Broers, *The Napoleonic Empire in Italy, 1796–1814* (Basingstoke: Palgrave, 2005); Alexander Grab, "Army, State and Society: Conscription and Desertion in Napoleonic Italy, 1802–1814," *Journal of Modern History* 67 (1995): 25–54.

24. Thomas Munch-Petersen, *Defying Napoleon: How Britain Bombarded Copenhagen and Seized the Danish Fleet* (Stroud: Sutton, 2007).

25. Matthew Levinger, *Enlightened Nationalism: The Transformation of Prussia's Political Culture, 1806–1848* (Oxford: Oxford University Press, 2000).

26. John Morgan, "War Feeding War? The Impact of Logistics on the Napoleonic Occupation of Catalonia," *Journal of Military History* 73 (2009): 83–116.

27. Gavin Daly, *The British Soldier in the Peninsular War: Encounters with Spain and Portugal, 1808–1814* (Basingstoke: Basingstoke, 2013).

28. Charles Esdaile, *The Peninsular War: A New History* (London: Allen Lane, 2002); "The Spanish Army of Napoleonic Wars," in *Armies of the Napoleonic Wars*, ed. Gregory Fremont Barnes, 188–213 (Barnsley: Pen and Sword, 2011); *Outpost of Empire: The Napoleonic Occupation of Andalucia, 1810–1812* (Norman: University of Oklahoma Press, 2012); and "Guerillas and Bandits in the Serrania da Ronda, 1810–1812," *Small Wars and Insurgencies* 25 (2014): 814–27.

29. John Gill, *1809: Thunder on the Danube; Napoleon's Defeat of the Habsburgs*, vol. 1, *Abensberg* (Barnsley: Pen and Sword, 2009).

30. John Gill, *1809: Thunder on the Danube; Napoleon's Defeat of the Habsburgs*, vol. 3, *Wagram and Znaim* (Barnsley: Pen and Sword, 2010).

31. Robert Epstein, *Napoleon's Last Victory and the Emergence of Modern War* (Lawrence, KS: University Press of Kansas, 1994).

32. John Gill, "'Those Miserable Tyroleans': Tactics and Alliance Politics in 1809," *Consortium, 2001*, 253.

33. Bruce McConachy, "The Roots of Artillery Doctrine: Napoleonic Artillery Tactics Reconsidered," *Journal of Military History* 65 (2001): 632.

34. John Kuehn, *Napoleonic Warfare: The Operational Art of the Great Campaigns* (Santa Barbara, CA: Praeger, 2015).

35. Carl von Clausewitz, *On War*, ed. Michael Howard and Peter Paret (Princeton, NJ: Princeton University Press, 1976), 340.

36. Jason Musteen, *Nelson's Refuge: Gibraltar in the Age of Napoleon* (Annapolis, MD: Naval Institute Press, 2011).

37. Robert Sutcliffe, *British Expeditionary Warfare and the Defeat of Napoleon, 1793–1815* (Woodbridge: Boydell and Brewer, 2016).

38. Kevin McCranie, *Admiral Lord Keith and the Naval War against Napoleon* (Gainesville: University Press of Florida, 2006).

39. Miranda to Robert, Viscount Castlereagh, June 10, 1807, BL. Loan Manuscripts 57/107 fol. 168.

SIX

New Wars, 1810–14

The key episode in this period, one as consequential as it was dramatic, was Napoleon's disastrous invasion of Russia in 1812. This was a major episode in, or for, the strategy of all the powers. These included Austria and Prussia, which took part as allies of France, and also Britain, which, separately, in another new war, was attacked in Canada and at sea by the United States that year. The latter, the "War of 1812," lasted until 1815. In turn, Russia won total success in 1812 as not only was the French invasion crushed, but the Russians were also to end successfully their separate war with the Turks. This success over the French resulted in 1813 in a new war, as first Prussia and then Austria changed sides and fought Napoleon, creating an anti-French coalition of unprecedented strength. Later in 1813, there was a fresh resetting of strategic goals as a result of the Battle of Leipzig, a resetting leading to a plan to drive Napoleon back into France. In turn, the failure in early 1814 of negotiations with France led to a new strategy focused on a determination to remove him.

WAR WITH RUSSIA

Despite his experience of Russian fighting quality at the Battles of Eylau (February 8, 1807) and Friedland (June 14, 1807), Napoleon had not been able to sustain his accommodation with Alexander I and their mutual guarantees, and thus concentrate his forces against Britain, let alone to turn Tilsit into a strong partnership. Napoleon's development of the Duchy of Warsaw as a French client state, nominally ruled by the pliable king of Saxony, who was made more pliable by this role, challenged Russia's position in eastern Europe. For over 250 years, Polish weakness had been a condition of Russian strength. Indeed, Austria, Prussia and Russia all raised large numbers of conscripts from their Polish territories and gained strategic buffers. To a degree, there was an equivalent to British concern over Ireland, although it was harder for foreign powers to intervene there.

Napoleon's refusal to accept a draft convention, negotiated in January 1810 by his ambassador to Russia, guaranteeing, as Alexander demanded, that the kingdom of Poland would not be revived, greatly increased Russian distrust of Napoleon about Poland and much else, and ensured that French actions were viewed through this prism. Napoleon was unable to sustain an alliance in which compromise played a role. Perfunctory alliances and limited compromise were his norm. Alexander's respect for Napoleon had encouraged him to try to build on their Tilsit agreement, but Napoleon's failure to reciprocate helped to wreck such hopes.

There was no true peace, and the French were very unenthusiastic about supporting Russian ambitions in the Balkans at the expense of the Turks, a position that continued that under the *ancien régime*. Matters were made worse in December 1810 by the French annexation of the northwest German Duchy of Oldenburg, which had dynastic links with the ruling Russian Romanovs and had been guaranteed at Tilsit. Meanwhile, the strategy of the Continental System was made tougher for others in 1810 when, in the face of large-scale evasion by means of smuggling, exports from Europe to Britain were only permitted if they passed through French ports or were carried on French shipping. The limited import of British colonial goods into France, but not elsewhere, was permitted, thus further increasing France's ability to act as the key economic force in continental Europe. The economic disruption that followed Napoleon's policies helped cause serious economic difficulties that sapped support for his system across Europe.

In December 1810, Russia left the French economic camp when it abandoned the Continental System, which was proving ruinous to the Russian economy. New regulations were announced for neutral shipping. Such a unilateral step threatened the cohesion of the French economic and political system and challenged Napoleon's insistence on obedience and his treatment of allies as servants.

Napoleon responded to Russian independence first with bluster, but also by greatly stepping up military preparations for possible war. He went east in part as an attempt to bring down Britain, in the same way as Hitler, in a different context, was to do in 1941. At the same time, both men were also motivated by a determination to control eastern Europe. French military preparations against Russia had already begun in October 1810, but, at that stage, they were designed for intimidation, not conflict. Napoleon, however, did not respond positively to Russian diplomatic approaches the following spring, approaches designed to make possible an armed neutrality and the avoidance for Russia of another war to add to that with the Turks.

Napoleon, indeed, was clearly thinking of war from the late summer of 1811 on, which would mean war in the 1812 campaign season. From October 1811, French military preparations were accelerated and, in January 1812, France's position in the Baltic improved with the occupation of Swedish Pomerania. More significantly, Napoleon forced an isolated Prussia to accept an offensive alliance treaty against Russia on February 24, 1812, and to dismiss reform figures such as General Scharnhorst.

However, the French were operating in a doubly precarious position. Any resort to war both risked provoking problems in their alliance system and also did not address the potential erosion of France's relative advantages. On land, the French lacked a lead comparable to that enjoyed at sea by Britain after its victory at Trafalgar. Moreover, the extent to which for Napoleon the warfare in 1807–9 had failed to shake the confidence arising from his victories in 1805–6 was serious.[1] Separately, the degree to which there was a capability gap between France and Russia is questionable, but, at any rate, the advantages of France's war-making strength were certainly under challenge. The Russian army had been significantly improved under Barclay de Tolly.

Having assembled a powerful coalition against Russia, Napoleon invaded on June 24–25, 1812. As on other occasions, the logic of his system demanded the curbing of his victim. Napoleon's closest advisers opposed the invasion, which was as unnecessary diplomatically as it was foolish militarily. Meanwhile, a perfunctory attempt to end the war with Britain had been made that April when Napoleon offered Britain peace, essentially on the basis of the status quo. Suspecting an attempt to divide Britain from her allies, the British government rapidly sought clarification on the future of Spain, as they were unwilling to accept its continued rule by Joseph. Napoleon did not reply,[2] and that ended the approach.

But for the invasion of Russia, the French might well have been able to send more troops, both French and allied, to Spain. This could have enabled them to beat their Spanish opponents while containing the British in Portugal, before defeating the latter. Instead, Wellington's major success at Salamanca on July 22, 1812, helped maintain British government backing for the idea of campaigning into Spain, as opposed to the very different strategy of only protecting Portugal.[3]

As with his earlier attacks on Austria, Prussia and Spain, and his planned invasion of Britain in 1805, Napoleon resolved to strike at the centre of his opponent's power, thus both gaining the initiative and transferring much of the logistical burden of the war to his enemy. In geographical terms, the centre meant an advance to Moscow and, thereby, cutting links between northern and southern Russia and establishing control over a symbolic place of power. The capital was St. Petersburg, which, however, was a difficult target overland. Indeed, on that axis, Étienne Macdonald was only able to advance as far as Jekabpils on the Western Dvina, but this brought no benefit. Riga, at the mouth of the river, was not captured, and this meant that there was no seizure of a port, a conceivable base and a possible negotiating chip. Further upriver, Nicolas Oudinot reached Daugavpils but did not exploit this advance. Nor was there any ability to use the northern axes of advance to take pressure off Napoleon's central axis. Instead, some of the Russian forces in the region moved eastwards to play a role in the resistance there.

Russia was a major naval power and, although he had ports in the Baltic, Napoleon lacked a navy able to give force to an amphibious attack on the capital. Sweden, moreover, was neutral. There was to be no equivalent to the Anglo-French fleet sent into the Baltic during the Crimean War (1854–56), let alone that sent to the Black Sea. This meant that Napoleon could not draw on the opportunities of naval support for land forces, including evacuation, comparable to that for the British during the Peninsular War, and what Napoleon had hoped for initially in his Egyptian campaign of 1798. Conversely, the scale of his force made such an option impossible. Yet, a naval dimension to his assault on Russia would have increased the pressure on Alexander I.

Napoleon invaded with over half a million men, many of whom were allied troops, principally German, Italian and Polish: two hundred thou-

sand were French, another one hundred thousand were from areas annexed to France since 1792, and the remainder were allied, including
thirty-five thousand Austrians, twenty-nine thousand Bavarians, twenty-
seven thousand Saxons and twenty thousand Prussians. This was unpopular military service with a vengeance, and notably so for the Italians.

The Russians fell back, denying Napoleon a decisive battle. Undoing
the results of the partitions of 1772–95, a Commission for the Provisional
Government of Lithuania was formed, and there was interest among
some of the nobility in a restored independent Grand Duchy of Lithuania
that was free from Poland as well as Russia. Nevertheless, Napoleon,
whose strategy lacked a political dimension, found little local support.
He considered proclaiming the freedom of the serfs, a measure the
French Revolutionaries in their radical stage would have pursued, but he
did not do so: such a move did not accord with his limited goal of forcing
Alexander to re-enter the Continental System.[4]

Like the Germans in 1941, the French were totally unprepared for the
nature of their task. Russian scorched-earth and guerrilla activity hit the
possibilities of obtaining supplies in the area of operations and of moving
them forward, while the French lost heavily both men and horses
through hunger, disease and fatigue. In 1812, despite the scale of logistical preparations, notably ammunition depots and supply trains with forty days' supply for the invasion,[5] grave logistical deficiencies when the
French invaded Russia, including a lack of smaller carts necessary for the
inadequate roads, combined with effective Russian scorched-earth and
guerrilla activity. Reports by the officers in the Italian units with Napoleon's army indicate a major concern with the nature of communications.
Roads were few, and those that existed were muddy and, in wooded
areas, affected by fallen timber which prevented rapid transportation.
Moreover, the high rate of the loss of horses created a major logistical
issue for these units. The French lost men as a consequence of logistical
problems and, more seriously, amidst the autumnal rain, lost operational
effectiveness and strategic rationale. Logistics became a matter of eating
the horses; and retreating from Moscow, eventually by the way they had
advanced, was to make the situation even more serious for the French.

The Dnieper was crossed successfully, but attacks on the Russian
forces defending Smolensk failed (August 17), and the Russians withdrew successfully, their divided and confusing command structure not
preventing their army from operating with some effectiveness. Finally, at

Borodino, seventy-five miles west of Moscow, on September 7, the Russians sought to stop the advance in prepared positions. In a battle of attrition that involved 233,000 men and 1,227 cannon, the indecisive Napoleon, who had far fewer troops at his disposal than in June, in part due to leaving them in garrisons, did not try to turn his opponent's flanks. Instead, he focused on breaking into and through the Russian position. The Russians resisted successive attacks and, when finally driven back, did so without breaking. Russian casualties were heavier, but Napoleon lost a quarter of his army without inflicting a serious defeat. Moreover, there was no damaging pursuit.[6]

Napoleon followed up Borodino by entering an undefended Moscow on September 14, but, instead of any meeting and negotiating with those he might intimidate and coerce, the largely deserted city was set ablaze that night, probably by the Russians. Whatever his views, the enormity of the task, logistical problems and the endurance of the Russian foes had in practice defeated Napoleon militarily before the difficulty of securing any settlement could thwart him politically. In line with his general problem of not knowing how to achieve peace, he had no terms to propose, faced an opponent who would not negotiate and could not translate his seizure of Moscow into negotiations.

At that point, strategy, operations and tactics came together with reference to whether, as some advised, Napoleon should winter in Moscow, taking advantage of the shelter and food available. During the Russian "Time of Troubles," the Poles had maintained a garrison in the Kremlin from 1610 to 1612, although, in part, this reflected support from some of the Russian *boyars* (aristocrats). Napoleon lacked that degree of support, and there was no equivalent to the divisions of the Time of Troubles, or even those of Spain during the Peninsular War. In the event, the Poles had been starved into surrendering in 1612.

Such a course in 1812 faced this risk but also others. Napoleon's army was not intended as the basis for a garrison but as a key field force, and that role would not be served if it remained in Russia. The example of 1799 suggested that Napoleon would be able to return to France, but that an army left behind might well be totally defeated. Moreover, it would probably not be as well treated as that defeated by the British in Portugal in 1808 but repatriated under the Convention of Cintra. By withdrawing his army, Napoleon would be able to shorten his lines of communication and supply, to fall back on and collect garrison forces and to remain in touch with Paris from which news of Malet's attempted conspiracy on October 23 arrived on November 6. Although weak and totally unsuccessful, the conspiracy underlined the political cost of Napoleon's military failure.

In the event, due to disease, heavy snowfalls, supply breakdowns and repeated Russian attacks, the retreat, which began on October 19, turned into a nightmare. The Russian attempt to cut Napoleon off at the Berezina River on November 26–28 failed, but the French rearguard suffered heavily there,[7] and the army that left Russia had had over five hundred thousand casualties, with savage losses also of horses and cavalry. Opposition to French hegemony required a skilful response, both military and political, but Napoleon had failed to provide this. Strategically, operationally and, at Borodino, tactically, he had totally mismanaged the 1812 campaign.

This was equally true once he had retreated from Russia with very heavy casualties. The year ended with Napoleon's demoralised and indifferently commanded forces retreating across Poland, very much against Napoleon's will, but reflecting his lack of understanding of circumstances and a new absence of grip over the army.[8] The commanders were in effect suffering from post-traumatic stress disorder, and the battering that the rearguard had received near Vilnius in early December contributed to the crisis of morale. In a repeat of his flight from Egypt in 1799, Napoleon had left his army on December 5 in order to return to Paris. Meanwhile, Napoleon's alliance system faced mounting difficulties. On December 30, Lieutenant General Ludwig Yorck von Wartenburg signed the Convention of Tauroggen with a Russian general, in effect neutralising the Prussian army. This was a step taken without the consent of the king.

Thereafter, there was no real attempt on the part of Napoleon to accept the military verdict and offer Russia terms that would assuage its hostility. Napoleon could neither conceive of a new ethos in French foreign policy or of a new system in eastern Europe. Both would have required compromise. This situation greatly contributed to Russia's determination to implement the decision in December 1812 to press on against France, and thereby put Prussia, which Napoleon had instructed to raise another thirty thousand men, in the front line. Moreover, Russia overrunning the Duchy of Warsaw ensured that France would not be able to raise troops there. For both sides, an offensive strategy appeared necessary to gain security.

Russia's position had been greatly strengthened in May 1812 by the Peace of Bucharest with Turkey, a peace that did not serve French interests. Although Russia did not obtain Moldavia, Wallachia or an alliance with Turkey, as had been hoped, previous wars had also ended in compromise, as was the norm, and Russia still gained both Bessarabia (modern Moldova) and an end to the war. However, there was still interest among Russian policymakers in stirring up the Balkan Slavs against both Turkey and Austria, and tensions continued with both powers. Napoleon, however, was unable to derive any significant value from them. Separately, Russian commanders suggested that their forces in the Balkans should cooperate with the British in the Adriatic or Italy, essentially reprising the War of the Second Coalition. The following year, the idea of a Russian contribution to the war against the French in Spain was raised.[9] This idea was fanciful given the Russian focus on operations in Germany, but it reflected the way in which Napoleon's defeat in 1812 opened up apparent possibilities.

DEFEAT IN GERMANY, 1813

The states that Napoleon had bullied into providing troops and resources were to abandon him, although some, such as Austria, which was more cautious, as well as exposed to French power, than Russia, took a while before attacking France. A wave of francophobia in the army and parts of the populace in early 1813 led Prussia to declare war on Napoleon in March, beginning the collapse of his grip on central Europe where he had long struggled to establish dominance and had come close to succeeding in 1809–12. In January 1813, Napoleon had harshly rejected Prussian terms and ordered the continuation of exactions. On February 28, in response, Prussia negotiated an alliance with Russia at Kalisz. This was followed, on March 19, by a convention at Breslau in which the two powers agreed on the liberation of Germany.

Napoleon fought back hard in Germany, aided by significant concerns about Russian and Prussian intentions among the German rulers, specifically the degree of Russian and Prussian support for a mass insurrection, while the Prussians themselves were concerned about Russian plans for Poland. Napoleon meanwhile rebuilt his army, but, unlike in 1792,

France's opponents were not outnumbered. Moreover, the new recruits from the conscript classes of 1813 and 1814 were more like the fresh troops of 1792 than the trained, experienced and physically fitter veterans of his earlier campaigns.

In broader strategic terms, there was also a political cost in 1813 when nine hundred thousand conscripts were called up. Evasion and desertion became far more serious, especially in the Auvergne and the southwest. Conscription and desertion became more obvious features of the social impact of war, while opposition to conscription contributed strongly to general war-weariness in France, a war-weariness that lessened the legitimacy of the regime.[10] There was a similar problem in France's occupied and allied territories, notably in Italy.

New levies, both French and German, helped Napoleon drive his opponents out of Saxony in May 1813, winning victories, but not crushing ones, at Lützen (May 2) and Bautzen (May 20–21). Bautzen led both sides to agree to an armistice. Napoleon's plans and moves reflected his continuing determination to take the offensive and to use that in order to gain strategic political and military outcomes. These could be unrealistic, but Napoleon was instinctively a gambler, and he was determined to force sequential warfare on his opponents. Moreover, as in other instances in history, for example for the Confederacy in 1862 and 1863, or for the Germans at Kursk in 1943 and the Ardennes in 1944, taking the offensive enabled the side with the smaller numbers to lessen the problem of knowing where to allocate forces in response to the prospect of an attack by their opponents.

There were also more specific factors. Thus, in early 1813, after Frederick William III declared war, Napoleon wanted to smash Prussia and use its space to raise supplies; to relieve the besieged French garrisons, notably at Danzig (Gdansk); and to impose himself on the Russians by forcing them to protect their lines of communication. Furthermore, operating into Prussia was designed to improve Napoleon's position in Saxony in a more lasting fashion, not least by weakening the political links between Prussia and Russia.

Yet, this proved an overcomplicated strategy, and one, in addition, that was flawed in implementation. Napoleon's strategy failed to pay sufficient attention to the possible, as opposed to desired, responses of others. Building on the Prussian failure in 1806, he underrated the Prussians and therefore was unwilling to give his subordinates sufficient forces to overcome them. Napoleon also did not adjust his strategy to his circumstances, notably his army ravaged by Russian defeat; his loss of horses in 1812, which hit the ability of the French to use the operational initiative; failings in intelligence; and a degree of command exhaustion.[11] Furthermore, as a result of Napoleon's seizure of Swedish Pomerania in January 1812, Sweden, where Bernadotte had become heir presumptive and, in effect, regent in 1810, not only did not join him against Russia that year, but also joined Napoleon's enemies in early 1813.

However, North Germany did not rise against Napoleon as had been anticipated. Indeed, Saxony rallied to Napoleon in May, while, concerned about Swedish aims on Norway, Denmark was to do so in July, having already helped the French regain Hamburg from Swedish forces. Concerned about their intentions, Austria refused to join Russia and Prussia but, instead, stopped fighting Russia, became neutral, mediated the armistice of Pleswitz on June 4, 1813, sought to arrange a more lasting peace, and proposed an independent central Europe, neutral towards both France and Russia. While mindful of the uncertainty and instability arising from Napoleon's essential character as a warmonger, Prince Clemens von Metternich, the Austrian foreign minister, was also hostile to Prussia and Russia, and, while ready to see him displaced,[12] was prepared to reach an agreement with Napoleon in order to obtain a partnership that would secure Austrian interests and re-establish Habsburg influence in Germany. In particular, Metternich regarded a powerful France as a natural and necessary counterweight to Russia. He sought stability rather than Austrian territorial expansion. Metternich offered Napoleon the left bank of the Rhine, co-guarantorship of a neutralised *Rheinbund*, non-interference over Spain and diplomatic support over colonial concessions from Britain, good terms, all of which were highly unwelcome to Britain. Indeed, the idea that the major port of Antwerp would be retained by Napoleon was regarded as particularly troubling.

Napoleon's response was totally unhelpful. Unwilling to see the end of his empire, the uncompromising Napoleon declared all France's annexations inalienable and began military preparations against Austria. Defeat had not curbed his instinctive bellicosity. Napoleon's refusal to negotiate peace, or to understand that it entailed compromise, delivered in person by an angry emperor to Metternich in Dresden on June 26, led Austria finally to join the anti-French camp: she declared war on August 11. This was a significant shift in strategic strength, one that Napoleon should have made more of an effort to thwart. Equally, his previous policy of holding on to his empire looked possible until Austria joined his opponents.

The league of the partitioning powers had been recreated, but, unlike in 1772, their target was a France that refused any limitations on its power. Moreover, again unlike in 1772, on June 8, 1813, Britain agreed alliance and subsidy treaties with Prussia and Russia. An alliance and subsidy agreement with Austria was reached on October 9. The French were also heavily outnumbered. Austrian, Prussian, Russian and Swedish forces exceeded 600,000 men, while Napoleon's total field army was only 370,000 and lacked the quality of the army he had commanded in 1805 and 1809 but had thrown away in Russia. Moreover, his German allies lacked enthusiasm.

French forces were defeated, Ney by the Prussians at Dennewitz on September 6. This was an aspect of the Allies' focus on attacking independently operating forces under Napoleon's subordinates. The limited ability of his marshals to operate as independent commanders, and their lack of supporting staffs comparable to that which supported Napoleon, cost the French dear. Furthermore, the marshals failed to cooperate to fulfil strategic objectives. Aside from Dennewitz, the Prussians defeated detached French forces at Grossbeeren (August 23), on the Katzbach River (August 26), and at Hagelberg (August 27), while the Allies won at Kulm (August 30). Only at Dresden (August 27) was Napoleon victorious, and this was not a triumph. Field Marshal Schwarzenberg, the Austrian commander of the Grand Army of Bohemia, while not a master of the art of war, was an adequate coalition arbitrator.

By failing to concentrate his forces, Napoleon had allowed their attenuation, and this had preserved neither the territory under French control nor the strategic advantage. Instead, it was Napoleon who had lost the initiative and was outmanoeuvred, his line of retreat threatened by the converging Allied forces. Attrition was thus combined, by Napoleon's opponents, with operational advantage, while their increased military effectiveness was also important. Threatened with Austrian invasion, and influenced by the French defeat at Dennewitz, Bavaria, long a stalwart of French interests, allied with Austria in October, repeating their alignment of 1745. This was a key blow to Napoleon: forces lost were now gained by his opponents. Pushed onto the defensive in Germany, Napoleon was affected not by geography or infrastructure but by having few draught horses and oxen, and those mostly of poor quality. French supply routes were also hit by attacks from German opponents and Russian light cavalry.

On October 16–19, at Leipzig, in the major battle of the year, one involving over half a million men, the heavily outnumbered Napoleon, unable to use interior lines to defeat his opponents sequentially, was severely defeated. Napoleon had got the decisive battle he sought, but badly mishandled it in a context in which he failed to appreciate the consequences of the shift in the qualitative balance of forces towards a more equal situation.[13] With this defeat, Germany was lost. Napoleon was no longer in a position to assist and exploit Frederick Augustus of Saxony, whose territories were now occupied by Prussia and Russia, and who now necessarily abandoned Napoleon. In addition, the kingdom of Westphalia was conquered and the *Rheinbund* collapsed.

Both then, and in 1814, Napoleon did not offer terms that would divide his assailants, despite the fact that, with the habitual tensions within coalitions, their agreement was based upon a shared foe but not joint objectives:[14] Austria distrusted Russia and Britain, and would have liked to retain a strong France, while the Russians sought a strong France in order to balance Britain. Their definitions of strength included a France territorially more extensive than in 1789, and, at least initially, they were willing to accept a continuance of Napoleon's rule; but his instinctive refusal to accept limits or half measures wrecked such schemes. Furthermore, repeated French assaults on other states for two decades had led them to adopt reforms that enhanced their ability to mobilise their resources. Thus, Napoleonic policies helped to close the capability gap between France and other states and also to end the subservient acceptance on which his imperial rule depended.

Moreover, with Napoleon now on the defensive, the practice of cumulative assault was working more successfully. Whereas, in 1809, Britain's Walcheren expedition was an unsuccessful diversion that did not help Austria, British successes in the Peninsular War in 1812–14 left France with fewer troops for operations elsewhere. Wellington certainly could not have fought his way to Paris in 1814, as he lacked the troops to do so, but Nicolas Soult's army that opposed him, fighting hard at Toulouse on April 10, was not available to help protect Paris from Britain's allies. So also with Suchet's army in Catalonia, which held a small British force and Spanish regular and irregular troops. Thus, the British had found a way to use their limited military power to maximum effect, something that had not been possible in the Low Countries.

Napoleon's distant management of the Peninsular War had, as before, proved flawed. It was understandable that he recalled veteran troops from Spain in 1813 to help build up his army in Germany, but he was unwilling to think through the consequences in terms of a viable strategy for Spain and therefore an appropriate place for the French forces in Spain in his overall strategy. Instead of encouraging a defensive strategy, Napoleon sent incompatible instructions, in that he both sought the defeat of the Spanish insurgents in northern Spain and also success in operating against Wellington, who was based in Portugal. Although he sought a sequential success, in practice there was a fundamental difficulty in accomplishing the two. The contrast was clear in Germany in that there was no comparable need to defend lines of communication back to France.

Wellington's total victory over Joseph at Vitoria on June 21, 1813, presented a demonstration to Britain's allies and potential allies that the Peninsular War had meaning. It therefore became an aspect of the struggle for alliance and influence in Germany in 1813. Napoleon ordered Soult to take command, and the latter launched a series of attacks on July 25, the so-called Battle of the Pyrenees. At this point, Wellington was cautious that Napoleon might be able to maintain relations with Austria and make peace with Russia and Prussia. As that fear was disproved, so Wellington was able to plan for an advance into France. Moreover, although most had earlier been moved to Germany, the remaining German units in Soult's and Suchet's armies were affected by the deterioration and then collapse of Napoleon's position in Germany.

THE COLLAPSE OF THE NAPOLEONIC EMPIRE, 1814

There were also changes in the international system in response to Napoleon. If Napoleon was immensely destabilising in terms of established notions of international relations, he also represented a culmination of the politics of "grab" exemplified by the Partitions of Poland. Indeed, Tilsit was in some respects another partition treaty with a different cast. Partly in reaction to the chaos and incessant conflict of such "diplomacy," a concept and culture of international relations emphasising restraint developed. It was seen in operation in the negotiations that led to and accompanied the anti-French coalition in 1813–15, in the Congress of Vienna and in the postwar attempt to maintain peace and order by the Congress system. Napoleon could not be encompassed in this new system, and his system and methods were made redundant by it as well as by his linked military defeat.

Napoleon was abandoned by former allies in 1813–14, losing for example Württemberg and Naples to Austrian alliances in October 1813 and January 1814, although the lesser states did not abandon him as speedily as is sometimes thought. Napoleon accepted the loss of Spain and made a peace treaty with Ferdinand VII, in part in order to free French troops for operations elsewhere. In contrast, Napoleon refused to surrender the kingdom of Italy, the Rhineland and the Netherlands as the price of a more general peace, and, instead, planned to invade Italy. The French forces abandoned Holland in November 1813, but Napoleon's attempts to divide the alliance, for example his response to the Austrian proposals of that month, failed.

In France, Napoleon was affected by falling tax revenues, widespread draft avoidance, a serious shortage of arms and equipment and a marked decline in the morale and efficiency of officials. The hounding of conscripts to depots was called the "blood tax" and left embittered communities and hatred for Napoleon. The economy was in a parlous state, hit by the British blockade and by the loss of Continental markets. Moreover, there was no winter break to campaigning, and this greatly lessened the French ability to mount an adequate response as well as hitting morale. Ironically, Napoleon's failure gave him a possible way out, as he could have probably won support from the exhausted public if he had agreed to a negotiated peace. That was certainly the opinion offered Napoleon by the secret police and the prefects. It flatly contradicted Napoleon's conviction that he could only save himself and France through victory.[15]

In early 1814, the Allies invaded France, with Prussia showing particular determination.[16] There were significant differences in strategy between the Allies, differences that, in one respect, were becoming more important as the shaping of the postwar world neared, but that had existed from the confused and difficult construction of the coalition only a few months earlier. Indeed, treating the coalition's history and strategy as a matter of sequential stages underplays consistent features throughout. Austria sought not the knockout blow against Napoleon offered by an immediate invasion of the Rhineland, but, rather (as in 1707, when invading Naples, instead of focusing on France), gains elsewhere, notably in 1814 in northern Italy. With "possession being nine-tenths of the law," it was crucially important for the Austrians that they regain Lombardy. To that end, an invasion of Switzerland was deemed necessary in order to cut or threaten French communication links with their forces in northeast Italy that blocked any Austrian advance there. This was a different operational version of the strategy adopted by the Allies in 1799.

The Austrians also proposed an invasion across the Rhine, not across the Middle Rhine aimed initially at Paris, as Prussia and Russia wanted, but across the Upper Rhine, in part in order to further secure Italy for Austria. This axis of advance also offered the possibility of cooperation with Wellington in southern France and of persuading Napoleon to negotiations—although there was scepticism among the military over both of these possibilities—while Alexander backed up the Swiss refusal to have their neutrality infringed, not that that had protected them earlier from Napoleon. As a result, the Austrians, having failed to bring to fruition a planned coup in Berne, increasingly focused their planning on an invasion north of Switzerland, with the Langres plateau and Metz being the initial goals. At the same time, for operational reasons of river crossing, the Austrians, with Swiss consent, but to the fury of Alexander, occupied northwest Switzerland.

While Napoleon discovered a willingness to negotiate, abandoning his earlier demands for a Rhine frontier and much of Italy, the Austrians did not press forward speedily to defeat Napoleon. Instead, Metternich wanted France left strong.[17] However, on January 25, Napoleon personally took control of his army. A lack of cohesion between the Allied forces, notably the Austrians and Prussians, helped the French, as it had done in 1792. However, overestimating the manpower at his disposal, Napoleon was outnumbered, and each battle reduced his veterans. Furthermore, victories, notably at Brienne (January 29), Champaubert (February 10), Nangis (February 17) and Montereau (February 18), as he manoeuvred with skill in order to destroy the most exposed Allied units, led Napoleon to return to his demands of the start of the year. These demands, however, were unacceptable to Austria, the power most willing to negotiate and to leave Napoleon in power.

The Allies agreed at Chaumont on March 9 not to conclude any separate peace with Napoleon and, instead, to continue the war and then join in maintaining the peace. Metternich was still interested in peace with

Napoleon, but the emperor's last proposals were unacceptable, and Metternich rallied to his allies. Thus, the cooperation that the Allies required was created by Napoleon, who produced on their part enough of a façade of unity to enable it to keep going.[18] There was no equivalent to the successful defensive strategy achieved by Louis XIV when confronting powerful coalitions, most obviously at the end of the War of the Spanish Succession (1701–14),[19] but also in the Franco-Dutch (1672–78) and Nine Years' (1688–97) Wars, a strategy of fighting on in order to provide opportunities to divide the coalition and win better terms via diplomacy.

In contrast, Napoleon, who was instinctively unwilling to accept limits or half measures, had lost touch with reality. His optimism and temperamental opportunism, or what might be termed an operational duplicity,[20] were no substitute for strategy. There was neither pragmatism nor rationality, enlightened or otherwise. This "complete misconception of reality"[21] was not one that was new to Napoleon at this stage as a result of the pressure of illness. Instead, it had been a consistent characteristic: diplomacy was not in Napoleon's toolbox.

Fighting in France itself, Napoleon was affected by a serious shortage of arms and equipment, as well as chaos in the Ministry of War. Having sought to benefit from chance and the creation of the options of chance, Napoleon in fact had had military and political chance increasingly imposed on him, while his options were removed. The French were defeated at Laon (March 9–10) and La-Fère-Champenoise (March 25), while Napoleon's manoeuvre failed at Arcis-sur-Aube (March 20–21). The French were heavily outnumbered. As the Allies bypassed Napoleon and advanced on Paris, where the French forces were weak and morale fragile, Napoleon's control over both regime and army crumbled. Marie-Louise left Paris on March 29 and the lacklustre Joseph Bonaparte, the head of Paris' Defence Committee, the next day. Marshal Auguste Marmont surrendered the forces defending Paris that day, but fighting continued until Allied occupation on the evening of March 31. A provisional French government, formed by Talleyrand on April 1, next day deposed Napoleon, who had advanced to Fontainebleau en route to Paris, and, with his marshals on April 4 telling him they were unwilling to fight on, Napoleon abdicated unconditionally on April 6, having failed to do so on behalf of his son and thus maintaining the fundamental dynastic strategic need, that of continuity. When he did so, the French were still in control not only of most of France but also of significant areas outside it, but

Napoleon's failure to accept the need for peace had wrecked the cohesion of the army as it had earlier done that of his empire.

The closing weeks and week of this war had shown Napoleon's long-established preference for manoeuvre and attack, rather than engaging in the defence of Paris or thinking strategically about his options. With the key exception of the defence of Paris, he proved operationally adroit, but to scant purpose in the face of the size and persistence of the invading Allied forces. This repeated his situation in 1813 and was a precursor of the strategic situation in 1815. In particular, Napoleon devoted little attention to reviving the National Guard.[22]

Louis XVIII, brother of Louis XVI (Louis XVII was the latter's dead son), returned to France on April 24, the only option for the government of France that did not appear to require Allied military support, and the choice of the foreign powers whose strategy for peace now rested on legitimist Bourbon rule. This was a reversion to the strategy of the early 1790s, one only made possible by success in war. Already, under the Treaty of Fontainebleau of April 11, Napoleon had been given the title of emperor, the small and vulnerable Mediterranean island of Elba as a principality and a revenue from the French government. Under the armistice signed on April 23, the Allies agreed to withdraw from France, and the French to evacuate their forces elsewhere. The armistice seemed the best way to consolidate Louis's position, and also reflected the extent to which occupation was not then either a necessary or a practical solution. The new government rapidly demobilised. Conscripts were ordered to return home on May 12, and over a hundred regiments were disbanded.

WAR IN NORTH AMERICA

In 1810, America established commercial restrictions on Britain or France if the other agreed to respect America's rights. This was cleverly manipulated by Napoleon[23] in order to turn American anger against Britain. An ambiguous response by Napoleon that summer was seen as favourable by President James Madison. As a result, another non-importation act was passed in February 1811. It prohibited British goods and ships, while permitting continued exports.[24] The British government correctly argued that the French repeal of measures against American trade was fraudulent and that Britain was being treated unfairly, but that argument had scant meaning in terms of the attitudes of the ruling group in America.

As a fundamental issue of strategic perspective, Jefferson and Madison failed to understand the nature of international relations,[25] overestimated American power after the 1803 Louisiana Purchase, and also mistook America's marginal leverage in the bipolar dynamic between Britain and France for a situation in which all three were major powers, which was not to be the case until later in the nineteenth century. There might seem to be a parallel here with the Prussian position in 1806, but that would be to underplay Russian caution and Napoleon's aggressiveness alike.

American leaders assumed that Britain would back down in the face of American anger and preparations for war, only to discover that they could not dictate the pace of events: Britain compromised, but inadequately, and too late for the Americans. To many of the latter, Britain's maritime pretensions, which were more pressing than those of France, a weaker naval power, were a true despotism. In retrospect, John Threlkeld of Georgetown was to attribute the "wicked war . . . to the leaning of our government to that of France" and, secondly, in a reminder of the vested interests always involved in strategy, to "the great desire of individuals to be general, colonel, captain, commodore, captain of frigates etc, privateers contractors etc."[26]

Once the war had begun, then it was also part of the cross-currents of wider strategic interests. The American invasion of Canada was very much geared to coincide with that of Russia, and depended on Britain being fully engaged. In turn, Alexander I of Russia was keen that Britain should not spread her efforts by fighting the United States and, instead, wanted her to be able to concentrate on their mutual enemy, Napoleon, a goal Alexander shared with Wellington, who wanted British forces focused on his efforts. Alexander also did not wish to bear the burden of the war with France while Britain was able to make transoceanic gains, a frequent theme from Britain's allies. Alexander's offer of mediation was accepted by the Americans,[27] who were affected by Napoleon's failure in Russia in 1812. Unwilling to be dependent on Russian mediation, the British rejected it and, instead, in November 1813, offered direct negotiations to the Americans, which were accepted by them in January 1814, although the negotiations that led to the Treaty of Ghent did not begin until August 9, and the war continued until the ratification of the treaty in 1815. That the talks were held in Ghent, Belgium, rather than Gothenburg in Sweden, the original intended location, underlined Britain's prominence: Ghent was garrisoned by British troops, and British ministers could easily go there.

Earlier in the war, the range of imperial schemes in this period as a whole included American expansionism, not that the Americans saw themselves in this light. Although Canada, which was unsuccessfully invaded in 1812, 1813 and 1814, provided the Americans with a clear strategic goal to permit the pursuit of imperial schemes, one designed to end British support for Native Americans, the Americans were unable to devise an effective means to obtain this goal. Aside from suffering generally from very poor generalship, the size of Canada (as then under British control) helped to make operational planning difficult for the Americans, as did the characteristics of the environment in the sphere of operations; the nature of contemporary communications, command and control; and also relationships between individual commanders. For these reasons, there was little prospect of coordinated campaigning, which would have been the best way to take advantage of the distribution of American resources. The alternative, their massing in a single concentration of power, was not possible for political reasons, as well as not being feasible in logistical terms. A deficiency in planning, moreover, accompanied the organisational and political limitations affecting the American war effort. Sectional differences were significant, with a reluctance by New England to fight and risk its trade and shipping.

The lack of an effective American strategy made it difficult to make use of tactical and operational successes: those comprised parts in a whole that was absent. More particularly, multipronged attacks were not coordinated and did not exert simultaneous or sequential pressure on the British. This would have been difficult to execute given the extent of operations, but functional problems alone were not responsible for the American failure of coordination. There were also serious political divisions in America over strategy. There was much support for a focus on the Lake Champlain corridor in order to divide Montreal and Quebec. However, Westerners were opposed to this emphasis and, instead, as part of their expansionist strategy, wanted to prevent British help to the Native Americans. This led them to press for operations further west, operations which, however, were difficult to support and coordinate.

Such a representative political culture was absent in France even during the Revolutionary period.

Napoleon's overthrow in 1814 enabled Britain to adopt the strategy of counteroffensive, but this strategy was totally different to that of America, as the British, although willing to consider a buffer for the Native Americans, were not seeking territorial gains. Despite reports to the contrary, New Orleans was not a British objective. Instead, their strategy was the very different one of forcing the Americans to stop the conflict. This strategy did not dictate any particular method. Instead, the British military strategy was means-directed, in the sense that the combination of troops advancing from Canada and making amphibious attacks were dependent not on any particular strategic logic other than the crucial one of where force was available. Furthermore, the strategy worked, not in the sense of making gains, for those were not the goal, but in increasing the costs of the war so as to oblige America to accept peace on the terms the British wanted. This was not an outcome due to British skill, but rather to the running out of the strategic road for America as a result of Napoleon's total defeat. In the eventual Peace of Ghent, there were no American territorial gains. Thereafter, despite periods of rivalry, even confrontation, the two powers never fought.

THE STRATEGIES OF GAINS

The strategic road had also run out for others dependent on Napoleon's success. In the case of Denmark, its vulnerability, already clearly seen in 1801 and 1807 to British naval attack, was now even more readily apparent due to the prospect of invasion overland from Germany. In territorial terms, Britain gained recognition of its capture of the North Sea island of Heligoland from Denmark in 1807, but the key loss was now the Danish possession of Norway to Sweden, a gain that Sweden had failed to achieve in the 1650s and 1710s. Yet that campaign also showed the heavy dependence of military success on political closure. Invading Swedish troops were defeated in 1814 at Lier and Skotterud, skirmishes which were Norwegian envelopment victories. Nevertheless, a Norwegian realisation of the strength of the experienced Swedish military was crucially coupled with the politics of the situation. Negotiations continued during the fighting, both aspects of a jockeying for position. Bernadotte had become heir presumptive to the childless and sick Charles XIII of Sweden from 1810, and in effect regent until he became king in 1818. His willingness to offer constitutional guarantees that met Norwegian concerns led to the end of resistance. The union, which was seen by Bernadotte as a more coherent and strategically wiser alternative than seeking to regain Finland from Russia, lasted until 1905 when it ended peacefully. A key contrast was a far less exploitative control of Norway than was seen under the French elsewhere in Europe under Napoleon. The British made no comparable efforts to annex the Faroes, Iceland, Greenland or the Danish islands in the Caribbean (since 1917, the American Virgin Islands). Denmark thus retained part of its far-flung overseas empire.

In the Peace of Paris of May 30, 1814, France got her frontiers of January 1792; and, as with previous treaties in 1697, 1714 and 1748, German hopes of regaining Alsace were not fulfilled. In March 1792, the British envoy in Berlin had suggested that in the event of war with France, Austria and Prussia would probably seek to gain and retain Alsace and Lorraine as indemnification for their expenses.[28] That, however, was not their goal then, or in 1814. Indeed, as a result of retaining control of enclaves seized by the Revolutionaries in 1792, Alsace was more under French control than after previous peaces.

However, a territorial consolidation on France's borders as part of the Vienna Peace Settlement greatly limited its chances of expansion. The kingdom of Sardinia (ruler of Savoy-Piedmont) was strengthened with Genoa, while Belgium and the Netherlands were united under the House of Orange, although its ruler's hopes of expansion in the Rhineland proved fruitless. Most crucially, Prussia regained the German territories it had lost under Napoleon, and gained much of Westphalia and the lower Rhineland, including Cologne, Coblenz, Münster and Trier. This was a major extension of Protestant rule over Catholics, and one that ensured that Prussia was now cast in the role of champion of German national integrity against France, as well as becoming coal rich. Whereas Prussia's military base in the region had, prior to the French Revolutionary War, been at Wesel, now there were Prussian forces placed to resist any French advance down the Moselle Valley, and to, and across, the Middle Rhine. The Prussian acquisition of so much more of the Rhineland and Westphalia than it had had previously led to a fundamental reorientation of Prussian policy westwards, not least as Poland was now stabilised as a largely Russian sphere of control, a situation that lasted until World War I. Prussia was also given an incentive to link its western and eastern possessions, first through economic means, and then ultimately through military and political unification, a key strategic outcome.

Prussia's gains helped to substantiate the Austro-Prussian dualism it sought in Germany. Yet, the Austrians were the predominant partner. The Holy Roman Empire was not recreated, nor were the Ecclesiastical Principalities. Germany was left with only thirty-nine states. The German Confederation, founded on June 8, 1815, a permanent union of sovereign princes and free cities, was placed under the permanent presidency of Austria. Moreover, Austria regained the lands ceded to Bavaria and France, although not the Black Forest possessions lost in 1805. Partly as a result of that, Baden and Württemberg were both strengthened, each acquiring significant Catholic minorities. Bavaria lost some of its Napoleonic gains, especially the Tyrol and Salzburg, both of which went to Austria. However, it kept others, notably Ansbach-Bayreuth (from Prussia) and Regensburg, which it had acquired in 1807, and now added Würzburg and part of the Palatinate, the latter producing a frontier with France on the left bank of the Rhine. These acquisitions also increased the extent to which Bavaria was a competing presence with Prussia, both in the Rhineland and due to its advance northwards into central Germany.

Hanover, which had ceased to exist during the wars, being gained, first, by Prussia and, then, by France, before part of it was granted to the kingdom of Westphalia, was restored, enlarged, notably with East Friesland, Hildesheim and Osnabrück, all gains George II (r. 1727–60) had failed to obtain. Hanover became the fourth-largest state in Germany, after Austria, Prussia and Bavaria (and the fifth largest in population), and in 1814 became a kingdom, joining Prussia, Saxony, Bavaria and Württemberg. This was a testimony to British power, and Hanover and Britain remained under the same monarch until 1837, when, on the death of William IV, Victoria could not succeed in Hanover, as only men could. However, the territorial gains were modest, and far less than those of Prussia. Indeed, Hanover remained only a regional presence, and even that had weaknesses: Lauenburg was lost to Denmark, while, far from Hanover absorbing neighbouring principalities, Hamburg and Bremen remained Free Cities (as did Frankfurt and Lübeck), and Oldenburg (the ruling house was linked to the Russian royal family), Brunswick, Lippe-Detmold and Schaumburg-Lippe continued to be independent.

The negotiators meeting at Vienna had sought to reconcile the variable strategies for gain of the victorious Allies. This was easiest for Britain, as it alone both wanted transoceanic gains and was in a position to secure them. The wartime gain of Mauritius, Tobago and St. Lucia from France, and Cape Town and coastal Sri Lanka from the Netherlands, was acknowledged. Other gains were returned, including Pondicherry and Réunion to France and Java to the Dutch, but their vulnerability was now clear. Possession by force was also important for Britain in the Mediterranean. It ensured the retention of Gibraltar (captured in 1704), and the recent wartime acquisitions of Malta and the Ionian Islands, but not regaining Minorca.[29] In a key strategic shift, peace with other European powers and, from the winter of 1814–15, the United States, also provided an opportunity for Britain to pursue transoceanic expansion, and in 1814–15, it was at war with the Gurkhas and, in 1815, finally successful in the interior of Sri Lanka.

The situation was more complex in continental Europe and more competitive. That which was overt was the need to avoid a French *revanche*. This strategic goal encouraged the strengthening of the frontier against France in the shape of a united Low Countries, a Rhineland under Prussia, a guaranteed Switzerland of permanent neutrality and a strengthened Piedmont. That which was more covert was a rivalry between Austria and Prussia.[30]

Peace also offered the prospect of new alignments within Europe. Indeed, initially, Metternich had hoped for an alliance of Austria, Britain and Prussia in order to check both France and Russia and, as a result, had been willing to see annexations as the price of Prussian cooperation against Russia. However, when Frederick William III rejected this policy of his minister, Karl August von Hardenberg, Metternich changed tack, and, in January 1815, Austria, Britain and France concluded a Triple Alliance, agreeing to oppose, if necessary by force, Prussia's wish to annex Saxony as well as Russian plans in Poland. Hostilities appeared possible, but, in May, in response in part to the need to address the new crisis posed by Napoleon's return, Frederick William, who had particularly wished to gain the city of Leipzig, backed down, although he was still ceded about 58 percent of Saxony. The diplomats at Vienna operated in a context of distrust. Thus, Sir Charles Stewart, the British envoy in Vienna, distrusted Metternich and also thought Talleyrand dishonest. The prospect of division leading to a breakdown or even strife was ended, however, by Napoleon launching what became the War of the Seventh Coalition, the last coalition, against him.[31]

NOTES

1. Harold Parker, "Why Did Napoleon Invade Russia? A Study in Motivation and the Interrelations of Personality and Social Structure," and Paul Schroeder, "Napoleon's Foreign Policy: A Criminal Enterprise," *Journal of Military History* 54 (1990): 131–46, 147–62.

2. *Annual Register* 54 (London, 1812): 420–503; Paul Coquille, *Napoleon and England, 1803–1810* (London, 1904), 270–71.

3. Joshua Moon, *Wellington's Two-Front War: The Peninsular Campaigns at Home and Abroad, 1808–1814* (Norman: University of Oklahoma Press, 2011).

4. Janet Hartley, "Russia in 1812. Part I: The French Presence in the *Gubernii* of Smolensk and Mogilev," *Jahrbücher für Geschichte Osteuropas* 38 (1990): 179–82.

5. Alexander Mikaberidze, *The Napoleonic Wars: A Global History* (Oxford: Oxford University Press, 2020), 531.

6. Alexander Mikaberidze, *The Battle of Borodino: Napoleon against Kutuzov* (Barnsley: Pen and Sword, 2007).

7. Alexander Mikaberidze, *The Battle of the Berezina: Napoleon's Great Escape* (Barnsley: Pen and Sword, 2010).

8. Frederick Schneid, "The Dynamics of Defeat: French Army Leadership, December 1812–March 1813," *Journal of Military History* 63 (1999): 7–28.

9. E. A. Mackenzie to — —, April 2, 1813, BL. Loan Manuscripts 57/7.

10. Alan Forrest, *Conscripts and Deserters: The Army and French Society during the Revolution and Empire* (Oxford: Oxford University Press, 1989).

11. James Arnold, *Napoleon 1813: Decision at Bautzen* (Lexington, VA: Napoleon Books, 2015).

12. Wolfram Siemann, *Metternich: Strategist and Visionary* (Cambridge, MA: Belknap Press, 2019).

13. Robert Epstein, "Aspects of Military and Operational Effectiveness of the Armies of France, Austria, Russia and Prussia in 1813," in *The Projection and Limitations of Imperial Powers, 1618–1850*, ed. Frederick C. Schneid (Leiden: Brill, 2012), 147.

14. John Kuehn, "The Reasons for the Success of the Sixth Coalition against Napoleon in 1813" (MA thesis, US Army Command and General Staff College, Fort Leavenworth, KS, 1997), 30–31.

15. Munro Price, *Napoleon: The End of Glory* (Oxford: Oxford University Press, 2014).

16. Gordon Craig, "Problems of Coalition Warfare: The Military Alliance against Napoleon, 1813–1814," in *War, Politics and Diplomacy: Selected Essays*, ed. Gordon Craig (New York: Praeger, 1966).

17. Michael Leggiere, "Austrian Grand Strategy and the Invasion of France in 1814," *Consortium, 2007*, 322–31.

18. Philip Dwyer, "Self-Interest versus the Common Cause: Austria, Prussia and Russia against Napoleon," *Journal of Strategic Studies* 31 (2008): 628–29.

19. Darryl Dee, "The Survival of France: Logistics and Strategy in the 1709 Flanders Campaign," *Journal of Military History* 84 (2020): 1021–50.

20. Harold Parker, "Toward Understanding Napoleon," *Consortium, 1997*, 208.

21. John Morgan, "Pragmatic Imperial Politics: The French Military Government in Catalonia, 1808–1810," *Consortium, 1997,* 343.

22. Michael Leggiere, *The Fall of Napoleon: The Allied Invasion of France, 1813–1814* (Cambridge: Cambridge University Press, 2007); Ralph Ashby, *Napoleon against Great Odds: The Emperor and the Defenders of France, 1814* (Westport, CT: Praeger, 2010).

23. Lawrence Kaplan, "France and Madison's Decision for War, 1812," *Mississippi Valley Historical Review* 50 (1964): 652–71.

24. Herbert Heaton, "Non-Importation, 1806–1812," *Journal of Economic History* 1 (1941): 178–98.

25. Peter Onuf and Nicholas Onuf, *Federal Union, Modern World: The Law of Nations in an Age of Revolutions, 1776–1814* (Madison, WI: Madison House, 1993).

26. Threlkeld to John Fisher, March 1, 1817, Exeter, Devon County Record Office, 1148 M/19/1.

27. Frank Golder, "The Russian Offer of Mediation in the War of 1812," *Political Science Quarterly* 31 (1916): 360–91.

28. Morton Eden to Grenville, March 3, 1792, BL. Add. 34441 fol. 403. See also Elgin to Grenville, October 2, 1792, NA. FO. 26/19.

29. Brian Vick, *The Congress of Vienna: Power and Politics after Napoleon* (Cambridge, MA: Harvard University Press, 2016).

30. Philip Dwyer, "The Two Faces of Prussian Foreign Policy: Karl August von Hardenberg as Minister for Foreign Affairs, 1804–1815," in *"Freier Gebrauch der Krafte": Eine Bestandsaufnahme der Hardenbergforschung,* ed. Thomas Stamm-Kuhlmann, 75–81 (Munich: Ouldenbourg, 2001).

31. Reider Payne, *War and Diplomacy in the Napoleonic Era: Sir Charles Stewart, Castlereagh and the Balance of Power in Europe* (London: Bloomsbury, 2019).

SEVEN

War without a Viable French Strategy? 1815

Although the new war involving Napoleon was totally unexpected, there was a degree of predictability about the strategies in the war of 1815. Indeed, because the Battle of Waterloo (June 18) speedily brought the conflict to a close, there was no reset of strategic goals, priorities and methods during it. Napoleon's return to France led to a strategy of crushing combination by the Seventh Coalition, while Napoleon, as was his norm, depended on sequential war fighting, but could no longer compel it, either strategically or operationally. He lacked a viable strategy.

Napoleon had been exiled by the victorious powers to Elba, an island between Corsica and Tuscany, but he was given sovereignty over it, as well as a revenue of two million francs from the French government, which, in the event, proved unwilling to pay up. He used the opportunity to improve the situation of the inhabitants, including by road building and educational reforms, but this was no long-term solution; instead, it was a frustrating lesson in impotence that mocked his greatly inflated sense of his own dignity.

As ever an opportunist, Napoleon escaped on February 26, 1815, evading two patrolling French ships and one British one. Having landed near Antibes on the Provence coast on March 1, he rapidly and decisively advanced on Paris, reaching it on March 20. In a classic instance of his strategy of risk, expediency and self-belief,[1] Napoleon overawed opponents, stage-managed confrontations where he prevailed, and, with support increasing and that from his opponent ebbing rapidly, moved speed-

159

ily on Paris, which was not held against him. Conversely, Louis XVIII directed a strategy of total failure. This failure reflected his more than uncertain control over the army, but also a lack of ability to mobilise opposition to Napoleon within France, opposition that was to be shown in subsequent rebellions against Napoleon's return. In part, this failure by Louis was a matter of a lack of speed, certainty and decisiveness; but the unpredictable nature of the task and the difficulties of the politics in this conflict were also significant. Indeed, this was conflict as civil war, one of the most significant, but most underrated, spheres of strategy.

The change of loyalty of much of the French army in the face of Napoleon's return to France was its second change within twelve months, as he had been abandoned the previous spring, albeit that was largely only a matter of abandonment by the commanders. Louis's fall, therefore, helped direct attention to a key element of strategic means and purpose, but one that is all too often ignored or underrated, that of retaining control over the military, and such that it could be used without qualification. This was an issue seen in the United States with the Newburgh Conspiracy in March 1783 and, more persistently, with General James Wilkinson in the 1800s. In Europe in 1815, there were also significant instances of disloyalty, lack of enthusiasm and fears of disloyalty, notably relating to Saxons and Rhinelanders newly in the Prussian army, and to the loyalty of the Dutch army, especially its Belgian units, many of whom had until recently fought for Napoleon.

Once in power, Napoleon promised other states that he would observe existing treaties, and he affirmed peace with the rest of Europe, but his rhetoric within France was hostile and bellicose. Armand de Caulaincourt, again Napoleon's foreign minister, was ordered to create a new league with the lesser powers, including Spain, Portugal, Switzerland and the minor German and Italian states, a testimony to Napoleon's lack of realism. So also was another aspect of his strategy, his confidence that the people elsewhere who had known his rule would reject war against France, whatever their rulers thought. This diplomacy to peoples, a throwback to the French Revolution, led Napoleon to order the publication of appeals to foreigners who had served in his forces to rejoin them. There were a large number of such foreigners, but the appeals were not heeded.

Napoleon's return anyway united the powers. On March 13, those assembled at Vienna declared Napoleon's invasion an illegal act and offered help to Louis XVIII. In a key aid to rapidity in strategic decision-making, the presence of Alexander I and Frederick William III alongside Francis II in Vienna eased tensions among the Allies and speeded deliberations. When he heard of Napoleon's escape, Alexander visited Metternich and promised solidarity, even though a few weeks earlier Alexander had threatened him with letting Napoleon loose against what he saw as a conspiracy of Austria, Britain and Louis XVIII.

On March 25, the powers renewed their alliance to overthrow the restored emperor, and, clearly differentiating between him and France, promised to support France against Napoleon and invited Louis to sign the treaty. This represented a deliberate reversal of the previous strategic perspective on Napoleon, that of him as a ruler with whom a war could not be waged on the premise of removal. The last had only changed in March 1814 after he rejected the Austrian attempt to negotiate a settlement, and thus there was a strategic continuity from then into 1815.

At Vienna, the powers agreed to field 600,000 troops. Austria, Britain, Prussia and Russia each promised to provide forces of 150,000 men, with Britain being permitted to provide some of its contribution with money to be used to subsidise the forces of allies or to hire troops from rulers lacking the necessary funds. This division of responsibilities was an appropriate recognition of the respective strength of the powers. Lesser states were also allocated contributions. Had Napoleon not been defeated by British, Dutch and German forces at Waterloo, other Allied armies would probably have rapidly defeated him. They were certainly pressing on France's other frontiers, such that a decision for combat by Napoleon would have been very swift in its outcome. There was no need for the advances of the range he had displayed in 1805, 1808, 1809, 1812 and, even, 1800.

In 1815, the Allies were not able to act sufficiently quickly to intervene in France on behalf of Louis before Napoleon took over. There was, however, a political dimension, with the British government feeling that such an act would make Louis more unpopular in France. The Dutch idea of occupying, with Louis's consent, the French frontier fortresses was militarily more viable, although also affected by Napoleon's speed. Such an occupation would have provided greater depth for the Allied position in the Low Countries, and produced defensive blocs on the road system. Yet, as a reminder of the complexity of strategic choices, such an occupation would also have tied up much of the Anglo-Dutch army in defensive positions and thus have given Napoleon greater opportunity to win any engagement in the field, leaving the garrisons redundant. Furthermore, the garrisons would not have been able to provide mutual support.

Instead, the Allies prepared to take the offensive. Wellington argued that the coalition should attack "when we shall have 450,000 men," and he was confident (with reason) that Napoleon could bring no more than 150,000 men to strike at any one point.[2] The need to attack was a prime point in Allied strategy, as it was seen as necessary both to protect the Vienna Settlement, and to prevent Napoleon from consolidating his position domestically and even internationally, and then invading his neighbours. International and domestic, political and military factors all converged. On April 6, Viscount Castlereagh, the British foreign secretary, told Parliament:

> It might be thought that an armed peace would be preferable to a state of war, but the danger ought fairly to be looked at: and knowing that good faith was opposite to the system of the party [Napoleon] to be treated with, knowing that the rule of his conduct was self-interest, regardless of every other consideration, whatever decision they came to must rest on the principle of power, and not on that of reliance on the man.

The Opposition amendment moved by Samuel Whitbread, who declared himself against a "new crusade" to determine the crown of France, was defeated by 220 votes to 37, a convincing majority.

As in 1813 and 1814, Napoleon had to defend his position, and, as then, he could have relied on a mobile defence. Because they were not building on a campaigning season, the coalition forces were less prepared for attack than in early 1814, and it would take time to deploy them. This situation gave Napoleon an opportunity to use the interior lines of his position in France to fight his opponents sequentially.

His strategic choice, instead, for attack, a key decision, reflected a range of factors. Attacking would enable Napoleon to strengthen his political position in France, notably Paris, consolidating his new regime on the basis of his old system. Napoleon was justifiably worried about his support in Paris. Indeed, in 1815, as in 1814, there was a widespread war-weariness that contributed to a marked lack of enthusiasm for Napoleon.[3] The weight of this factor deserves attention.

Attacking would also provide Napoleon with the strategic opportunity of disrupting the opposing coalition, as well as the operational support of being able to raise supplies from conquered territory, and the tactical ability to use French skills in the assault. By concentrating on part of the opposing Allied forces, Napoleon could hope to translate his overall numerical disadvantage and weaknesses in logistics into a local superiority in numbers.

Such a strategy required the choice of an area of advance. Napoleon had won success in 1796–97 and 1800 attacking in Italy, but this was very much not the centre of gravity of the coalition, while doing so would expose Paris to attack from the Allied forces in nearby Belgium. There was even less point to contemplating Spain. Napoleon could have moved east into Germany against the advancing Austrian and Russian forces. However, again, Paris would have been exposed. Instead, attacking into Belgium gave Napoleon an opportunity to win the war sequentially, both militarily and by unpeeling the coalition. He hoped that the parliamentary Opposition would benefit politically in Britain from his success, forcing a change in policy there.

To defend Belgium without knowing the likely axis of French advance, the standard problem for a defending force, the British, Dutch and Prussians had to deploy their forces over a large area in order to cover the possible routes of attack. In practice, the French advance would depend on a paved road, notably in order to transport the artillery, but, compared to most of Europe, there were a large number of roads that could be used. Moreover, the Allies had a number of places of interest to defend, including the Belgian North Sea ports, notably Ostend and the naval base at Antwerp, as well as the court of the exiled Louis XVIII at Ghent, the Belgian capital at Brussels and the strategic positions on the river Meuse: Namur, Liège and Maastricht, which could open the way for the French into both Germany and the eastern Netherlands.

In practice, from the perspective of both sides, all of these positions were instrumental, with the operational subordinated to the strategic level. As Napoleon's principal objective was the rapid defeat of the opposing armies in Belgium so that he could then turn against the Austrians and Russians who were advancing towards eastern France, in contrast, the preservation of these armies in Belgium was the key objective for the Allies. Their location there was a form of forward defence comparable to that of the Austrians in southern Germany in 1805. In 1815, there was no real possibility for the Allies to combine against Napoleon on exterior lines, as that would have risked the British and Dutch moving away from their key area of operation in Belgium. In 1815, however, Napoleon did not attempt the outflanking he managed in 1805 at the expense of Austria. Indeed, there was no outflanking then on his part at the operational or the tactical level, or, indeed, arguably the strategic equivalent of being able to persuade one of his would-be opponents not to fight.

The places mentioned above were secondary goals for both sides, establishing the geography of the conflict and its initial character as the interplay of places and armies, with both sides manoeuvring in order to pursue primary and secondary goals. Thus, in an instance of the prioritisation that was so important in operational and strategic geography, Napoleon's opportunity rested on the degree to which the Allied protection of secondary goals, in particular of lines of communication, provided him with an opportunity to secure his primary goal of defeating their forces, with the consequent strategic benefits. In Napoleon's mind, there was none of the confusion between securing key positions and inflicting defeats that was to be seen with many offensives, for example with Hitler and his unsuccessful invasion of the Soviet Union in 1941, or, to a degree, with the Allied advance in France and the Low Countries in 1944.

For the Allies in 1815, in turn, while the strategic necessity was preserving their alliance, it was important in an operational mode to get within the French decision loop (the OODA loop [observe, orient, decide, act] in modern parlance). A rapid response to French moves would enable them to concentrate their forces and to engage the French from a position of numerical superiority. This response would also let the Allies protect the places that were deemed essential. Moreover, in terms of a rapid response, any Allied concentration that was not near the frontier, if followed by a battle that left Napoleon able to advance, would pose a challenge, as one or another of the Allies' armies would probably find it difficult to retreat along secure lines of communication, or would do so but leave themselves separate and vulnerable, as with the Austrians and British after the Battle of Fleurus in 1794.

The choice of a place of concentration dramatised the military geography at issue. Initially, the Prussians proposed that the Anglo-Dutch and Prussian armies retreat to Tirlemont, about twenty-five miles east of Brussels, a position that would take the Prussians nearer to their lines of communication to the east. Wellington, however, thought this proposal militarily and politically unwise, the two combining in the anxiety that the French would be able to take Brussels and, as a result, that the loyalty of the Belgian forces (part of the Dutch army only since 1814) would be affected. Such a concentration would also risk the French conquest of western Belgium and cut Wellington off from the port of Ostend and the sea route to Britain, the route for both supplies and retreat.

Alternatively, had the Prussians concentrated there, and the British to the south of Brussels, then Napoleon would really have been able to defeat the two armies separately. As a result, Wellington pressed for a deployment by both armies south of Brussels, which, however, was very close to France. The Prussian commander, pending the arrival of Field Marshal Gebhard von Blücher, was Lieutenant General Count August von Gneisenau, who had served in Canada on behalf of George III in the Ansbach forces in 1782–83. Keen to cooperate with Wellington, he agreed, a decision that was to be of great importance for the campaign.[4]

Because they both, in the event, deployed south of Brussels, the Allied armies, however, were close to the French frontier and therefore vulnerable to attack, as was to be shown on June 16, 1815, the day after Napoleon invaded, in the Battles of Ligny and Quatre Bras. More specifically, as the events of that day were to indicate, these armies risked contact engagements, which they did not want, prior to concentration. The concentration, both of the individual armies and of the two together, moreover, would require marching across the axis of French advance. Complicating the situation for both Allied armies, and providing additional opportunities for Napoleon, the Prussian I Corps blocked the French advance north of Brussels via Charleroi, the crossing point he chose over the river Meuse. Yet, instead of Prussian forces to the north of this corps' area of deployment, there was Wellington's reserve round Brussels, ensuring a southwest to northeast division between the armies. This division meant that the I Corps was not protecting Prussian positions to the north and, linked to this, suggested that the axis of Prussian concentration, and, if necessary, withdrawal, would be east-northeast along the Prussian lines of communication and towards where the other Prussian units were located, thus opening up a gap with the British forces. This was reminiscent of the start of Napoleon's 1796 Italian campaign, in which he had attacked between the Piedmontese and Austrian forces, causing each to withdraw along their separate lines of communication and enabling him to defeat each in turn.

By invading Belgium on June 15, 1815, Napoleon gained the strategic advantage, which he aimed to do in order to defeat separately the Prussian army and the British-Dutch-German force under Wellington. Both were attacked on the 16th, but, although the Prussian army was hit hard at Ligny, the two armies survived and thwarted Napoleon on the 18th. At Waterloo, the defensive firepower of Wellington's army beat off successive French frontal attacks. Alongside the destruction of the French Old Guard in the last attack, the arrival of Prussian forces on the French right spelled the end. Waterloo was a double defeat for Napoleon: he failed on the offensive and was then defeated on the defensive. This was a far more serious defeat than that inflicted on the Russians at Borodino in 1812.

It is unclear that Napoleon's grand strategy was sustainable anyway. Ever the gambler, he had won battles in 1813–14, but without winning the war. In 1815, large Allied armies, especially Austrian forces, were approaching France from the east. Napoleon's army was weak, and he lacked his former energy and the earlier range of effective subordinates. Yet, Waterloo was not a strategic irrelevance. Napoleon was crushed, and the war in truth ended beyond any hopes that events leading to Allied divisions would provide him with opportunities.

Nevertheless, Napoleon, as ever, continued to be fertile in his strategic conceptions, and there is much to be gained from seeing how leaders adapt to failure. He ordered a concentration of forces at Laon and Rheims, a concentration designed to hold off the Anglo-Prussian invaders until a new army could be gathered. In part, this was a matter of ancillary forces and conscripts, but there was also a determination to call on French regular forces from the Vendée and the Rhine.

Additional strategies were urged by others in Napoleon's circle. His brother Lucien and Louis-Nicholas Davout, the minister of war, pressed him to dissolve the hostile Chamber of Deputies and rule as a dictator, possibly also calling on the Parisian workers for support. However, the tired and defeated Napoleon was no longer the general of 1795, ready to order cannon fired on opponents in the streets of Paris. Nor was he willing to lead the forces that Davout wished to regroup and build up, eventually, once Paris had been lost, beyond the river Loire. There was no equivalent to the circumstances, or resilience, of Alexander I in 1812.

By June 26, 1815, about sixty thousand French troops were at Laon, but Napoleon had already totally lost control of the politics of Paris, which he left the previous day. Moreover, the British and Prussian forces that had invaded France on June 21 did not advance against Laon, where the army appeared to them to be irrelevant. Instead, they agreed that they must focus on Paris, a repetition of the strategy eventually followed by the Allies in 1814, and one that again demonstrated its value. Furthermore, the advancing Prussians got between the major French force and Paris. Napoleon meanwhile continued to think of military moves, on June 29 considering trying to defeat, first, Blücher and then Wellington, who were advancing separately. There was still fighting, notably on June 28, but not on a major scale. A French attack on the Prussians outside Paris was repulsed on July 3, after which Davout agreed that the French army would evacuate Paris and retire behind the Loire. Napoleon's regime had depended on his main battle army and his prestige; but, resting on these fragile, and now weak, foundations, the regime rapidly collapsed. As William, Lord Cathcart, the British representative at the Austrian headquarters, had noted, "It seemed to be the received opinion that Bonaparte's hopes and expectations depended greatly on the results of his first battle."[5] That was a repetition of the situation with Marengo in 1800, but now his position was far worse.

A British naval blockade was also an important aspect of strategy.[6] It was designed to end the possibility of Napoleon escaping to fight again, as Simón Bolívar did from Spanish forces in Latin America. Thwarted of his plan of escaping to America, Napoleon surrendered to a British warship on July 14 at the Atlantic port of Rochefort, and was exiled to distant St. Helena, a British possession in the South Atlantic, to die in 1821 and to return to France only as a corpse.

Louis XVIII, in contrast, had returned to Paris on July 8, 1815. France was occupied after Waterloo as a strategy of rapidly ending resistance and restoring Louis, in cooperation with local Royalists, took effect. An important aspect of the strategy of defeating Napoleonic support was the crown's tolerance of a popular "White Terror" that summer. Subsequently, that was to become, with the restored monarchy, a more formal process of restrictions and surveillance designed to limit radicalism. In opposition, there was to be no equivalent to the rebellion in Spain in 1808 in terms of the reaction in France against the Bourbons and the occupying Allied troops.

The war of 1815 also saw British forces capture anew Guadeloupe and Martinique from the French. Moreover, that year, the British, in a forward strategy in the South Atlantic, annexed Ascension Island and, in 1816, Tristan da Cunha and Gough Island, in order to prevent their being used as a base for a rescue attempt for Napoleon, although none of substance was made. St. Helena was fortified and defended with a significant garrison.

British naval power was also demonstrated in the only area in Europe outside France where Napoleon had significant support: Naples. A squadron of British frigates entered the Bay of Naples and threatened to bombard the city unless the pro-Napoleonic navy surrendered within forty-eight hours. It did, mirroring a successful British naval intimidation of the city in 1742. This was a culmination of the role of British naval power in the crisis, which included a presence off Ancona and Gaeta, as well as protecting Sicily.

Further north, the Austrians had initially been pushed back by Murat, the king of Naples, who had invaded the Papal States on March 19, seizing Rome and Florence, and defeated an Austrian force at Cesena on March 30. Murat benefited from the extent to which many Austrian units were north of the Alps and, at Rimini on March 31, he issued a proclamation to all Italians, calling for a new order and a "war of independence for Italy." However, Murat suffered from the unpopularity of Napoleon's rule, which undermined his political strategy, and from the effective response of the Austrians, who were able to concentrate sufficient forces to capture Bologna on April 16 and Cesena on April 21, and to defeat Murat at Tolentino on May 2–3. This defeat led to the dissolution of Murat's army. British marines and Austrian troops subsequently occupied Naples on May 23. Murat had failed to heed Napoleon's advice to wait before acting. Had he done so, there could have been a combination in timing with the invasion of Belgium on June 15, and this might have left northern Italy more vulnerable to Murat. However, the campaign underlined the limitations of success (or failure) in secondary theatres and, therefore, their strategic inconsequence, at least in so far as the bigger picture was concerned.

The Second Treaty of Paris, that of November 20, 1815, stipulated an occupation of northern France for five years, an occupation, to be paid by France, that was a key aspect of the new Allied strategy of pacification and a protection for Louis XVIII. This occupation was also to secure a large indemnity of seven hundred million francs, and when that was paid in late 1818, the occupation came to an end.[7] The treaty also entailed the cession of Beaumont and Bouillon to the Netherlands, Saarlouis to Prussia, and Landau to Bavaria. This was in part a matter of weakening French frontier fortifications, a process also seen with the demolition of those of Huningue near Basle that had successfully resisted attack in 1814 and 1815. The loss of the Saar and Sambre coalfields has been regarded as a serious blow to France's industrial development. Rumours of more substantial Allied acquisitions, however, proved groundless. There was no equivalent to the loss of Alsace-Lorraine to Prussia in 1871.

Louis XVIII rang the changes by abolishing the Imperial Army on August 9, 1815, which led to the demobilisation of its troops. In October, a committee was established to assess the behaviour of officers during Napoleon's return. There were punishments, including trials and shootings, for those deemed unacceptable, notably Ney on December 7, which was a way to ensure the army's future loyalty.

By the Quadruple Alliance of November 20, 1815, the four great powers—Austria, Britain, Prussia and Russia—renewed their anti-French alliance for twenty years, a step designed to limit the chances of France disrupting the alliance. Napoleon had failed, totally. In his place had come an attempt to develop a practice of collective security through a congress system, along with Tsar Alexander's Holy Alliance of Christian monarchs, or at least those of Russia, Austria and Prussia, designed to maintain the new order.[8] This was very much a strategy of using power to affect the balance of force.

NOTES

1. David Bell, *Men on Horseback: The Power of Charisma in the Age of Revolution* (New York: Farrar, Straus and Giroux, 2020).

2. Wellington to Charles, Lord Stewart, Ambassador to Vienna, May 8, 1815, BL. Loan Manuscripts 105 fol. 9.

3. Charles Esdaile, *The Eagle Rejected: Napoleon, France and Waterloo* (Barnsley: Pen and Sword, 2016).

4. John Holland Rose, "Sir Hudson Lowe and the Beginnings of the Campaign of 1815," *English Historical Review* 16 (1901): 517–27.

5. Cathcart to Castlereagh, June 21, 1815, ed. Charles, Marquess of Londonderry, *Memoirs and Correspondence of Viscount Castlereagh* (London: Henry Colburn, 1849), 2:382.

6. Admiral George, Viscount Keith, Commander-in-Chief in the English Channel, to Rear Admiral Sir Henry Hotham, July 10, 20, 1815, Hull, University Library, Hotham papers, DDHO/7/8.

7. Christine Haynes, *Our Friends the Enemies: The Occupation of France after Napoleon* (Cambridge, MA: Harvard University Press, 2018).

8. Paul Schroeder, *The Transformation of European Politics, 1763–1848* (Oxford: Oxford University Press, 1994), is the best guide to scholarship on this period.

EIGHT

Strategic Assessment

Your sovereigns born to the throne may be beaten twenty times and still go back to their palaces; that cannot I—the child of fortune: my reign will not outlast the day when I have ceased to be strong, and therefore to be feared.

—Napoleon to Metternich, June 26, 1813[1]

How powers assessed problems, goals and capabilities was crucial to the strategic world of the period. There was scant institutional structure for this process, but rather a matter of *ad hoc* decision-making in which instinct drew on information. At the same time, both instinct and information involved the perception of contexts and opportunities. Far from being fixed, this perception was affected by the impact of ideological suppositions on the assessment of how the international system did, could and should operate. Dynasticism and nationalism, and, more generally, the varied character of international rights and interests, were all forced through, and redefined by, the prism of war.

Ancien régime international relations had seen aggressive opportunism, as with Louis XIV, Frederick the Great and the Partitions of Poland. These had all been carried out by sovereign rulers. To a degree, in contrast, generals who lacked inherited rulership came to the fore in France in the 1790s, and notably so with Napoleon, in a pattern not seen in eighteenth-century Europe, but one that was to become very common in Latin America and Haiti. This pattern contrasted with the situation in the United States, where, from George Washington on, former generals came to power through democratic means. The weakened control of the

171

Revolutionary French government over their generals from the mid-1790s, combined with the extent to which French policy focused on territorial expansion and strategic opportunism, ensured that powerful generals became key figures in a foreign policy that was distinctly not diplomatic. Neutrals, for example, were systematically bullied. French military successes also gravely limited the extent of rival diplomatic systems, as powers intimidated by France were obliged to break off relations with its enemies.

Napoleon proved a prime instance of this process of the general as policymaker, first in command in northern Italy, where, against the wishes of the Directory, he forced Austria to accept the Truce of Leoben in 1797. There, and later elsewhere, Napoleon proved particularly adept at the principle of compensating victims at the expense of others, the strategy of a chain of victimisation subsequently followed by both Hitler and Stalin.

The pressures generated by the Second Coalition prepared the ground for Napoleon's seizure of power in a coup in November 1799. At one level, this coup reflected a return to *ancien régime* patterns of diplomatic activity, notably as the inexorable scope of Napoleon's ambition, and his vainglorious capacity to alienate others, can readily be seen to repeat those of Louis XIV (r. 1643–1715), whose stance similarly became so unacceptable that extensive coalitions were established in order to fight him. Moreover, just as Napoleon's regime marked a limitation of radicalism within France, so it also reflected, and sustained, the abandonment of (French) Revolutionary objectives and methods in international relations already anticipated with the Thermidor reaction in 1794. In particular, the open diplomacy of revolutionary forums was replaced by the secrecy of opportunistic pragmatism.[2]

This shift would suggest that a fundamental divide occurred in international relations, and the strategic context it posed, not with the (two) overthrows of Napoleon and the Vienna Peace Settlement, all in 1814–15, but rather with Thermidor in 1794 and Napoleon's rise to power in 1799. Such an approach can be taken further by arguing that, therefore, there was a fundamental continuity throughout the nineteenth century, one, indeed, that lasted until the Russian Revolution of 1917 introduced a totally different pattern in thought in a major power.

Such a continuity, however, did not mean that the return of France to a monarchical format from 1799 and, under, eventually in 1804, Emperor

Napoleon I, entailed a reversion to an *ancien régime* system of strategy. Instead, one major development that continued was the focus on the nation, although this focus had had pre-Revolutionary anticipations, notably in the discussion of foreign policy from the late 1750s.[3] This focus was true both of the French, whether Revolutionary or Napoleonic, and of their opponents. Moreover, nationalism was understood by French policymakers both as a positive force for identity and cohesion, one that led strategy in a certain direction and, in addition, gave it particular force, and yet also as a negative, even xenophobic, response. The latter attitude was directed by the French against other states, both dynastic multiple monarchies, most obviously the Habsburg amalgamation, and other nation states. However, in turn, the French were affected by hostility to incorporating international forces, most obviously Napoleonic France, as in Spain from 1808.

Partly as a result of such nationalism and xenophobia, the very process of strategy took part in a more volatile context than that prior to 1792, volatile as that could be. For example, in 1797, the residence of the French envoy in Rome was occupied by papal police during a riot; the rioters had taken refuge there. In the ensuing disorder, General Léonard Duphot, an aide to the French envoy, was killed. Given, however, that the French had sought to provoke a revolutionary uprising, their conduct was less than exemplary, while the crisis was exploited by Napoleon in order to occupy Rome in February 1798, overthrowing papal rule, and to proclaim a Roman republic. In 1798, the tricolour flag of the French embassy in Vienna, prominently displayed on an Austrian national holiday by a provocative envoy, led to a crowd demonstration. Leaving Vienna, the envoy demanded reparation. Such a use of diplomatic symbols and incidents as the occasions for complaint and action represented a repositioning of the long-established concern for status, seen for example in controversies over precedence, away from dynastic monarchy, as with Louis XIV in the 1660s, and towards, instead, a new concept of the state. This had been prefigured from the 1750s but became more common in the 1790s.

As a reminder that chronologies of change were (and are) complex, alongside nationalism in the 1790s and 1800s came, in the 1800s, on the part of Napoleon, a very traditional dynastic aggrandisement, although one that proved provocative to nationalist feeling outside France. Dynastic prestige played a major role in Napoleon's creation of kingdoms and principalities for his family. Having made himself president of the Italian Republic (a renaming of the Cisalpine Republic) in 1802, Napoleon, as a result of refusals by his brothers Joseph and Louis, named himself king of Italy in 1805, being crowned on May 26, with his talented stepson, Eugène de Beauharnais, already arch-chancellor of the French empire and commander of the imperial crown, as viceroy from June 1805 until 1814. In 1806, Eugène was adopted by Napoleon and declared heir presumptive to the king of Italy in the absence of Napoleon having a second son. On January 14, 1806, he also married Princess Augusta, the eldest daughter of Maximilian I Joseph of Bavaria. She had been promised to Charles, the heir to the Duchy of Baden, but Napoleon had this engagement blocked. Instead, Charles that April married Stéphanie de Beauharnais, Napoleon's adoptive daughter, a cousin of Eugène. As part of the endless merry-go-round that continued until the end, Eugène in October 1813 added the Grand Duchy of Frankfurt, although the Allies occupied it from December.

In 1806, Napoleon replaced the Batavian Republic created in 1795 with the kingdom of Holland under his brother Louis. In 1810, Louis fell out with his brother, who found him insufficiently ductile and overly keen to identify with Dutch interests. Louis abdicated in favour of his son Napoleon-Louis Bonaparte (1804–31), who became King Louis II for only ten days. French forces invaded, and the kingdom was annexed to France. Louis I had fled to Austria.

Another brother, Joseph, became ruler of Naples in 1806. In 1808, after Louis turned it down, Joseph was given the Spanish crown, and was, in turn, replaced in the Sicilies as co-rulers by his younger sister Caroline and her husband Joachim Murat, a leading commander who had been made Grand Duke of Berg in Germany in 1806. Berg was a Bavarian territory that included Prussian territories. After Murat went to Naples, Berg was ruled by Napoleon in a personal union before in 1809 being given to the infant Napoleon-Louis Bonaparte, Louis II of Holland, who held the status of duke until December 1813. Another brother, Jerome, became king of Westphalia, a new state created by Napoleon that reflected his dominance of Germany and was designed to help maintain it. Westphalia also proved a significant source of troops and funds for Napoleon.[4]

The eldest surviving sister, Elisa, became Princess of Piombino and Lucca in 1805 and Grand Duchess of Tuscany in 1809. Another sister,

Pauline, became Duchess of Guastalla, and her husband, Prince Camillo Borghese, was made governor general of the French *départements* in northern Italy. A non-family member, Louis-Alexandre Berthier was made sovereign prince of Neuchâtel in 1806, replacing Frederick William III of Prussia; while, that year, Bernadotte became the sovereign Prince of Ponte Corvo, part of the kingdom of Naples formerly subject to the pope. Talleyrand was made Prince of Benevento, another sovereign principality.

Far from these new rulers serving the cause of their nations (although Louis, to Napoleon's irritation, sought to do so), these rulers were all subordinate to Napoleon, in a form, in effect, of vassalage. He not only deployed the force and intimidation that maintained them in position but also was senior to them as emperor, a status he had awarded himself in 1804. This was important, as status was a means to affirm and regularise position. As such, it was appropriate to his status that his marital diplomacy culminated in 1810, when Napoleon married into the Habsburgs, now the Austrian imperial family, as the Holy Roman Empire had been extinguished in 1806. His bride, the Archduchess Marie Louise, was a spoil of war from Austria's defeat by Napoleon in 1809. She was intended to cement Austria's new relationship with France, as well as to provide an heir who would carry through this relationship. In the event, there was an heir, Napoleon II, the king of Rome, but he was never to rule, despite Napoleon's interest in abdicating in his favour when defeated in 1815. Marital diplomacy was also used by Napoleon to link his family into other ruling families, as when Jerome Bonaparte was married in 1807 to Princess Katharina Friederike of Württemberg, the daughter of Frederick I of Württemberg, a marriage which had been agreed in 1803. Frederick had been made king by Napoleon in 1805 as an aspect of the process by which, alongside bullying and intimidation, Napoleon also offered benefits to his German allies in the shape of grander titles, internal autonomy, protection from Austria and Russia and expanded territories. So also with the Beauharnais marriages with the ruling houses of Baden and Bavaria.

Napoleon's family aggrandisement helped produce a strategy that was at once dynastic and imperial, one matched by the creation of an imperial nobility. Thus, Soult was made Duke of Dalmatia; Oudinot was made Duke of Reggio in Naples; Ney, Duke of Elchingen; and another marshal, Macdonald, became Duke of Taranto in 1809. There were multiple titles, such that Berthier, already Prince of Neuchâtel, also became Prince of Wagram in 1809. Napoleon created about 2,200 titles, as well as the *Légion d'honneur*. Large grants of money were distributed, a pattern later to be seen with Hitler. There was also imperial nobility in the British world, but one that had greater longevity and therefore legitimacy.[5]

Napoleon's imperial strategy was characterised by very uneven relations, including with his family, such as those also seen between Napoleon and states that were clients or that he saw as clients. Living his own myth of decisiveness, Napoleon certainly sought to direct and, even, conduct matters in person. Unlike most rulers of the period, he travelled considerable distances, notably to central and eastern Europe in 1805–7, 1808–9 and 1812–13, to Spain in 1808 and to Russia in 1812. However, as his government, strategic direction and diplomacy were intensely personal, a government of personal empire rather than of France, the policy-making process, as with other military sovereigns, was an adjunct of his travels, rather than being greatly hindered by them.

Yet, Napoleon was a total failure at the diplomatic aspects of strategy. As under Louis XIV, the problem of European alliances was evaded because neither ruler really sought allies on the basis of equality, however conditional. Instead, they were interested in clients: powers that could be manipulated, if not controlled, and the manipulation was frequently in the form of bullying and intimidation. Indeed, as the threat of force was central to Napoleon's means, diplomacy was an adjunct of strategy. When Napoleon, like Louis, was given the challenge of sustaining an alliance in which compromise played a role, he failed; and, failing to learn, he did so repeatedly. Alexander I of Russia's respect for him encouraged Alexander to try to build on their agreement at Tilsit in 1807, but Napoleon's repeated failure to reciprocate or to contain the resulting tensions helped to wreck such hopes.

Napoleon, who owed everything to a "boldness of determination,"[6] was happiest with a strategy of force. His character, views, ambitions and ambience did not lend themselves to accommodation, other than as a short-term device. Instead, Napoleon's will and attitude ensured that peace treaties were imposed and that, once they were made, the French sought further benefits, while their defeated opponents felt only resentment and a determination to reverse the settlement. Napoleon's will to dominate was both personal and a continuation of that of the Revolution, as was a refusal to countenance limits in the shape of diplomatic conventions. Thus, treated as spies, foreign envoys were embarrassed, threatened and imprisoned. Sir George Rumbold, the British chargé d'affaires to the Hanse towns, was seized by French troops in 1804, although in independent Hamburg. Typically, Napoleon, in contrast, expected his own envoys to be well treated.

It was indicative that Napoleon took further the tendency, already seen both with *ancien régime* France and, even more, France in the 1790s, to employ soldiers in diplomatic roles and as heads of missions abroad.[7] Alongside the dismissal of experienced diplomats earlier in the decade, for example Auguste de Choiseul-Gouffier from Constantinople in 1791, this ensured a worrying lack of understanding of other states as a basis for diplomacy. However, both the Revolutionaries and Napoleon ignored this issue. For them, broadcast rather than receive was the tone and means of strategic formulation.

The tendency to employ soldiers contributed to an increasing militarisation of the conduct of French policy. Thus, General Count Antoine-François Andréossy was sent to Austria to enforce a diplomacy of bullying after Prussia had been defeated at Jena in 1806, while General Anne-Jean-Marie-René Savary, the envoy sent to St. Petersburg in 1807 after the Peace of Tilsit, was arrogant and difficult. The following year, Savary was sent to Madrid to prepare for the French seizure of power. General Jacques-Alexandre-Bernard Law de Lauriston succeeded Caulaincourt (the most "diplomatic" of Napoleon's generals) in St. Petersburg in 1811 and failed to maintain the latter's careful and cautious approach to relations with Russia, an aspect of the damage-control Napoleon made necessary. Indeed, it was Napoleon who was responsible for the failure of the Franco-Russian entente established in 1807 at Tilsit. The French were not alone in employing generals in this fashion, but Napoleon appeared particularly attuned to it.

An interesting contrast was Robert, Viscount Castlereagh, British foreign secretary from 1812 until 1822. He had been a lieutenant colonel in the Irish militia deployed against the risk of French invasion in 1796, but his "military" background was essentially administrative and political, which proved to be a more useful contribution. Chief secretary of Ireland in 1798–1801, at the time of the 1798 rebellion, Castlereagh became president of the Board of Control for India in 1802–6 and secretary of state for war and the colonies in 1805–6 and 1807–9.[8]

The use of generals was not new for France, and was seen with other powers, such as the Austrians Schwarzenberg and Bubna, but this use became more insistent under Napoleon. It was also an important aspect of a failure to appreciate that an effective diplomatic service must produce reports and ideas that might be challenging, and, at the very least, explain the views and capabilities of other powers. In contrast, Austria followed what might be termed a diplomatic-intensive strategy, as in 1813 when it joined the coalition late and thus maximised its political advantage as well as military security.

Darwinian ideas of the operation of international systems suggest that developments by one power are matched by others as they compete to survive and succeed. Yet, as with the example of Napoleonic warfare, it is unclear how far this process operated, as opposed to an alternative process in which the *ancien régime* states essentially followed their existing practices with continued, less or greater effectiveness. The latter interpretation would put less of an emphasis on any transformational results from the French Revolution or Napoleon, and this conclusion seems pertinent if the composition, institutions and character of the strategies and diplomacies of France's opponents are considered. The principal changes they had to address were those of war. The length of the warfare beginning in 1792, but in eastern Europe in 1787, and, in particular, the major changes in alliances, as coalitions were created and brought low, led to a tempo in diplomacy that was notable, as it was very much the adjunct of strategy. War, its presence, changes and consequences, set the pace for the diplomacy of all states. Much of this diplomacy became a matter of keeping coalitions together and weakening those of opponents.

The major powers continued, and under the same dynasties, with the exception of France and Spain, for which the breaks in continuity came in 1792 and 1808, but there was considerable change at the level of the secondary powers. States disappeared, notably Poland, Venice and the Netherlands, while others, particularly Naples (in 1806) and Spain (in 1808), saw a change in dynasty as a result of conquest. Thus, many of the players and pieces were removed from the board, and this removal constituted a major change in the strategic context.

Not all of this change, however, was a consequence of the actions of France. Poland was partitioned out of existence in 1795 by Austria, Prussia and Russia, completing a totally opportunistic and violent process that had begun in 1772. Moreover, Austria played a major role in the territorial changes in Germany and northern Italy, as (for Germany) did Bavaria, Hesse, Prussia, Saxony and Württemberg. Nevertheless, France took an instrumental role in many of these German and Italian changes and became the dominant player in ensuring them in the 1800s.

At the same time, the possibility of change was also checked. Most obviously, the calls for national risings for liberty that, albeit often cynically, had characterised the 1790s became less common. Napoleon called on the Hungarians to rise for independence from Austria in 1809, talked of an Italian national spirit in the kingdom of Italy, and sought to profit from Polish nationalism and anti-Russian feeling in the Grand Duchy of Warsaw; but, in general, he focused, albeit often with great incompetence, on a highly instrumental approach to politics. This was very much seen with his allies. In 1806, Napoleon did not consult his ally Spain, even when proposing to cede the Balearic Islands to Ferdinand of Naples, while, in 1808, Florida was offered to the United States as an alliance bribe, again without considering Spanish views. Neither proposal was followed up, unlike the French acquisition of Louisiana from Spain.

It would, however, be mistaken to conclude with Napoleon, and that for several reasons. First, in studying strategy, there is only so much to be gained from considering failure rather than success. Secondly, Napoleon neither mastered strategy nor even rose to its challenges of understanding the interests of all the key players, and the possibilities and prioritisation this entailed. Thirdly, and related to both of these points, a focus on Napoleon leads to attention being concentrated on Europe, rather than the wider strategic dimensions of conflict and consequence. The latter dimensions direct attention both to the specifics of the longer-term Anglo-French struggle outside Europe, and also to the interaction between that struggle and other conflicts, notably in India, Latin America and North America. To a degree, there was such an interaction, alongside the autonomy in particular strategies and their implementation.

The end result of Napoleon's efforts, and those of the other powers, had been greatly to enhance British maritime and Russian land power by 1815. Both states were on the edge of Europe, and thus more able to protect their home base than other European countries, yet also capable of playing a major role in European politics. The tactical and operational proficiency of their forces (in the British case in particular of the navy, the most powerful and successful in the world[9]) was matched by a strategic advantage stemming from their ability to deploy considerable resources

and from a base that was difficult to conquer. The extent of these resources was important; the scale of warfare, and the simultaneity of commitments (a product of "tasking") and operations on many fronts, were
such that war posed formidable demands on the countries and states
involved. The response to these demands required not simply resources
in aggregate, but also organisational developments and cooperation between governments and political elites. Again, this was not new, and
could be seen over the previous centuries, but the greater scale of warfare
was notable compared to the major conflicts in 1756–63 and 1775–83.

The problem of mobilising resources, however, was lessened by the
widespread increase in the European population from the 1740s, a development that, like the recovery from the "Little Ice Age,"[10] helped make
Napoleonic warfare sustainable. Indeed, population increase was a key
factor in aggregate Western military capability. Numbers helped states
accommodate heavy casualties and yet continue fighting. France did so
not only through conscription but also from extending its empire from
which it raised troops. Russia suffered possibly 660,000 military casualties between 1789 and 1814, many due to disease and poor diet, while its
army may have received as many as two million recruits between 1802
and 1812. Despite suffering terrible losses in Russia in 1812, while also
fighting an intractable and now unsuccessful war in Spain, Napoleon was
able to raise fresh forces the following year, albeit at the cost of weakening his regime by lessening its popularity, which affected the stability of
the Napoleonic system in both 1814 and 1815. Indeed, the consequences
for the Napoleonic system of raising this manpower was an instance of
war weakening the state, a frequent occurrence, and one that contrasts
with the general, but misleading, portrayal of war as strengthening
states.

Britain and Russia represented extensive economic systems. Britain
drew not only on its own resources, which had been considerably enhanced by population growth and agricultural, industrial and transport
improvements, each generally termed revolutions, but also on the global
trading system that it was best placed to direct and exploit thanks to
naval strength and maritime resources. Russia similarly benefited from
scale and resources, not least grain production and its metallurgical industry, although administrative sophistication, entrepreneurial initiative
and fiscal capability and efficiency were each far less in evidence than in
Britain. Moreover, geopolitically, each state was able to repel Napoleon,

as the British showed with the affirmation of their naval mastery in 1805, culminating in victory at the Battle of Trafalgar, and the Russians in their unbroken and ultimately successful resistance to the invasion by Napoleon and his allies in 1812.

Their militaries also improved, which ensured that France did not benefit from any lasting capability gap. The pace of reform greatly accelerated during the war, as serious deficiencies, already apparent in the case of Britain from the War of American Independence,[11] were highlighted by repeated failure. In Britain, in part as a response to the failures in the War of American Independence, the rise of the War Office, under the secretary at war, from 1783, especially from 1809 to 1828 under Henry, 3rd Viscount Palmerston, a Junior Lord of the Admiralty from 1807 to 1809 (and later prime minister), and, above him, under the secretary of state for war from 1794, provided a larger and more effective bureaucracy for the conduct of overseas operations. The secretary of state for war had a lot of power over operational planning, but the army commander-in-chief, situated in the Horse Guards, administered personnel.[12] This process of administrative reform was taken further from 1806 with the appearance of the first of a number of reports by the newly established Commission of Military Enquiry.

Improvement was due in large part to the efforts of George III's second son, Frederick, Duke of York, who became commander-in-chief in 1795 and was a more effective administrator than he was a field commander, the latter clearly demonstrated by his failure in Holland in 1799.[13] In the face of defeat, the army needed to be revived, and York took particular care to raise the quality of the officers. York's changes can be seen as part of a period of national reform, one that included the introduction of income tax (1799), parliamentary union with Ireland (1800–1801) and the national census (1801).

York encouraged schemes for military education. A military college that would train cadets was opened in 1802 at Marlow and developed into the Royal Military College at Sandhurst, and one to train staff officers opened in 1799 at High Wycombe. York was successful due to governmental support as well as that of an officer corps that was interested in thinking about war as well as learning it on the job. Wellington was not the only up-and-coming officer who read widely on military matters and was, in effect, part of a British branch of the Military Enlightenment.[14] York was also a supporter of the standardisation of drill.[15]

Consistency was a standard theme, and this emphasis helped to turn a collection of regiments into an army, a development from which Wellington was to benefit greatly in so far as his British units were concerned. Consistency aided the transfer of officers, troops and equipment between units, and improved tactical and operational flexibility. While presiding over a significant increase in the size of the army, from 40,000 men in 1793 to over 250,000 in 1813, York addressed the conditions of the ordinary soldiers, including chaplaincy services,[16] food, accommodation (by means of building barracks), medical care, punishment regimes and the provision of greatcoats to keep out the cold.

York was a supporter of the cause of light infantry, one associated in particular with Colonel John Moore (1761–1809), who, in 1803, was appointed commander of a new brigade at Shorncliffe Camp in Kent, which was designed to serve as the basis of a permanent light infantry force. Moore had been much impressed by the system of training and manoeuvring light infantry developed by Major Kenneth Mackenzie the previous decade. Particular emphasis was placed on marksmanship, which was aided by the use from 1800 of the Baker rifle, a flintlock produced by Ezekial Baker. Colonel Charles Manningham and Lieutenant Colonel William Stewart were key figures in developing the Experimental Corps of Riflemen, established in 1800, later the 95th Rifles (1802) and then the Rifle Brigade.

Moore's force was to become the Light Brigade and, subsequently, the Light Division. His career showed the possibility of rapid promotion for the talented son of a Scottish doctor. As a lieutenant general, Moore was killed at the Battle of Corunna on January 16, 1809, while managing, in the face of stronger French forces, the successful evacuation of a force he had led into Spain in a failed attempt to thwart the French conquest of the country. More generally, the risk of conflict, both of combat and disease, lessened the availability of talent, and Wellington's career was eased by the death of alternatives, notably Ralph Abercromby (1801, Egypt) and Moore, who were killed in conflict, and Sir Gerald Lake, who died in 1808 as a result of sickness, having returned from India the previous year. In turn, Wellington exposed himself to considerable personal danger, notably at Argaum in 1803, but also at Waterloo. Similarly, in the War of 1812, Major General Isaac Brock was killed in action at Queenston Heights in 1812.

Public support for war, which was far less coerced than in France, was important in Britain, where the French challenge focused a strong patriotism. On August 1, 1814, when a national jubilee was held to celebrate peace with France, the London parks were opened to the public, as an inclusive step.[17]

With their very different politics, Britain and Russia saw off Napoleon, exploiting his inability to provide lasting stability in western and central Europe, and thus thwarted the last attempt before the age of nationalism to remodel Europe. Britain won at Waterloo, but Russia was then the longstop or final resort to block Napoleon on land. Their success ensured the reversal of the trend towards French hegemony which had reached its height in 1812, when France had been greatly expanded—Rome, for example, was annexed in May 1809 and Hamburg in December 1810—while large parts of Europe were under French satellites or allies, such as Bavaria and Saxony.

Although Austria was the key power in Germany and, even more, Italy, the success of Britain and Russia was to define Europe and the postwar world. Britain remained the leading maritime and imperial power until succeeded by the United States in the 1940s, with Russia the dominant state on the Eurasian landmass for the remainder of the nineteenth century and until the crises of 1905–20, although Prussian victory over France in 1870–71 had lessened its relative power. The British and Russian armies had an ability to engage not simply in conflict with other Western states, but also with non-Western powers. As a result, Britain and Russia made major territorial gains in the quarter-century beginning in 1790 and also thereafter, which set the basis for their future competition in the "Great Game" for dominance of South Asia and neighbouring regions. This process continued in the twentieth century, albeit in a different form, and with the United States eventually replacing Britain as the opponent of the Soviet Union.

In 1814–15, Europe was returned by Napoleon's victorious opponents to the multiple statehood that distinguished it from several of the other heavily populated regions of the world, most obviously China, but also Southwest Asia. This return was as much a consequence of Napoleon's political failure as of the absence of a lasting military capability gap in favour of France. These, moreover, were structural factors that took on meaning in war and on the battlefield. By 1815, victory in an individual battle or even campaign seemed of scant weight beside the massive resources deployed against France by the coalition and its unity. The scale was different from that of the challenge faced by Frederick the Great (Frederick II) of Prussia in the mid-eighteenth century, as was the "miracle" required for Napoleon to be able to follow Frederick in surviving attack. Alongside continued limitations on the part of all powers in the scale and processes of strategy formulation,[18] the difference in scale of resources also reflected the transition in Napoleonic warfare. This was from the battles of 1792–1807, when, to a considerable extent, the French had engaged opponents using more traditional tactics and force structures, to those of 1809–15. Then the opposing forces were more similar to those of France, which was also faced with more extensive deployment of resources by her opponents.

The political will that was critical was not only that of Napoleon, but also that of the French population, much of which was politicised as a result of the Revolution and its consequences, notably long-term conscription. In 1814 and 1815, Napoleon discovered that his assessment offered to Metternich in 1813, and quoted at the beginning of this chapter, was correct, and that support from the population was fragile. The comparable situation for France's opponents was also very important. Public support was a key factor in any evaluation of strategic capability and choices, one that is overly neglected but was still an important factor in both strategic context and strategic conjunctures.

NOTES

1. Richard von Metternich, *Memoirs of Prince Metternich, 1773–1815* (New York, 1880), 185–87.

2. Marsha Frey and Linda Frey, "'The Reign of the Charlatans Is Over': The French Revolutionary Attack on Diplomatic Practice," *Journal of Modern History* 65 (1993), 740; Marc Belissa, *Repenser l'ordre européen (1795–1802): De la société des rois aux droits des nations* (Paris: Kimé, 2006).

3. Edmond Dziembowski, *La France face à la puissance anglaise à l'epoque de la guerre de Sept Ans* (Oxford: Oxford University Press, 1998).

4. Sam Mustafa, *Napoleon's Paper Kingdom: The Life and Death of Westphalia, 1807–1813* (Lanham, MD: Rowman and Littlefield, 2017). For a weaker support, see Jacques-Olivier Boudon, ed., *Les provinces illyriennes dans l'Europe napoléonienne, 1809–1813* (Paris: Editions SPM, 2015).

5. John Severn, *Architects of Empire: The Duke of Wellington and His Brothers* (Norman: Oklahoma University Press, 2007).

6. Carl von Clausewitz, *The Campaign of 1812 in Russia* (London: Stackpole, 1992), 260.

7. Edward Whitcomb, *Napoleon's Diplomatic Service* (Durham, NC: Duke University Press, 1979); Margaret Chrisawn, "A Military Bull in a Diplomatic China Shop: General Jean Lannes' Mission to Lisbon, 1802–1804," *Portuguese Studies Review* 3 (1993–94): 46–67.

8. John Bew, *Castlereagh: Enlightenment, War and Tyranny* (London: Quercus, 2011).

9. For the army, see Jeremy Black, *How the Army Made Britain a Global Power, 1688–1815* (Oxford: Casemate, 2021).

10. Geoffrey Parker, *Global Crisis: War, Climate Change and Catastrophe in the Seventeenth Century* (New Haven, CT: Yale University Press, 2013).

11. Andrew O'Shaugnessy, *The Men Who Lost America: British Command during the Revolutionary War and the Preservation of the Empire* (New Haven, CT: Yale University Press, 2013).

12. Roger Knight, *Britain against Napoleon: The Organisation of Victory, 1793–1815* (London: Allen Lane, 2013), 104.

13. Derek Winterbottom, *The Grand Old Duke of York: Life of Prince Frederick, Duke of York and Albany, 1763–1827* (Barnsley: Pen and Sword, 2016).

14. Ira Gruber, *Books and the British Army in the Age of the American Revolution* (Chapel Hill: University of North Carolina Press, 2010); Christy Pichichero, *The Military Enlightenment: War and Culture in the French Empire from Louis XIV to Napoleon* (Ithaca, NY: Cornell University Press, 2017).

15. Mark Gerges, "Those Complicated Maneuvers of Dundas: British Cavalry Doctrine, 1793–1814," *Consortium, 2006*, 240–51.

16. For initial strength and weaknesses, see Michael Snape, *The Royal Army Chaplain's Department, 1796–1953: Clergy under Fire* (Woodbridge: Boydell and Brewer, 2008), 29–32.

17. Edwin Marrs Jr., ed., *The Letters of Charles and Mary Anne Lamb* (New York: Cornell University Press, 1975–78), 3:96.

18. Rory Muir and Charles Esdaile, "Strategic Planning in a Time of Small Government: The War against Revolutionary and Napoleonic France, 1793–1815," *Wellington Studies* 1 (1996): 1–90.

NINE

Later Strategic Scrutiny

In September 1815, in a dramatic display of power, Alexander I reviewed a parade of 150,000 Russian troops east of Paris, in the Russian occupation zone, alongside Francis I of Austria and Frederick William III of Prussia, each of whom was also dressed in Russian uniform. Earlier, on July 10, the three monarchs had entered Paris. The fact of power was readily apparent, and, with it, the total failure of both the Revolutionaries and Napoleon. In each case, their strategic goals and means had been deeply flawed and lacked resilience. The Revolution collapsed as a result of the events of 1799, while Napoleon, in turn, could not survive defeat. If there was no perverted *Götterdämmerung* equivalent to the Berlin bunker of 1945 for Hitler, Napoleon discovered hell in his own terms, impotent, bar in his anger and spite, on an isolated island in the storm-tossed South Atlantic.

JOMINI AND CLAUSEWITZ

The strategies of remembrance bound up in the war were overwhelmingly political, rather than being concerned with learning supposedly objective lessons on military capability. These strategies related to legitimation and delegitimation, and both sought to capture for political purposes the need to remember and celebrate. In France, contesting the Napoleonic myth was to the fore, while in Germany and Italy, debating different roles in the wars served to provide a means to contest politics, notably in its most potent forms of identity and symbolism.

The French Revolution provided a long-lasting republican account of the valour and value of citizen soldiers.[1] Separately, Napoleon nevertheless provided Western commentators with the ambition and apparent need to explain success in war, because the challenge he posed, or had posed, focused attention and required assessment. The drama, length and severity of the French threat excited interest, while most military figures for decades after had served in these wars. The apparent need to understand the Napoleonic Wars reflected not only his repeated successes in the 1800s but also the extent to which the international system did not change greatly until Prussia's defeat of Austria in 1866. Indeed, France was to find itself at war, separately with powers that had fought Napoleon: Russia (1854–56), Austria (1859), and Prussia/Germany (1870–71), and close to war with Britain. The battlefields in the wars with Austria and Prussia were those fought over under Napoleon, who still seemed relevant, and especially so because the "empty battlefield" of lethal firepower did not develop till late in the century.

Confronting the legacy of Napoleon encouraged a bold attempt to write about a science of command, which has long proved a major route to discussing strategy. This was ironic, as Napoleon's belief in the genius of the leader, or rather of himself as leader and genius, a kind of Romantic superman, did not lend itself to copying. Indeed, Napoleon did not endorse a science of war of the Enlightenment time, as he believed that his genius had both superseded and smashed what he saw as the mechanistic narrowness of such a science.

Jomini and Clausewitz were to be the major figures in this discussion.[2] The key rule master for long proved to be the Swiss-born Antoine-Henri Jomini (1779–1869). He served in the French army as chief of staff to Marshal Ney before switching, in 1813, to the Russian army, being made a lieutenant general by Alexander I, the central figure in Napoleon's overthrow. Jomini's influential works, which included the *Traité des grandes opérations militaires* (1805–9) and the *Précis de l'art de la guerre* (which appeared first in a very partial and elementary form in 1810 as the conclusion to the *Traité*), aimed to find logical principles at work in warfare, which was seen, by Jomini, as having timeless essential characteristics. In particular, Jomini sought to explain the success of Frederick the Great and then of Napoleon, who was the subject of his *Vie politique et militaire de Napoléon* (1827).

Jomini, like Clausewitz, a more difficult writer to confront, wrote in the shadow of Napoleon, and self-consciously so. Jomini had to address the topics of his sweeping success and of his subsequent complete failure, although his explanation of this failure was rather lacking. Jomini's focus was operational, not strategic. To him, building on the tradition of much eighteenth-century consideration of conflict, as well as on a method and ethos of explanation in mechanistic terms, the crucial military point was the choice of a line of operations that would permit a successful attack. Napoleonic operational art was discussed in terms of envelopment—the use of "exterior lines," and, alternatively, the selection of a central position that would permit the defeat in detail (separately) of opposing forces—a position which was described in terms of interior lines. The corps gave Napoleon, he argued with reason, a "force multiplier," one that greatly increased operational effectiveness.

By focusing on decisive battles, Jomini emphasised battle winning as decisive, rather than the wider consequences of social, economic and technological change.[3] He was, for example, critical of the Spanish guerrilla warfare against French occupation, which he himself had witnessed, and he spent very little time discussing it.[4] Napoleon himself devoted scant interest in 1814 to the possibility of guerrilla resistance to the Allied invaders. Separately, like Clausewitz, Jomini paid insufficient attention to the British.

Jomini's emphasis on battle on land continues to be widespread in the discussion of Napoleonic generalship. It can be seen, for example, in the focus on the Battle of Waterloo, or on the operations of the campaign of June 15–18, when considering the events of 1815, and not, as it should also be, on the political contexts for Napoleon's strategy, notably his diplomatic isolation, which helped force him onto the attack, nor on his failure to inspire widespread support within France after the battle. Jomini's influence remained strong into the 1860s, including in the United States[5] and in Britain, as in *The Operations of War Explained and Illustrated* (1866) by Edward Hamley, the new professor of military history at the new Staff College at Sandhurst. Moreover, although the successes of Prussia from the 1860s focused attention thereafter on Clausewitz, in practice Jomini's operationally focused reading of strategy has remained important in America to the present.[6] Jomini was interested in practical lessons. His was really a "how-to" approach, one of lessons allegedly to be learned from a relevant past.

The Prussian Carl von Clausewitz (1780–1831), in contrast, sought to train the minds of commanders and statesmen and emphasised a broad approach, most notably stressing the inherent political nature of war and, therefore, the balance of political determination. A young man of talent, Clausewitz fought in 1793 in the Prussian army against the French, being promoted to ensign and then in 1795 to second lieutenant. In 1801, he applied to the Institute in the Military Sciences for Young Infantry and Cavalry Officers, then under its new director, Gerhard Scharnhorst, who was eager to understand and teach changes in the nature of war. This institute became an important forcing house for Clausewitz's intellectual development. In 1804, he drafted a short work entitled *Strategie*, which covered a range of topics. Unpublished, this study emphasised the importance of securing the object of a war, and, to that end, the value of battle.[7] The campaigns he took part in influenced his views.[8] They also reflected the changeable nature of international relations. Having served with the Prussian army on the Rhine in 1793–94, Clausewitz was kept from action by Prussian neutrality until, in 1806, he was captured in the defeat at Jena. Opposed to Prussia's subsequent alliance with Napoleon, Clausewitz fought for the Russians in 1812–13. Rejoining the Prussian army, Clausewitz served at Ligny and Wavre in the Waterloo campaign. In his posthumously published, but important, account of Napoleon's Russian campaign, Clausewitz presented the French strategy in 1812 as one of victory in campaign enabling the dictation of a peace that was to be aided by creating dissension between a weak government and the nobility.[9] In about 1827, Clausewitz also wrote *Feldzug von 1815: Strategische Uebersicht des Feldzugs von 1815* (The campaign of 1815: Strategic overview of the campaign),[10] an assessment that was unsympathetic to Wellington and which the latter countered.

The nature of Clausewitz's approach has been subject to a variety of interpretations. The assessment is based largely on *Vom Kriege* (*On War*), an unfinished work, although also usefully drawing on his other writings. This process has been encouraged by the somewhat opaque nature of much of the text, by his plentiful use of passive tenses and subordinate clauses, and by issues concerning the meanings of particular phrases and words. Clausewitz's early education in philosophy was reflected in his work, but, affected by the tension between the Enlightenment-era thought seen with Jomini and that of the period of Romanticism, Clausewitz was not always systematic in his argumentation.[11] Approached differently, the interplay of passion, reason and possibility (all elements in motivation analysed by the classical Greek writer Thucydides) found in his thought scarcely allowed Clausewitz to be systematic. Indeed, it is possible to "re-read Clausewitz in these climatic terms of Romantic self-conception," one in which atmospheric terms best capture the psychological transformation caused by war. [12]

Clausewitz had read extensively in military history, believed in its significance, and produced historical studies from his years at the institute. [13] More significantly, he addressed the issue of the nature of war in history, focusing on the problem of the significance of change during his military career, a process for many contemporaries centered on France, and on the question of whether there was going to be more change. The validity of both offence and defence was one dichotomy altering in time that concerned him. His use of strategy was primarily in terms of how battle was employed for the purpose of war, a question that was at once operational and strategic. At the same time, in both respects, the context and content of strategy in reality greatly depended on the nature of the opponent.

The moral character of military forces was important for the eighteenth-century commentators, and not only those of the American and French Revolutions, with their stress on citizen virtues. Clausewitz, indeed, can be located in this tradition of assessing the moral character of military activity as an aspect of understanding and placing how war works, so that commanders would best be able to evaluate and respond to situations. Clausewitz and Jomini addressed the changes stemming from the mobilisation of society seen with the French Revolution and, later, in opposition to Napoleon, with the German War of Liberation of 1813, and also the changes arising from the high-tempo offensive war-making developed by Napoleon. Neither commentator, however, devoted equivalent attention to naval warfare, or the technological changes and, in part, industrialisation of warfare that became more insistent and incessant during the nineteenth century, and they were particularly weak in covering non-Western militaries, and therefore seeing, for example, Napoleon as but one among several horseback monarchs of the period. [14]

Already, a sense of the potency of the industrial new can be glimpsed in Major General Thomas Grosvenor's account of the British bombardment of Copenhagen in September 1807. On the 2nd, he wrote:

> Began the bombardment of Copenhagen at sunset, three mortar batter-
> ies of twelve each all opened at the same time. . . . The Congreve arrows
> [rockets] made a very singular appearance in the air. Six or seven com-
> et-like appearances racing together. They seemed to move very slow.
> The town was set on fire.

Three days later, Grosvenor added, "The Great Church was on fire to the
very pinnacle of the steeples. The appearance was horrifyingly grand."[15]

Alongside the idea of the novelty, however, comes the significance of
continuities. Moreover, these continuities challenge the idea that Napoleonic warfare was somehow new because given to manoeuvre operationally and to decisiveness strategically. In practice, neither of those were
new goals nor methods, and only a limited understanding of pre-1792
warfare can suggest otherwise.

THE LANGUAGE AND PRACTICE OF STRATEGY

The works of Jomini and, later, Clausewitz, each of which was translated
into other languages, were to affect the developing use of the term and
concept of strategy. The use of both term and concept spread in the early
nineteenth century. For example, in Russian, the linkage with Greek ensured that the term had been present for a long time, but that it reflected
Byzantine usage, as in *strategos* or stratagem. In addition, *stratig* (military
leader) was long-standing. Suvorov, the impressive commander against
the French in 1799, wrote a work, *The Science of Victory* (1796), that focused on combat rather than strategy. In contrast, the modern sense of
"strategy" was acquired at the end of the eighteenth century, and the
Napoleonic Wars helped Russians to get a better sense of the term. By the
1820s, it was well established.

Although the word "strategy" was coming into use, many commanders did not employ it to describe the strategy that they certainly had.
Thus, the Prussian general Gebhard Leberecht von Blücher (1742–1819)
was more generally typical in understanding the concept of strategy, but
without using the word.[16] During earlier periods, generals had understood the concept of strategy but employed other terms. For example,
when they formulated the strategy to follow during the seventeenth century, they used terms such as "the policy to follow," "the requirements of
your Majesty," "the needs of the Monarchy" and "to maintain the reputation." As the language became more modern, the semantics changed.

"Strategy" as a term was employed in Britain in a military context from the 1810s. The term "strategy," however, was not employed in British official or private correspondence of the period when referring to strategic concepts, thinking and intentions. In 1808, Wellington used the word to refer to what is today understood as tactics or organisation. John Wilson Croker, a pro-government MP who handled for Wellington the latter's business as chief secretary for Ireland, recorded of a discussion, that the general said: "Why to say the truth, I am thinking of the French that I am going to fight. . . . They have besides, it seems, a new system of strategy, which has out-manoeuvred and overwhelmed all the armies of Europe."[17] It is not certain, however, that this memorandum was made at the time.[18] At any rate, it is unclear whether Wellington's reference is to the French corps system, the use of infantry columns or effective combined arms practices and structures. These would not be seen today as constituting strategy, although they capture the contemporary focus on specific tactical matters when assessing effectiveness.

In Britain, government policy or plans were often cited when referring to what we would term strategy. "Prospects" or "plans" with respect to Spain, Austria or other powers were other terms. "Arrangements with nations" was another often-used phrase. It was chiefly the employment of the word "government" that was used to signify a strategic concept. The "art of war" was another commonplace term. Wellington's 1806 memorandum on British plans for South America and his 1809 memorandum on the defence of Portugal definitely articulated the concept of strategy. In 1806, he scotched a plan to deploy forces simultaneously on the east and west coasts of South America, while in 1809 he clearly explained how the British army should be used to defend Lisbon, how this would facilitate the defence of Portugal and how it might even enable the British to go onto the offensive in Spain. The means to accomplish this were thirty to forty thousand British troops, the retraining of the Portuguese army, and the construction of the defensive Lines of Torres Vedras to ensure that Lisbon supplied by the navy was a secure base.[19] These lines saw off the subsequent French advance on Lisbon in 1811–12, and this defensive success was followed by an advance into Spain that led to a major victory over the French at Salamanca; although that, in turn, had to be followed by retreat into Portugal.

As with many other commanders, Wellington was somewhat less keen on strategy when it clashed with his interests. This was an issue

Napoleon could ignore by directing French strategy so that it was a matter of his interests, although that practice proved to have serious limitations. Wellington did not appreciate that his reiterated calls during the Peninsular War (1808–13) for resources, both military and naval, had to align with other governmental concerns. In particular, although he appreciated that he fundamentally received the naval support he required, Wellington's demands on it could be inappropriate. They were repeatedly rejected by the Admiralty, which drew attention to its extensive other commitments, which had been increased by the outbreak of the War of 1812.[20]

Although the navy could cover both contingencies, this situation underlined the problems posed by power projection, and by independent army and navy structures, but also the existence of key questions of commitments and resources, irrespective of the nature of the organisational system. The implementation of one strategy could close down strategic options elsewhere, and was in large part intended to do so. Thus, strategy was a multilevel process, and, as it remains, a process as well as an outcome.

WORLD WAR COMPARISONS

Very briefly visiting Paris in 1940 after his total victory over France, Hitler, also a veteran of World War I, found time to visit the tomb of Napoleon in the Invalides, as if he, Hitler, was a latter-day Alexander the Great seeking to contemplate the tomb of Achilles. The strategic legacy of the French Revolutionary and Napoleonic wars, indeed, was not solely a matter of the influence on later military thought, and especially so through the significance of Clausewitz. There was also the extent to which these wars served as a point of reference for considering the conflicts of the twentieth century.[21] That year, Winston Churchill wrote a foreword for an edition of William Pitt the Younger's wartime speeches.

Linked, but separate, there is the question of whether the later conflicts can provide a point of departure for a consideration of the warfare of 1792–93. The contrasts in the material technology, operational means and tactical methods of conflict are certainly very notable. Large forces continued to advance by marching, but logistics were transformed first by rail and then by the internal combustion engine, while the nature of the war at sea was radically different, and that of war in the air was invented and rapidly developed. These changes, however, left (and still leave) unclear the extent to which strategic parallels can be found. Here, the major one, at the level of what was once termed "grand strategy," is the contrast between the land-based empire and its maritime rival, a contrast that goes back to Sparta and Athens in Thucydides's account of the Peloponnesian War (431–404 BCE), and forward to the Cold War between the Soviet Union and the United States (1945–91).

This emphasis is one that presents a perspective that might be unwelcome to many specialists on warfare in 1792–1815, as it places the focus on the naval struggle and on the strategies of global power: we should look at Trafalgar as well as Austerlitz for 1805, and maybe downplay Austerlitz accordingly. In this perspective, the key, and consistent, theme indeed puts the Anglo-French struggle foremost, with Spain also being an important naval power, while, correspondingly, Austria and Prussia, at least relatively, become less significant. As Prussia spent much of the period neutral, other than an interlude in which it was heavily defeated in 1806, that is possibly appropriate for Prussia. Indeed, seeing it as strategically significant reflects more its later success from 1864 to 1871 as a military power than the situation even in 1813–14, when it was very much secondary to Russia and Austria.

If the focus is on Britain and France, then the conclusion is that neither the Revolutionaries nor Napoleon could work out and implement a viable and effective strategy towards Britain, whether the focus was (or is) on conflict, economics, diplomacy or subversion. Assaults on Britain in the shape of invasion preparations and attempts failed, as did blockades. Moreover, victories on the Continent did not determine the outcome. Thus, while, in 1941, Hitler failed to get at London by marching to Moscow; in 1812 Napoleon reached Moscow, but he was totally unsuccessful in his wider strategy and did not know how to prevent Russia from subsequently overwhelming his earlier successes. Although Napoleon got to Moscow, his forces had left Russia by the close of the year. In contrast, Hitler did not reach Moscow, but his forces retained until 1944 enough territory to serve as a buffer against further Soviet expansion. General success for France came closer in 1797 and 1806, when there was British interest in negotiations, and in 1802, when a treaty with Britain was agreed, while Russia and Austria had already made peace with France. However, on no occasion did Napoleon devote sufficient effort to the task of negotiating and sustaining peace with Britain. This proved a key strategic failure. The Russians regard their conflicts of 1812–15 as "a patriotic war and campaigns for the liberation of Europe," which is also how they see World War II.

Comparisons of Napoleon with Hitler[22] anger many, as they seem to lessen the horror of the latter while providing a degrading as well as unfair comparison for Napoleon. That is not my intention. There are obviously comparisons that can be made between these empire builders, especially as both these individuals were narcissistic and megalomaniacal; but the contrasts are readily apparent, and they emerge from the process of comparison. Napoleon reintroduced slavery into the French overseas empire in 1802, but there was no comparison to Hitler's genocidal policy towards Jews and Roma.

Strategy, however, attracts comparison between the two, both in order to probe parallels and so as to clarify through contrasts. Hitler had none of the tactical or operational command experience of Napoleon, and was incapable of drawing on this, as well as on an understanding of command skills, in order to evaluate his generals. Moreover, Napoleon was able to take a much more assertive command line, not least because he was in direct command of the largest army. He brought together the military and political sides of strategy more completely than Hitler, and also lacked the latter's obsession with minutiae.

Their contexts were also very different, not least in the ability of air warfare to challenge the security of areas otherwise under control. So also with the ability of the United States to intervene in Europe and thus give substance to amphibious invasion to a degree that was lacking in 1792–1815. Yet, there were also many similarities between the two men as strategists: in goal, content and process, and in the interacting nature of the three. The highly transactional nature of the politics and the untrustworthiness of the relations with other states were matched with conquered areas by the failure to try to ground control in consent, by the readiness to oppress and exact and by the extremely harsh response to opposition. In military terms, there was a marked preference for sequential war-making and a preference, indeed desire, to take the offensive. As strategists of, and in, defence, both Napoleon and Hitler were highly flawed. Defence was seen solely as the basis for a manoeuvrist counteroffensive, as in 1813–14 or July–August 1943 (Battle of Kursk) or December 1944 (Battle of the Bulge), but the strategic underpinnings were delusional. Ultimately, indeed, that is the most appropriate term. Others may offer rationalisations, even defences, for this delusional thinking and response, both as far as individual episodes and the overall prosecution of the war are concerned, but the net effect in each case was a strategy of folly that led to disaster.

CONCLUSIONS

Debate over Napoleon continues,[23] but it is notable that criticism of his generalship has become more striking in recent decades.[24] In many respects, this book comes in that tradition, although with more of an emphasis on his strategy. At the same time, it is necessary to assess differing views. Thus, in 1997, David Gates argued that "Napoleon's brilliance as a military commander has rarely been equalled, let alone surpassed."[25] Yet, at the same time, had the factors of distance and weather in 1809 when attacking Austria been comparable to those Napoleon faced when invading Russia in 1812, it is possible that the failure of the Napoleonic system would have been dated earlier.

Separately, the eventual number of Napoleon's opponents was obviously important, and was a product of political as well as military failure. He suffered from his unwillingness to compromise, and thus to bring stability to the inherently unstable French hegemony across much of Europe, and from his ultimate inability to defend this hegemony. Gates suggested that Napoleon lost sight of the politics that war was supposed to further, ensuring that his marshals abandoned him in 1814. This was Napoleon as strategic failure, which is an appropriate conclusion.

The French lacked a position and lead comparable to that enjoyed by the British at sea after Trafalgar, and the circumstances of land warfare were not such as to permit a replication of a lead of this type. The combination of this military precariousness with political opposition to French hegemony required skilful management, both military and political. His apologists notwithstanding, Napoleon could not provide this and did not learn how to do so.

NOTES

1. Alan Forrest, *The Legacy of the French Revolutionary Wars: The Nation-in-Arms in French Republican Memory* (Cambridge: Cambridge University Press, 2009).

2. For comparisons, see Michael Handel, *Masters of War: Sun Tzu, Clausewitz and Jomini* (London: Frank Cass, 1990).

3. Ami-Jacques Rapin, *Jomini et la stratégie: Une approche historique de l'oeuvre* (Lausanne: Payot-Lausanne, 2002); Lawrence Crowell, "The Illusion of the Decisive Napoleonic Victory," *Defense Analysis* 4 (1988): 329–46.

4. Beatrice Heuser, "Lessons Learnt? Cultural Transfer and Revolutionary Wars, 1775–1831," *Small Wars and Insurgencies* 25 (2014): 864.

5. James Morrison, *The Best School in the World: West Point, the Pre-Civil War Years, 1833–1866* (Kent, OH: Kent State University Press, 1986).

6. Bruno Colson, *La culture stratégique américaine l'influence de Jomini* (Paris: Economica, 1993).

7. Carl von Clausewitz, *Strategie: Aus dem Jahr 1804, mit Zusätzen von 1808 und 1809*, ed. E. Kessel (Hamburg: Hanseatische verlagsanstalt, 1937), 37–82.

8. Donald Stoker, "Clausewitz's Lost Battle: Sehestedt 10 Dec. 1813," *Military History Monthly* 68 (May 2016): 40–46.

9. Carl von Clausewitz, *The Campaign of 1812 in Russia* (London: Stackpole, 1992), 253. Clausewitz also commented on campaigns in which he was not present: Clausewitz, *Napoleon's 1796 Italian Campaign*, ed. Nicholas Murray and Christopher Pringle (Lawrence: University Press of Kansas, 2018).

10. Christopher Bassford, Daniel Moran, and Gregory W. Pedlow, eds. and trans., *On Waterloo: Clausewitz, Wellesley, and the Campaign of 1815* (Clausewitz.com, 2010).

11. Azar Gat, *The Origins of Military Thought, from the Enlightenment to Clausewitz* (Oxford: Oxford University Press, 1989).

12. Thomas H. Ford, "Narrative and Atmosphere: War by Other Media in Wilkie, Clausewitz and Turner," in *Tracing War in British Enlightenment and Romantic Culture*, ed. Neil Ramsey and Gillian Russell (Basingstoke: Palgrave Macmillan, 2015), 182–84, quote 184.

13. Peter Paret, "*On War* Then and Now," *Journal of Military History* 80 (2016): 481–82, and "The Function of History in Clausewitz's Understanding of War," ibid., 82 (2018): 1055.

14. Jeremy Black, *Plotting Power: Strategy in the Eighteenth Century* (Bloomington: Indiana University Press, 2017), 194.

15. BL. Add. 49059 fols 27, 30.

16. Michael Leggiere, *Blücher: Scourge of Napoleon* (Norman: University of Oklahoma Press, 2014).

17. Croker's memorandum, June 14, 1808, *Memoirs, Diaries and Correspondence of the Right Hon. John Wilson Croker*, ed. Louis Jennings, 3 vols. (London, 1884), 1:12–13.

18. See commentary, http://www.lifeofwellington.co.uk/commentary/chapter-fourteen-dublin-and-westminster-october-1807-july-1808#sthash.pylldowVD.dpuf, accessed April 17, 2016; Martin Robson, "Sir Arthur Wellesley as a Special Advisor, 1806–1808," in *Wellington Studies*, vol. 5, ed. Christopher Woolgar, 38–60 (Southampton: Hartley Institute, University of Southampton, 2012), esp. 39–54.

19. Second Duke of Wellington, ed., *Supplementary Despatches . . . of Duke of Wellington*, 15 vols. (London, 1858–72), 6:35; Colonel John Gurwood, ed., *The Dispatches of . . . Wellington*, 8 vols. (London, 1844), 4:261–63.

20. Kevin McCranie, "Perception and Naval Dominance: The British Experience during the War of 1812," *Journal of Military History* 82 (2018): 1067–91.

21. Andrew Liaropoulos, "Revolutions in Warfare: Theoretical Paradigms and Historical Evidence—The Napoleonic and First World War Revolutions in Military Affairs," *Journal of Military History* 70 (2006): 363–84; Jeremy Black, *Strategy and the Second World War* (London: Robinson, 2021).

22. See, for example, Paul Schroeder, *Transformation of European Politics , 1763–1848* (Oxford: Oxford University Press, 1994), 392–93.

23. For a brief introduction, see Clare Siviter, "Napoleon: Two Centuries of Life after Death," *History Today* 71, no. 5 (May 2021): 28–41.

24. Paddy Griffith, *The Art of War of Revolutionary France, 1789–1802* (London: Greenhill, 1998), 11; Owen Connelly, *Blundering to Glory: Napoleon's Military Campaigns*, 2nd ed. (Wilmington, DE: Scholarly Resources, 1999).

25. David Gates, *The Napoleonic Wars, 1803–1815* (London: Edward Arnold, 1997), 259.

TEN

Conclusions

> The possibilities of manoeuvre have once more reached a pitch of development that has not been seen in Europe since the days of Napoleon. Coming so quickly on the heels of the long stagnation, which was the feature of the war on the Western Front during the Great War [1914–18], the antithesis is all the more striking.
>
> —Major General Sir Percy Rawcliffe,
> director of military operations, 1920[1]

Commenting on the wide-ranging and fast-moving Polish-Russian struggle, Rawcliffe also threw light on a continual fascination with Napoleon as a commander who had been able to deliver mobility and manoeuvre. In practice, that operational capability did not always produce strategic achievement, but it was easy, as later with *blitzkrieg*, to be deceived by the wrapping, and that very much remains the case today.

For long, the major theme in the discussion of strategy was of improvement through institutionalisation, notably by means of the introduction and use, on the Prussian model, of General Staff systems from the late nineteenth century. The development of an explicit conceptual isation for strategy, and of related literature, doctrine and historical analysis, was also part of this mindset, and Clausewitz was much mentioned. Unsurprisingly, this analysis was pushed particularly hard by those involved. Indeed, there was a circularity, with those writing about strategy asserting its importance, and thereby receiving due encouragement, a situation that has continued to the present.

Readers will have their own views on the matter. Here it may be helpful to note that strategy in the modern world is not some abstract

201

process that is politically neutral, which is the desideratum in democratic political systems, but, instead, it is heavily shot through by political and cultural assumptions, and by service, institutional and individual ambitions and rivalries. It is a little unclear how a world in which key strategic players include, or have recently included, Erdogan, Modi, Putin, Trump, and even the more measured Xi Jinping can be discussed in terms of improvement, or the thesis frequently advanced of a careful distinction between policy and strategy, with the latter, furthermore, supposedly directed by optimal military considerations in a non-political atmosphere.

Thus, the many limitations of Napoleon as a strategist, as opposed to his skills (and failures) in command of campaigns or battles, and notably in operational art,[2] do not appear so out of keeping with the modern world. Nor do the problems we can readily see in Napoleon's strategy, especially the difficulty he confronted in avoiding the rush to action or in finding viable limits, necessarily appear so striking, as the latter assessment frequently only becomes apparent in hindsight. Instead, it is easier to note that Napoleon, like many military figures, including many of his opponents, found the recourse to force rational and necessary, as well as attractive and status affirming. This situation encouraged him to assess circumstances and rationality accordingly, although his belief in his own genius and mission (a belief shared by Hitler) clearly affected his assessment of the endemic risk and chance of war.[3]

Moreover, Napoleon was able to see the example of the past as offering assurance of the wisdom of fighting. He was also prone to see any disagreement from a hostile, if not paranoid, perspective.[4] Again, there is nothing here that we could not have seen, not only over the last century, but indeed over the last thirty years. Crucially, any "rationalisation" of Napoleon, as though drives such as ambition, pride and status seeking were secondary to him, or war and strategy were forced on him by aggressive other powers, does violence to the reality of the man, of the context he arose from and created[5] and of the continuing role of such factors.

With Napoleon's France, as for other powers, there is also the question of how far to look when considering strategic players, those domestic elements that played an active role in strategic formulation and/or implementation. In Britain, public politics meant that other views could be publicly expressed, as in May 1798 when the parliamentary Opposition unsuccessfully pressed for a separate peace with France. That, how-ever, did not mean there was not also extra-ministerial politics in other countries, nor that war was not discussed. However, in France, such politics did not really affect strategy under Napoleon.

If the strategic context and culture of Napoleonic France was unsur-prising, then the same point can be made about the response of other powers. In particular, there was a concern, for all of them, about the value of responding either with force or with compromise. Each strategy had limitations and was dependent in part on the possible domestic impact, but, more particularly, on the unpredictable nature of the response by other powers, notably, due to the risk involved, that by Napoleon.

For those considering opposing France, there was the unpredictability of the cohesion and longevity of the alliance system directed against that power, an unpredictability driven home by the history of coalitions over recent and earlier decades. There was not the equivalent of the uncondi-tional surrender policy of World War II, which was designed to hold the Allies together. Instead, a key strategic element in 1792–1815 was that each of the coalitions lasted at most five years and then collapsed, until that of 1815, which, in the event, only had to hang together for a brief period.

Moreover, despite the mutual pledge of the coalition of 1815 at Vien-na, Napoleon was hopeful that victories for France would lead to a col-lapse of the alliance, maybe with the Opposition forcing a change of policy in Britain. That might seem implausible, but the course of 1794–95 had brought a more striking change, and coalitions against France had subsequently collapsed in 1797, 1800–2, 1805–7 and 1809, as, conversely, had Napoleon's coalition system in 1813. In addition, the willingness of Austria to negotiate with France during the campaign season in 1814 very much underlined the need for powers to be able to handle total transfor-mations in the strategic situation: Metternich proved better able to do so than Napoleon, which was a measure of the latter's serious limitations both in understanding the situation and in responding.

This need, indeed, was one of the key characteristics of the situation, and it is all too easy to lose sight of the awareness of this factor when assessing the decisions that were taken about strategy and its implemen-tation. The conservation of force(s) became more important in that con-text, as it was unclear that reliance could be placed upon the aggregate strength of an alliance, and, if so, what reliance entailed. Thus, Britain in early 1814 had to face the danger that it might be left isolated anew if Austria, and then others, settled with France.

More generally, aside from the conservation of force(s), resources were an abiding issue in strategy. This was not least because the wars with France were only part of the widespread military commitment of Britain and Russia. Moreover, in assessing strategic options, and in considering what success against France accordingly would mean, all other powers would have to consider how best to confront the challenges of subsequent years. Indeed, in 1823, French forces invaded Spain in cooperation with King Ferdinand VII, who was suppressing Spain's liberals, while Austria acted against liberalism in Italy in 1820–21.

Resources were a significant factor in strategy, but a variable one. At sea, they were a matter of warships, trained crew, and support systems, notably bases, and these could not readily be accumulated rapidly. On land, the situation was more complex, in part because of the ability of troops with limited training to play a role, as in Spain during the Peninsular War (1808–14), when the regulars of the French army were in part tied down by the need to confront, alongside Spanish regulars, Spanish irregulars.[6] Separately, troops were easier, generally much easier, to recruit, deploy and supply than fleets, and this contrast helped ensure that generals did not appreciate the particular constraints affecting admirals. This was a particular issue with Britain's allies, but also with Napoleon. With navies, a loss of ships meant total strategic nullity, not least if the lost ships were incorporated into the opposing fleet. With armies, it tended to be defeat, and not destruction, that was crucial. Indeed, as Austria exemplified, those who were defeated could, despite attempts to limit forces, frequently fight again, and that was understood from the outset. Again, that factor affected the nature, goals, course, and contemporary verdicts of strategy.

The contrast between contemporary and subsequent verdicts on strategy is one that offers an appropriate topic for conclusion. The nature of contemporary judgement was a factor in achieving, measuring and sustaining success, and was notably so with reference to the ability to set the agenda, to win by imposing will, and to lubricate prestige accordingly. This process was required not only in so far as opponents were concerned, but also with respect to allies and neutrals. Indeed, victories were frequently even more designed to maintain alliances than to defeat opponents, or, at least, the latter was intended to ensure the former. The role of victories on land in building European coalitions therefore ensured that these victories appeared consequential and, as a result, necessary.

In truth, The Hague, Turin, Rome, Vienna, Berlin, Madrid, Paris and Washington (capitals captured in that order from 1795 to 1814) were only seizable by land, which was what happened to each in turn. Vienna had been threatened by French advances in 1704 and, even more in 1741, but it fell in 1805 and 1809. Few capitals, principally Constantinople, Copenhagen, Lisbon, London, Naples, Stockholm and St. Petersburg, were subject to naval attack, which was a far from easy process, although Copenhagen and Naples suffered it in this period. Thus, from the perspective of European powers, the undoubted significance of naval success on a global scale appeared of lesser importance than at that of Europe. This contrast helped to produce a strategic disjuncture, which is not unusual. The same was the case in World War II and, to a degree, in Anglo-French conflicts between 1689 and 1763.

The balance of assessment now will vary, just as it did at the time, with various analyses offered both of strategy and of Napoleon. The key factor, the one to the fore in this book, is to avoid easy judgement. For example, alongside the emphasis on Napoleonic battles as decisive and planned, and thus as an adjunct to strategy and a demonstration of operational capability, has come the realisation that, in addition, they consisted of a number of smaller combats which added up to a more or less coherent engagement. This situation was far from new. Instead, such combats were generally decided by local circumstances, notably the number and quality of the troops on each side, their tactics and morale, the advantages conferred by terrain, command responsibilities and, as with Marengo in 1800, luck. If one army was consistently successful in the early phases of a battle, it would rapidly gain a moral and a tactical ascendancy. What mattered was not the body count, but the destruction of the enemy's cohesion and will to fight. A successful surprise flank attack could be very important in this. Yet, most battles contained much indecisive fighting, particularly long-range skirmishing, as well as half-hearted advances which petered out before reaching the enemy lines.[7] This situation scarcely matched often glib later remarks about the operational and tactical values of strategic moves.

Instead of easy judgement, it is repeatedly necessary to understand the complexity of the subject, and, in large part as a result, the extent to which multiple, different and changeable assessments are valid. Indeed, these characteristics were an important aspect of the strategic context and the strategic outcome. Certainty in subsequent judgement is inappropriate and does violence to the uncertainties of the past. Here, there is a critical assessment of Napoleon, but it is necessary to note that not all share it.[8]

Furthermore, it is too easy to assume mistaken clarities in the linkages between causes and consequences. This study, nevertheless, is helpful in establishing some consistencies in general terms with respect to the relationship between operations and strategy. The crucial ones offered are, first, the need to distinguish between operational art and strategic skill, rather than asserting the latter in terms of a demonstration of the former. Secondly, in order to appreciate operations, you have to understand strategy and the objectives, priorities and political will and structures that are all involved in it.

NOTES

1. NA. WO. 106/6238, p. 19.

2. Claus Telp, *The Evolution of Operational Art, 1740–1813: From Frederick the Great to Napoleon* (London: Cass, 2005).

3. Although somewhat confusing and not really about Napoleon, Anders Engberg-Pedersen, *Empire of Chance: The Napoleonic Wars and the Disorder of Things* (Cambridge, MA: Harvard University Press, 2015).

4. Ambrogio Caiani, *To Kidnap a Pope: Napoleon and Pius VII* (New Haven, CT: Yale University Press, 2021).

5. Adam Zamoyski, *Napoleon: The Man behind the Myth* (London: Collins, 2018).

6. Charles Esdaile, *Fighting Napoleon: Guerrillas, Bandits and Adventurers in Spain, 1808–1814* (New Haven, CT: Yale University Press, 2004).

7. Rory Muir, *Tactics and the Experience of Battle in the Age of Napoleon* (New Haven, CT: Yale University Press, 1998).

8. For a far more sympathetic assessment, see Andrew Roberts, *Napoleon: A Life* (London: Allen Lane, 2014).

Selected Further Reading

Necessarily selective, as even the most superficial of lists will take a volume, the focus here is on readily accessible works. Earlier works can be found in their bibliographies. To stay up in the anglophone literature, readers are recommended to subscribe to the *Journal of Military History*.

Adams, Michael. *Napoleon and Russia*. London: Hambledon Continuum, 2006.

Bartlett, Thomas, ed. *1798: A Bicentenary Perspective*. Dublin: Four Courts Press, 2003.

Bell, David. *The First Total War: Napoleon's Europe and the Birth of Warfare as We Know It*. New York: Houghton Mifflin, 2007.

Bertaud, Jean-Paul, and Daniel Reichel. *Atlas de la Révolution française: L'armée et la guerre*. Paris: Ecole des hautes études en sciences sociales, 1989.

Bew, John. *Castlereagh: A Life*. Oxford: Oxford University Press, 2012.

Bickham, Troy. *The Weight of Vengeance: The United States, the British Empire and the War of 1812*. Oxford: Oxford University Press, 2012.

Black, Jeremy. *The War of 1812 in the Age of Napoleon*. Norman: University of Oklahoma Press, 2009.

Branda, Pierre, ed. *La saga des Bonaparte*. Paris: Perrin, 2018.

Branda, Pierre, and Thierry Lentz. *Napoléon, l'esclavage et les colonies*. Paris: Fayard, 2006.

Bregeon, Jean-Joël, and Gérard Guicheteau. *Nouvelle histoire des guerres de Vendée*. Paris: Perrin, 2017.

Broers, Michael. *Napoleon: Soldier of Destiny*. New York: Pegasus, 2014.

Browne, Haji. *Bonaparte in Egypt: The French Campaign of 1798–1801 from the Egyptian Perspective*. London: Leonaur, 2012.

Bush, Robert. *The Louisiana Purchase: A Global Context*. New York: Routledge, 2013.

Clark, Christopher. *Iron Kingdom: The Rise and Downfall of Prussia, 1600–1947*. Cambridge: Cambridge University Press, 2006.

Colson, Bruno. *Leipzig: La battaile des Nations, 16–19 octobre 1813*. Paris: Tempus, 2013.

Cooper, Randolf. *The Anglo-Maratha Campaigns and the Contest for India: The Struggle for Control of the South Asian Military Economy*. Cambridge: Cambridge University Press, 2003.

Cuccia, Phillip. *Napoleon in Italy: The Sieges of Mantua, 1796–1799*. Norman: University of Oklahoma Press, 2014.

Das, Amita. *Defending British India against Napoleon: The Foreign Policy of Governor-General Lord Minto, 1807–1813*. Woodbridge: Boydell and Brewer, 2016.

Davey, James. *In Nelson's Wake: The Navy and the Napoleonic Wars*. New Haven, CT: Yale University Press, 2015.

———. *The Transformation of British Naval Strategy: Seapower and Supply in Northern Europe, 1808–1812*. Woodbridge: Boydell and Brewer, 2012.

Davis, John. *Naples and Napoleon: Southern Italy and the European Revolution*. Oxford: Oxford University Press, 2006.

Duffy, Michael. *Soldiers, Sugar and Seapower: The British Expeditions to the West Indies and the War against Revolutionary France*. Oxford: Oxford University Press, 1987.

Dwyer, Philip. *Napoleon: The Path to Power*. New Haven, CT: Yale University Press, 2008.

Epstein, Robert. *Napoleon's Last Victory and the Emergence of Modern War*. Lawrence: University of Kansas Press, 1994.

Esdaile, Charles. *The Peninsular War: A New History*. London: Allen Lane, 2002.

———. *Napoleon's Wars: An International History, 1803–1815*. London: Allen Lane, 2008.

———. *The Wars of the French Revolution, 1792–1801*. Abingdon: Taylor and Francis, 2018.

———. *The Wars of Napoleon*. 2nd ed. Abingdon: Taylor and Francis, 2019.

Eysturlid, Lee. *The Formative Influences, Theories and Campaigns of the Archduke Carl of Austria*. Westport, CT: Praeger, 2000.

Feldbaek, Ole. *The Battle of Copenhagen 1801: Nelson and the Danes*. Barnsley: Pen and Sword, 2002.

Finley, Milton. *The Most Monstrous of Wars: The Napoleonic Guerrilla War in Southern Italy, 1806–1811*. Columbia: University of South Carolina Press, 1944.

Gill, John. *1809: Thunder on the Danube*. Barnsley: Pen and Sword, 2008.

Glover, Gareth. *The Forgotten War against Napoleon: Conflict in the Mediterranean, 1793–1815*. Barnsley: Pen and Sword, 2017.

Grainger, John. *The Amiens Truce: Britain and Bonaparte, 1801–1803*. Woodbridge: Boydell and Brewer, 2004.

Hagermann, Karen. *Revisiting Prussia's War against Napoleon: History, Culture and Memory*. Cambridge: Cambridge University Press, 2015.

Hall, Christopher. *British Strategy in the Napoleonic War, 1803–15*. Manchester: Manchester University Press, 1992.

Hayworth, Jordan. *Revolutionary France's War of Conquest in the Rhineland: Conquering the Natural Frontier, 1792–1797*. Cambridge: Cambridge University Press, 2019.

Hughes, Michael. *Forging Napoleon's Grande Armée: Motivation, Military Culture, and Masculinity in the French Army, 1800–1808*. New York: New York University Press, 2012.

Jones, Colin. *The Great Nation: France from Louis XV to Napoleon*. London: Allen Lane, 2003.

Jorgensen, Christer. *The Anglo-Swedish Alliance against Napoleonic France*. Basingstoke: Palgrave Macmillan, 2004.

Knight, Roger. *Britain against Napoleon: The Organisation of Victory, 1793–1813*. London: Allen Lane, 2013.

Krajeski, Paul. *In the Shadow of Nelson: The Naval Leadership of Admiral Sir Charles Cotton, 1753–1812*. Westport, CT: Praeger, 2000.

Leggiere, Michael. *The Fall of Napoleon: The Allied Invasion of France, 1813–1814*. Cambridge: Cambridge University Press, 2007.

———. *Napoleon and the Struggle for Germany*. Cambridge: Cambridge University Press, 2015.

Lieven, Dominic. *Russia against Napoleon: The Battle for Europe, 1807 to 1814*. London: Allen Lane, 2009.

Mackesy, Piers. *War without Victory: The Downfall of Pitt, 1799–1802*. Oxford: Oxford University Press, 1984.

McGrew, Roderick. *Paul I of Russia: 1754–1801*. Oxford: Oxford University Press, 1992.

Mikaberidze, Alexander. *The Napoleonic Wars: A Global History*. Oxford: Oxford University Press, 2020.

Muir, Rory. *Britain and the Defeat of Napoleon, 1807–1815*. New Haven, CT: Yale University Press, 1996.

———. *Wellington, I: The Path to Victory, 1769–1814*. New Haven, CT: Yale University Press, 2013.

Mustafa, Sam. *Napoleon's Paper Kingdom: The Life and Death of Westphalia, 1807–1813*. Lanham, MD: Rowman and Littlefield, 2017.

Paret, Peter. *The Cognitive Challenge of War: Prussia, 1806*. Princeton, NJ: Princeton University Press, 2009.

Planert, Ute, ed. *Napoleon's Empire: European Politics in Global Perspective*. Basingstoke: Palgrave, 2016.

Popkin, Jeremy. *A Concise History of the Haitian Revolution*. Oxford: Oxford University Press, 2012.

Price, Munro. *Napoleon: The End of Glory*. Oxford: Oxford University Press, 2014.

Rapport, Mike. *The Napoleonic Wars: A Very Short Introduction*. Oxford: Oxford University Press, 2013.

Roberts, Andrew. *Napoleon: A Life*. London: Allen Lane, 2014.

Roider, Karl. *Baron Thugut and Austria's Response to the French Revolution*. Princeton, NJ: Princeton University Press, 1987.

Ross, Steven. *Quest for Victory: French Military Strategy, 1792–1799*. New York: A. S. Barnes, 1973.

Rothenberg, Gunther. *The Art of Warfare in the Age of Napoleon*. Bloomington: Indiana University Press, 1978.

———. *Napoleon's Great Adversary: Archduke Charles and the Austrian Army, 1792–1814*. Bloomington: Indiana University Press, 1992.

———. *The Emperor's Last Victory: Napoleon and the Battle of Wagram*. London: Weidenfeld and Nicolson, 2004.

Schneid, Frederick. *Napoleon's Italian Campaigns: 1805–1815*. Westport, CT: Praeger, 2002.

———. *Napoleon's Conquest of Europe: The War of the Third Coalition*. Westport, CT: Praeger, 2005.

———, ed. *European Armies of the French Revolution, 1789–1802*. Norman: University of Oklahoma Press, 2015.

Schroeder, Paul. *The Transformation of European Politics, 1763–1848*. Oxford: Oxford University Press, 1994.

Severn, John. *Architects of Empire: The Duke of Wellington and His Brothers*. Norman: University of Oklahoma Press, 2007.

Simms, Brendan. *The Impact of Napoleon: Prussian High Politics, Foreign Policy, and the Crisis of the Executive, 1797–1806*. Cambridge: Cambridge University Press, 1997.

Ward, Peter. *British Naval Power in the East, 1794–1805: The Command of Admiral Peter Rainier*. Woodbridge: Boydell and Brewer, 2013.

Yapp, Malcolm. *Strategies of British India: Britain, Iran, and Afghanistan, 1798–1850*. Oxford: Oxford University Press, 1980.

Zamoyski, Adam. *Napoleon: The Man behind the Myth*. London: Collins, 2018.

Index